MW00811497

The Inquisitive Christ

The Inquisitive Christ

12 Engaging Questions

Cara L. T. Murphy

New York Nashville

FaithWords
Hachette Book Group
1290 Avenue of the Americas, New York, NY 10104
faithwords.com
twitter.com/faithwords

First Edition: March 2020

FaithWords is a division of Hachette Book Group, Inc. The FaithWords name and logo are trademarks of Hachette Book Group, Inc.

The publisher is not responsible for websites (or their content) that are not owned by the publisher.

The Hachette Speakers Bureau provides a wide range of authors for speaking events. To find out more, go to www.hachettespeakersbureau.com or call (866) 376-6591.

Library of Congress Cataloging-in-Publication Data

Names: Murphy, Cara L. T., author.
Title: The inquisitive Christ : twelve engaging questions / Cara L.T. Murphy.
Description: New York : FaithWords, 2020. | Includes bibliographical references. | Summary: "There is an incredible truth about the nature of Christ: the Son of God is a curious God who asks. And His questions are life changing. The answer to your need for connection, to your spiritual doubt and restlessness, can be found by examining God's questions. Scripture reveals that Jesus asked over 300 questions to teach, engage, and invite us closer. Now, experience an intimate and transformative conversation with the Son of God by exploring twelve of the most powerful questions from the Gospels. Through Christ's questions, you'll journey deeper into a Kingdom existence and be taken by the truth of His love and desire to walk in union with you, His Kingdom preparations for you, and the relevance of His promises in your life. Let Jesus ask-and He'll ignite your imagination, intellect, heart, and soul"-- Provided by publisher.
Identifiers: LCCN 2019041813 | ISBN 9781546038375 (hardcover) | ISBN 9781546038382 (ebook)
Subjects: LCSH: Jesus Christ--Miscellanea. | Questioning. | Jesus Christ--Teachings.
Classification: LCC BS2415 .M87 2020 | DDC 232--dc23
LC record available at https://lccn.loc.gov/2019041813

ISBNs: 978-1-5460-3837-5 (hardcover), 978-1-5460-3838-2 (ebook)

Printed in the United States of America

LSC-C

To the true Irish few:
You have joined me at the feasting table of questions,
blessing the appetite and still hungering for more.

Contents

Acknowledgments

"Acknowledge" is such a pale word for what must happen on this page. I can acknowledge many truths, but the Gospel has taught me that gratitude springs from a deeper place. It is to this place I go.

To Jimmy Murphy—fellow pilgrim and Kingdom Son. You saved me from falling off Mount Brandon, and you've saved me every day since. The fruit is now ripe. We knew one day it would be.

To Mom and Dad. You could see who I was becoming, and you never lost that vision. We share together in what's to come.

To MGW and JCRF. Your stories are beautiful, and so are your lives. Thank you for sharing them with the world and with me. I love being your mom.

To the first readers—Alison Kline, Lisa and David Sosin, Caroline White, and especially my *anam cara* Sacha Layman. Your eyes were safeguards to every word that God had planned. I'm grateful these words found a home with you.

To my agent, Scott Lamb. Your unflappable patience made me believe anything was possible. Indeed, it was. Thank you for seeing me and believing in what you saw.

To the team at FaithWords and HBG, especially my amazing editor, Virginia Bhashkar. Your collaborations have polished every rough edge. Thank you for making me a part of your family.

To my Irish friends. *Feicfidh mé thú go luath*, Lord willing. *Sláinte.*

And to the Inquisitive Christ. The glory and my heart belong to you.

The Inquisitive Christ

Introduction

I towered far, and lo! I stood within
The presence of the Lord Most High,
Sent thither by the sons of earth, to win
Some answer to their cry.
"The Earth, say'st thou? The Human race?
By Me created? Sad its lot?
Nay: I have no remembrance of such place:
Such world I fashioned not."

—Thomas Hardy,
"God-Forgotten"

In a few hours' time, everything would change. Their plans and hopes would collapse on the hillside of Calvary. Their faith would shatter like glass into a million shards.

Jesus knew this. He knew his friends were walking into crisis and perceived abandonment. In the deepening shadows of Passover, he also knew what they did not—that in his physical absence, his presence would remain. His care for them, his preparations, would be specific, individualized. He'd told them so, many times.

But they didn't trust the promises he'd made to them that night or any other. Their doubt, long embraced, would not allow them to risk believing in the dark.

He passed through Jerusalem's twilight streets, their fear and unbelief the landscape he was passionate to navigate. In the pause of this holy night, in the gap of their mistrust, he entered with a question.

"If [my intimate preparations] *weren't so, would I have told you that I'm on my way to get a room ready for you?"*

John 14:2

His question, though somewhat chiding, was meant to expose the deep-rooted lie attached to every heart since the Garden gates clanged shut in Genesis 3. This lie fuels human doubt like gasoline, compelling us to wander our green-and-blue planet, fending for ourselves and searching for a home we are afraid we'll never find.

This lie wraps itself around our souls with clinging tenacity: *God has forgotten me.*

But Jesus's question, posed to his disciples and extended to all, kindly reminds us that the lie, while loud, has never been true. We are not abandoned. We are not unseen. We are not "God-forgotten."

Something in each of us needs to be pointed repeatedly toward these truths. The questions of Jesus serve as the signposts, showing us the way.

In the year I turned thirty, I desperately needed these signposts. That year, my husband, Jimmy, and I first stepped American feet onto Ireland's dark loam, our ancestral soil. We'd been married for ten years and had begun to observe something unsettling. This unsettling thing had crept into our lives quietly, unnoticed. While we'd been busy making a life for ourselves, we had accidentally embraced a paradigm of mistrust. Like the disciples, we were doubting the relevance of God's promises for us and our messy lives.

We had slowly transitioned from living as beloved children to forgotten ones, and in the midst of this subconscious belief, *we* ended up forgetting *God.* It's easy for an orphan to make that leap of doubt.

We had forgotten him, his desire to walk with us in union, his intimate preparations on our behalf. On the outside, I'm sure we seemed content, and we were pleased with this appearance. The truth was that contentment was far from us. We were restless and dissatisfied.

Dissatisfied in our comfort.

Dissatisfied with the relational status quo.

Dissatisfied with the dryness of our slumbering Christianity.

Painfully dissatisfied with the small story we'd written for ourselves.

This is where the invitation to risk more with God entered, into a place just empty and quiet enough that the echo of something unexpected could be heard. From this experience of deep dissatisfaction, of needing to both remember and *be* remembered, we did something completely outside our carefully crafted twenty-year plan. With urgency nipping at our heels, we decided to throw our lives into the air like confetti, watching where the pieces would float next. We wanted to shrug off the protective cloak we'd worn over our tiny world, the covering that kept us cloistered within, and God with all his wildness out.

In other words, we decided to move to Ireland.

Both Irish in ancestry, we desired to see the land of our forebears, perhaps finding true contentment there. I had known that ancient Celtic tradition calls Ireland "the Terrible Beauty," and, by instinct—although I didn't understand it—I knew I needed exposure to something unapologetically wild. I wanted to remember the God who had once caught my imagination and intellect, my heart and my soul.

But I was scared I'd become even more dissatisfied.

Ireland isn't a large country, by any means. Although only the size of Indiana, it is certainly big enough to overwhelm two untested American parents, responsible for our daughters, Macy and Jo. We knew this wouldn't be a sightseeing vacation. It would be a pilgrims' voyage, an answer-seeking course correction, done with a five- and six-year-old in tow.

It felt like we were walking blind into a minefield.

We narrowed our focus to County Kerry, the largely rural southwestern border of Ireland. We threw a dart at the county map, picking a peninsula. I spun Jimmy seven times with his eyes closed, and he poked the village of Caherciveen with a tack.

We scolded ourselves for our ridiculous behavior, for moving forward with this irresponsibility. We prayed fervently, argued and kissed, emoted like maniacs, and obsessively researched the Internet.

Kerry, or as its people call her, "the Kingdom," sits at the westernmost edge of Europe, and we liked that. We'd heard there were more sheep there than people. As introverts, this statistic appealed to us. We wanted soul-quiet, and our world at home had gotten loud with people, places, and things.

This predictable family of four did what no one predicted, stepping off the edge of our lives. We closed our home in Virginia, put the house on the market, and gave our key to a real estate agent, never planning to return. With four enormous suitcases, we said goodbye to everything we'd ever known. Sitting on the runway, Jimmy and I held hands, our trusting little girls waving goodbye to America from the windows of the plane.

After two flights, a five-hour drive across country, and several Dramamine, we arrived—frazzled and believing we may have made the biggest mistake of our lives.

We were wrong.

Pulling onto the gravel drive, our Irish cottage peeking around the next bend, we could sense immediately that God was there waiting, a huge grin on his face. Glimpsing the fresh-catch fishery across the street and the newborn lambs mewling around the outer courtyard, we knew he was there, antsy like a kid at a party, itching to finally yell, "Surprise!"

We had not been God-forgotten.

As he'd said in John 14, he spoke the same over us: In spite of our wrestling, everything would be okay. He was preparing something special all along.

"Would I have said it if it weren't true?"

We had traveled with so many personal questions, expecting them to be met by either God's certainty or his silence. In reality, he gave us very few answers, but he was not silent.

Instead of the answers we craved, we got something else,

something unexpected and infinitely better. God surprised us with his inquisitive nature. He met us with holy conversation and tailor-made dialogue.

God gave us *his* questions.

In County Kerry, he revealed his desire to draw us near by asking us a host of soul-penetrating, Gospel questions, abundant as Irish rainfall. As with the disciples, his questions pointed the way along the winding path to intimacy with him.

We thought we understood questions—we'd been asking them our whole lives. But we discovered we'd been taught the Socratic method by the wrong teacher. There is a motivational chasm between fallen questions asked by fallen humanity and these unexpected questions offered by God.

Fallen questions accuse. The questions of God invite.

Fallen questions mask what's hidden beneath. The questions of God are revelation.

Fallen questions stifle discussion. The questions of God breathe life into conversations with him.

The deep-rooted lie that we're God-forgotten in turn compels us to question God, to forget him *before* we can be forgotten. But through his questioning, he gently offers us a safe place to lay down our doubt, sitting with us in the unknown space between inquiry and answer.

We all are making the risky and bewildering journey to our ancestral Home. We have so many decisions to make from what feels like far, far away.

His presence, however, is closer than we think.

Jesus isn't spending eternity concentrating on his own personal comfort. At this very moment, we are on his mind. His plans for us are both grand and individualized. He dwells with us, and he doesn't miss a thing.

We all throw darts at the spiritual map. Our best efforts are stumbling in the dark. But we are not forgotten for even one second. He walks with us, always available, always present, providing the questions that point the way forward.

While not limited to a dozen, this book explores twelve of

those questions in the Gospel narratives. To engage what he asks will take patience. It will take stillness. It will take courage. His preparations are in place even now, beginning with his questions.

Godspeed to you, friend, on the road paved with Gospel questions.

PART I:

BREACHING THE BARRICADE OF DOUBT

CHAPTER ONE

"Where Is Your Faith?"

Drowning in the Current of Mistrust

Why can't you see
What you're doing to me
When you don't believe a word I say?

—Elvis Presley,
"Suspicious Minds"

"O you of little faith, why did you doubt?"

—Jesus Christ,
Matthew 14:31, ESV

On the western edge of Ireland, the Atlantic rushes from North America like a refugee in flight. Despite the promises made by the Gulf Stream, at the height of an Irish summer, the temperature of Kerry waters huddles in the mid-forties. The air temperatures don't cross into the seventies save a miracle, and there's always the breeze that bites.

Nevertheless, the Gaeltacht Irish are sailors and fisherfolk and lovers of the sea. The cold does not keep them landbound any more than it does the native sea mammals that soak in the chill tub of Ireland's bays. Even wee Irish children swim in these waters.

The Murphys were not going to be put to shame. When in Rome, and all that nonsense.

We determined not only to get our feet wet—we were going to submerge. We were going to swim to the local fishing pier and back, the length of three football fields in one direction. We decided to do this great feat the next warm, sunny day. That day came and went, and we found a legitimate reason to back out.

Despite the sun's warmth, the water was still cold—iceberg cold.

We waited a few more days until the forecast called for a June heat wave, when the air temperature would reach a whopping 68 degrees Fahrenheit. That day came, and that day it rained.

We procrastinated until evening, knowing the beach would be empty. When we arrived, the only other person crazy enough to swim was an older man from the village, wearing nothing but a tragically small suit and a swim cap. He swam belly up, lazily backstroking near the shore like driftwood. He waved as we picked our way down the stony beach.

Reluctantly dropping our towels, we stepped into the water, holding hands. Jimmy and I stood there, hopping from one foot to the other, shrieking like distressed animals. The next moment, Jimmy Murphy dropped my hand and ran like a wild man into the crashing surf.

I followed. We were going to touch that pier if it killed us.

When I first dove under the water, I thought with shocking ire: *The Atlantic has betrayed me.* This water was for penguins and Antarctic explorers—not for normal swimmers. Instantly, it felt like every ounce of breath was sucked from my body, and every muscle strangled itself seeking warmth. We were gasping and swallowing water all while trying to move shocked limbs that were furious at our brains. Somewhere in the distance, I heard the whoops of my children.

Within steps, the rocky bottom gave way, and we were well beyond our depth—the fishing pier still far in the distance. I rolled over on my back, concentrating. I needed to regulate my labored breathing. Thick, tan seaweed, ten feet long or more, danced just beneath my back and legs. It tickled and bumped against me. We knew whale life was abundant in Kerry. I was picturing what mammoth sea creatures were watching me from the weeds below. I tried imagining that I was simply swimming in a backyard pool. This did not work.

Jimmy and I reached the pier at the same time, but the waves were too rough to climb the narrow concrete stairs to the platform high above. They were slick and algae-covered, and I imagined my head cracking like a waterlogged melon with the next thrashing roll. We touched the pier with our toes in defiant joy and kicked off in a rush, turning to go what felt like miles back to shore.

What we didn't realize was that our swim to the pier had been in cooperation with the current. Now this same current opposed us, violently, and we drifted quite a bit as we fought with heavier limbs toward shore. We were completely numb. For the first time, I thought of how dangerous this was, how easy it would be for one of us to lose control, carried into the sea beyond from sheer exhaustion. When we finally hauled ourselves onto the shoreline's slimy rocks, white as sheets and panting for breath, I thanked Jesus. Our girls, first-grader Macy and kindergartner Jo, ran to us, cheering, unaware how precarious life had just been.

We'd been naïve, foolish.

We bundled up in our towels and drove home to our tiny Euro shower, where American heads and shoulders stuck out above the curtain. We hunched under the hot flow for an extravagant amount of time, uncaring that we had to pay extra for hot water. Jimmy stoked the peat bricks in the grate. I made scalding mugs of instant coffee. It took us several hours, a heap of Irish blankets, and a nap to feel warm again.

The Irish Atlantic water is an untamed environment, unfriendly for play, dangerous for extended immersion. We stayed in too long, we swam out too far, and we'd come close to true peril. We were way out of our depth.

Each of us is irresistibly compelled to make this foolish swim daily, never expecting that we won't be able to return to shore when we've had enough. What many would never choose for our bodies, we force upon our souls. This self-inflicted peril is the universal story of our time.

There is an ancient wound in the beating heart of the world, a wound that spreads doubt like toxins into every exchange. There is a Mariana Trench down the center of the cosmos, a rift as dark as death itself. In reaction to the taunts of betrayal, corruption, and the evasion of truth we live with every day, we've all plunged into the ever-moving current of suspicion.

We, the image-bearers, do not trust the image we bear. God, the image-giver, is deeply misunderstood. We keep seeing through the eyes of betrayal, expecting to find him exposed as a divine fraud.

We trust nothing, doubt everything. Questions and mistrust are as involuntary as sweating in the heat or shivering in the cold.

This swim we're in is not a hospitable environment. Our limbs are numb, slothlike in a sea that feels more like mud than saltwater. We forget how cold we are, thinking we're safe, but we're not. We've just lost feeling, we've lost control, and the current is steering.

SCHOOL DAYS

Being deceived by someone in authority, someone meant to protect and uphold truth, is not a moment easily forgotten. My parents were teenagers during Nixon's America. They both remember where they were when they watched the highest official in the land shake his head and swear he was not a crook. They can also remember the day this same president was caught in his lies and corruption.

My generation remembers its own moments. It was the mid-nineties, the decade of MTV and Doc Martens, when young millennials first began to learn that our world was full of questions, an unsafe place for us to grow. This was a world where a famous football player allegedly committed a double homicide, walking free when so many thought him guilty. This was a world that broadcasted the Somalian genocide alongside news of Julia Roberts's latest beau. This was a world where the United States government quibbled fiercely over what constitutes Oval Office perjury.

At the same time I was taught "Just Say No" to sex and drugs, my president was lying about his abuse of them. My peers and I watched the media coverage in our social studies classrooms. We were being educated by our country's humiliation and exposure from the top down.

It wasn't just a political problem, nor could all the blame be assigned to Hollywood or sports organizations alone. The worldwide church fared no better. From the Vatican to the Bible Belt, pastors and priests fell like dominoes in the game of tawdry vices. The dress of Christ's bride was being dragged through the mud at an alarming rate, and corruption was leaking out everywhere. Televangelists, prosperity gospels, false healings, and big hair became the face of the church. Thanks to modern media, the church could no longer hide its mess.

The doubting world watched with rising anger, growing in proportion to the current's magnetic pull on our homes and families.

At that time, I wanted to be a lawyer or a writer when I grew up. In my idealistic youth, both occupations were held by defenders of justice, culturally appointed truth-tellers. I'd heard it asked in the televised trials we watched at school: "Do you swear to tell the truth, the whole truth, and nothing but the truth, so help you God?"

The appropriate response is to put hand to Bible and promise, "I do." It reminded me strangely of a wedding. But like many marriages around me, I found that the vows could be broken before they'd even been made. It seemed no one was capable of telling the *whole* truth. My formative teenage years were saturated with these small betrayals. This awakening to the fragility of trust took the yielding material of childhood clay, spinning and shaping us until we all understood what must be done: Trust no one. Doubt everything.

We were being schooled in the most important lesson of our times—the value of the question. This was not simple rhetoric or healthy analytical processing. We weren't being taught simply to think—we were taught to doubt, to mistrust.

We were choking down the salty seawater of mistrust because that was the thing to do. To survive, suspicion and doubt would be my allies. Questions and cynicism would chart the course like glittering holes in the black sky.

SLIGHT MOMENTS IN PUBLIC RESTROOMS

All stories end the same. Sooner or later, every kid realizes that the world isn't a safe place to grow up.

For some, one traumatic event defines the insecurity of the individual position. For others, it's a series of frightening disappointments, slight moments that leave us feeling small and scared in a world of mean giants. These moments create in each of us a capacity that we were not born possessing: the capacity to mistrust. It's this world-bred capacity that teaches us that to survive we must be tough. We must not trust. We must question the people around us and suspect the things they say. None of us escape this capacity for self-protection.

As a parent, I thought I could shield my daughters from such a capacity. I could not and cannot still. This painful discovery, fraught with a maddening helplessness every parent understands, was made certain when my oldest daughter, Macy, was seven. This girl is a fierce, ninja-warrior princess. Macy is strong and brave and full of wonder, but even Macy is not immune to the increasing capacity for mistrust.

The slight moments found her out, just like the rest of us.

We were in Killarney, the city closest to our home village on the Kerry peninsula. It was less than a couple of hours away, but we didn't go there often. It was a different kind of beauty than the coast—a manicured, civil beauty that lacked the raw wildness drawing us to the seascape. In Killarney, there is an old estate, Muckross House, surrounded by an Old World park with clipped lawns and gardens, a lake, and a closely trimmed wooded path. The times we visited, it reminded me of Central Park—overrun with tourists, people taking pictures and buying souvenirs. We hadn't been there long when Macy tugged my sleeve with an urgent need to find a restroom. We followed the signs and found what we needed.

One thing important to know about Irish public restrooms is that there are no stalls—not in the same way we have them in America. Each toilet area is a tiny room, much like a broom closet. There is no crawl space under or over the door. When the door is shut, the occupant has barely any room to move, let alone remove the necessary clothing. Elbows touch the sides of the walls, and knees press against the door, shut to freedom.

Macy didn't like the look of it, but her need was pressing. These small, cramped rooms designed for relieving oneself threatened my own adult sense of personal security. She asked if I would go in with her, but there simply wasn't room. I remember impatiently urging her to go in, that everything would be fine.

Everything was not fine.

When she tried to get out, she found that she couldn't turn the doorknob. The rusted lock had stuck, and the door was jammed. It took exactly one second for my sweet, trusting daughter to get hysterical. She started shrieking and sobbing, pushing the door, pulling the door, kicking the door with her pink rubber Crocs. She jiggled the knob as hard as she could. I could hear her muffled fists pounding on the solid wood. She couldn't hear me trying to calm her down. I was starting to get hysterical myself. Irish women were staring helplessly.

I didn't know what to do. Macy didn't know what to do. Never had I felt so far from all that made me feel safe and in control. I'm sure my daughter felt the same. We both just did the one thing that the moment called for: panicked twisting of the lock and the doorknob.

I'm not sure how long we did this. It could have been two minutes or twelve. Eventually, something clicked into place and the knob turned. She burst from the stall into my arms. I'll never forget her flushed, sweaty face, the matted hair plastered to her forehead, her terror-filled eyes.

From that point on, Macy was terrified to shut the bathroom door. Any bathroom door. Even when we returned to the States, with our wonderful, wide, roomy stalls, Macy had been so traumatized by the bathroom's betrayal that she could not close herself inside any restroom.

What could be simpler, safer than a child using the bathroom without fear? It's at the basic level of our core human need to have domain over our own bodies. Even in the simple things, however, we are daily confronted with how precarious our situation remains. Not even the bathroom is a given.

The slight moment had found her, and her own young capacity for mistrust was born.

I tried to reassure her that she was safe, that she could trust me and other bathrooms—but in one instant, Macy had learned the lesson the world loves to teach, the lesson we all learn early and keep learning along the way.

Trust is for children and fools.

NOTHING NEW

We are all Macy in the bathroom—trapped, betrayed by false promises of safety in a reality that seems unsafe. At a deep level, we are all unable to escape the frightening world that surrounds us on a daily basis. Therefore, we can see only two options for getting out of bed every day. We can either live in constant fear or we can choose to embrace mistrust. Ironically, making this choice eradicates neither. Day after day, we find we're still stuck with both fear and doubt.

However, the culture at large still believes it has a choice, and we tend to choose the latter. "Doubt has become a virtue," warns author John Eldredge, "a means of rejecting intolerance and oppression."[1] Popular opinion idolizes the unbeliever. Cynicism is prized over belief, suspicion over faith. Skepticism is our strongest asset. Accusations are our cultural companions. So much is wrong with the world, and we want to uncover it with questions.

We are born looking for who we can trust, but we're nourished on the milk of suspicion.

We want to trust. It's not that we want to be infested with doubt, but we've been burned too often and too long. We watch and wait for those around us to fail, to fall, to disappoint us yet again. After a while, we take a strange sort of satisfaction in being proven right. We may even hope we will be disappointed, because knowing we cannot trust is at least the one thing we can trust.

This generation of questioners is not unique. What looks like a twenty-first-century problem turns out to be a human problem. Scandals and media-delivery systems come and go, but the capacity for doubt is at the core of every civilization.

Doubt is our silent inheritance from the culture before us, and they before them.

What was will be again, what happened will happen again. There's nothing new on this earth. Year after year it's the same old thing.

Ecclesiastes 1:9

Words penned by a cynical king, this verse reminds us of the damage the world does to each successive culture. Remove social media and satellite television, and all cultures share "the same old thing" in common: doubt and mistrust. We've been drifting in these twin currents since the snake first whispered into humanity's upturned ear, and we've long since forgotten how to use legs on dry land.

FIRST-CENTURY JEWS AND MILLENNIALS

Religious exploitation. Political unrest. Social injustices and human atrocities. An unseen God who has been silent for so long one forgets he was ever capable of speech. The New Testament reads more like a journalistic exposé than first-century Judaic culture.

Yet, this *is* the culture into which the incarnate God entered. This is the culture he enters still.

The doubt *du jour* centered around Messianic expectation and a desire to break the yoke of foreign tyranny. Galilean and Judean Jews had lived lifetimes of moments, both slight and graphic, moments designed by a Roman dictatorship and corrupt Jewish governance to break spirit and will. Mothers and fathers watched in enraged horror as Jewish babies were ripped from cradles, slaughtered. Families, already struggling to fill stomachs, were stripped of the little money and property they had to fill Rome's fat coffers. This was a world ripe with the stench of crucified bodies that could be seen from holy walls.

The Jews could not trust their government.

The Temple in Jerusalem—a spiritual gathering place that was to be their refuge—took more from the people than it would give. The religious elite led the people with the shepherd's rod of guilt, intending to beat the law into the hearts of their broken flock. Theft, corruption, and bitter accusation filled the Temple courts alongside the thick smell of animals' spilled blood.

The Jews could not trust their religious leadership.

And Yahweh. Where *was* he? Why had he sent no prophet? Why did he keep silent? Why did he allow his holy city to be overrun with pagans? Like our time, the faithful remnant was choking on questions that remained unanswered by heaven. They cried out for saving, for God's burning wrath to fall on their enemies like fire and rain. They cried for Messiah. They watched for Messiah. They put all the remaining fragments of hope like Fabergé eggs in the militant hands of a Messiah-to-come.

But the longer they waited, the harder it was to hope. Their own capacity for doubt in Yahweh eventually blinded most Jews to all but their own ideas of God's plan for salvation.

Almost no one expected the Messiah they got.

Under twilight's blanket, Jesus slipped quietly into their world, thwarting expectations in a way that felt like betrayal. He spoke treasonous words. He shattered widespread expectation like grandmother's crystal, and he didn't apologize for it. He seemed to belong to no political party, no factional affiliation, no alliance that had been established for generations. Many ignored him. Some looked on with mild curiosity. A few risked trust, believing he was who he said, and he took their trust right to a Roman cross.

They weren't ready for this Messiah. They didn't want this Messiah, and the stink of suspicion only thickened in the sticky, Middle Eastern air.

They called him a law-breaker. They insinuated demon possession was to blame. They told bawdy jokes with him as the punchline, calling him drunkard, glutton, at home with the shady element. The greedy looked for a magician to entertain them. The confused wanted a rabbi with all the answers. Almost everyone cried for *basileus* (bä-sē-lyü's)—a king greater than Caesar.[2] They sneered at this Nazarene carpenter who didn't play by their rules, wanting instead a political mastermind or military zealot.

What they got was Jesus. The long-awaited Messiah was not who they'd been waiting for at all.

They had been wrong to wait, to expect God to send a savior. They'd been wrong to fight against the world's current of doubt. They'd been wrong to trust. Because they didn't want him, they hated him. Like a thankless child at Christmas, disappointment in the reality gave birth to wayward thought. Doubt makes hatred of the undesirable easy as breathing.

As they watched him die, they knew how wrong they'd been to believe his claims, and they kicked themselves for it. Misplaced faith. Abandoned expectations. The same message inundating our culture also swallowed theirs.

Trust has always been for children and fools.

AFTER DINNER

They rowed from shore with full stomachs, the first they could remember in weeks. As they maneuvered their open vessel through calm waters and light breezes, they could almost feel the smile of God cresting on each wave, sea-foam teeth and a wide, glad grin riding bareback on watery haunches. At this moment, the God who could bridle the sea was real. He had filled their gullets with fish and their bowels with bread.

They trusted because they had tasted.

He'd insisted they go ahead without him. He'd promised to catch up, but nobody knew how. They had the boat. They had the crew. Jesus had nothing with him but his own two legs, not even an old donkey to plod the narrow path that skirted the lake. They took their time on the evening crossing, thinking they'd surely need to return and fetch this absent-minded rabbi.

As evening crept into the sky, the twinkling mischief of the day grew to an offended sea of growing crests and troughs. The last of the sinking sun wiped the smile of God from the water. The men dropped the mainsail and stowed their meager gear. They didn't like the hostile expression of the sky.

They spent the night bailing the boat, trying to keep the sea in the sea where she belonged. The relentless battering caused her to spin like a top. A few of them leaned white-knuckled over the side and fed to the fish the contents of a miraculous dinner. Even in fear, Peter smiled to himself. "All fish return to the sea," he muttered, remembering his graying father saying the same.

By wee morning, they were clinging to gnarled ropes and oars and the hope of the coming sun. They rowed and rowed their boat, and they were no closer to either shoreline. The hour grew darker than ever, and with it the sea. The skiff rose and sank, matching the rhythm of waning belief. Peter wondered why Jesus had sent them on, if this was some test from an eccentric schoolmaster.

It was with those questions that he first spotted something

odd in the water. No, it was something odd *on* the water. It was too small to be a vessel. What kind of sea creature could swim upright? The others saw it, too, and a common scream of terror and wonder leaped from the boat and was carried off by the hungry wind.

They stared hard into the distance. It looked like a bearded man, crowned with sea spray, billowing with wind-whipped robes like a sail. Someone cried out, "It's Neptune!" and they all howled with fright and disbelief.

So much for orthodoxy.

As the god came nearer, they saw that he meant to pass them on their stern. He hadn't even looked in their direction. Peter squinted against the salty bite of wind. He'd know that profile anywhere.

"It's the Lord!" Peter bellowed, standing so fast that he knocked his head on an unsecured oar that slammed against the gunwale in a wild drumbeat. When he looked again, Jesus was looking back. He couldn't discern the expression in the dark, but Jesus's eyes were glowing with a piercing question.

The figure called out to them, speaking their names as one who knew them. It sounded like him. It looked like him. They couldn't know for sure.

"If it's really you, then ask me to come to you," Peter heard himself shout. He wished afterward that he'd just kept his flapping trap shut.

"*Come on then,*" Jesus replied, as if inviting Peter for an evening's leisure stroll.

Steadying himself with an oar, he balanced on the rocking lip of their skiff. The breath before he jumped, he wondered what he was doing. He was suspended above himself, watching the whole moment and yet unable to intervene.

When he leaped, he expected immersion. What he got was glistening earth, so solid it jarred his knees and knocked the breath from his lungs. He looked at Jesus, then back at the boys, then back at Jesus, a huge Peter-grin splitting his face in two. He roared with laughter. Jesus roared back. He picked up one foot and stomped it down as a test. He didn't even make a puddle's splash.

He started to walk toward the laughing Jesus, one surreal step at a time. He was halfway there when he felt the pulsating current beneath his feet. One gnarly wave rolled between them, and for a moment, he lost sight of Jesus.

Seeing was always believing. He mistrusted what supported his enormous frame. Just as if the ground had dropped away, he felt emptiness beneath his feet and seawater choking his throat.

"*Help!*" he coughed as he surfaced.

In the next moment, he was grabbed with a steel grip and found himself standing beside God-Made-Flesh. He was completely dry.

> Jesus didn't hesitate. He reached down and grabbed his hand. Then he said, "*Faint-heart, what got into you?*"
>
> Matthew 14:31–32

When Peter jumps from the boat into the water, we see a man ready to reverse his own capacity for doubt. He leaped from the safe womb of a wooden skiff into the volatile belly of a thrashing sea storm. We see someone impetuous but also willing to risk trust. Peter did a very brave and very strange thing in a vote of God-confidence. What were his actions if not trust in this gravity-defying Son of Man? But Jesus's reprimand of Peter seems disproportionate, harsh even.

Jesus's response surprises us, because it is not how we would respond. The response of God's Son is not directed toward Peter's glorious and impulsive moment of faith. He focuses in dogged determination on the doubt plaguing Peter's heart about the goodness of God.

He wants to address not the trust we possess, but the trust that we've lost.

In the addressing, his strategy is most unexpected. His rescue came with a question.

SURPRISED BY QUESTIONS

Meek and mild Jesus. The stained-glass portrait of a simpering Savior, wearing a lamb upon his shoulders as a woman might wear a mink stole. Jesus—eternally patient, forever unflappable. We, too, may have some misplaced expectations about the Messiah we've got.

What he asked Peter is difficult and *seems* impatient, with a tone that would alarm the symbolic lamb from his shoulders. If we listen intently, we hear with surprise that he is addressing all his disciples.

He is questioning the current-caught church. He is questioning you and me.

"Where is your faith?"

Like Peter, as Christians we still have not escaped this capacity for mistrusting the heart of God. None of us can. We see this in the frustration of John the Baptist. The first prophet in four hundred years, this mouthpiece of Yahweh did not expect the Messiah he got. In the wake of misunderstanding, mistrust came to dwell in this New Testament prophet.

> John, meanwhile, had been locked up in prison. When he got wind of what Jesus was doing, he sent his own disciples to ask, "Are you the One we've been expecting, or are we still waiting?"
>
> Matthew 11:2–3

Even John, the locust-eating Baptizer, had the capacity to ask from a place of doubt lodged deep in his hairy breast.

As much as we'd like, let's not make doubt into something mental, some deficiency of our doctrine. The solution to wrong doctrine is simply more self-sufficiency. We study harder, we read more, but the problem lies much deeper, within the soul.

What is authentic lack of faith but our hearts telling God that he is not trustworthy? That we will not believe him? More facts will not cure what ails us. Each one of us must be rescued from the relentless current of suspecting God of foul play.

When we continue to be carried along by mistrust, we are choosing rebellion against the Messiah we got. We are choosing to tell him he's not worthy—or *trust*worthy.

Let's call a spade a spade. Jesus does.

A.V.I.R. SYNDROME

We require rescuing. We cannot be children of God and adrift in this current of doubt and mistrust. The two are mutually exclusive in a world that hardens us, keeping us ignorant of our peril. Both the individual and the culture are in grave danger, and we don't realize what's coming next.

Drowning. We are drowning, leaving behind an ever-growing capacity for mistrust.

We were not designed for this current. Our legs were meant to walk, run even, on the firm ground of true faith, experiential faith. We were created to know in the core of our beings that the One who gave us breath and life is really, truly good. He is trustworthy. He desires, above all else, to have deep communion with each one of us in the current.

The invitation of the Gospel is to walk on firm footing, to give up this life of treading water, but we can't. We are in a state of drowning, hopelessly tangled in lines of clammy seaweed. We've made the sea our home, and to climb out and dry off would be too risky. Besides, we're not even sure we can. Our limbs don't work like they once did.

The irony is that we would fight any would-be rescue. Anyone who would jump into the water would inevitably drown as they tried to save us. We see this concept played out in the tragic scenarios of physical drowning statistics. Scientists and first responders name this high rate of double drownings and failed rescue attempts the aquatic victim-instead-of-rescuer, or A.V.I.R. syndrome. According to the *International Journal of*

Aquatic Research and Education, "Attempting an in-water rescue, especially by untrained bystanders, is notoriously dangerous with the significant likelihood of death."[3]

Our politicians cannot rescue us. Our celebrities and athletes cannot rescue us. Our pastors, ministers, and priests also cannot, for all are swimming in this current alike. We cannot put our trust in any of these, for none have the power to save. We are stuck as perilous companions in this ancient sea, and the rescue cannot come from any mortal drawing breath.

There are no heroes when the whole world is drowning. We end up dragging one another down.

What we need is Someone free of the water, Someone strong enough to pull us out of the current in which we're trapped.

AN INQUISITIVE CHRIST

Victims ensnared in this current cannot be convinced of personal trustworthiness by manipulation or persuasion. For God to enter our world, holding out his hands, shouting, "I AM not a liar!" won't work. Seeming evidence to the contrary is constantly flung in our faces. His shouts would only entrench us further into mistrust. Like Peter, we have a Savior who walks by us on the water, not assuming we're ready to stop treading.

A sledgehammer doesn't integrate hearts but shatters them. Compulsion never succeeds, and, frankly, is undesirable. Voluntary trust can never be forced. Belief cannot be demanded. To woo the frightened animal from the cage, once abused and cruelly betrayed by those meant to protect it, a different approach must be taken.

His methodology of resolution is curious. Once again, he shatters our paradigm as we drift toward disaster in the current. His tactic for dealing with the traumas and slight moments that have created this capacity for suspicion, doubt, and mistrust is clever and kind. A complex problem must be provided a complex solution.

How does God pursue the hearts of a culture that celebrates doubt and avoids pursuit?

He asks questions.

At all times, he sees the trust-to-mistrust ratio with laser accuracy. At all times, Jesus knows where our faith is. He knows where the doubts are, too. If mistrust has punched holes in our faith, an authentic encounter with the questioning Christ will quickly make the holes known. He knows it better than we do, but he invites us to observe the nature and true placement of our faith by asking us questions. It is in his severe mercy that he exposes doubt in us. He is jealous for our whole hearts, all our trust. He is passionate to rescue our hearts from this posture. He pursues us with a holy and fierce pursuit, and he wants our faith to rest in him alone.

Jesus is the only One ever to live without this capacity for mistrust. In all times, and in all ways, he never stuck one toe in that dizzying current. Yet he doesn't observe our plight from a safe distance. He sees us and is overcome by what he sees. He knows we are struggling with wanting to trust. He understands we've been betrayed by all but him.

He walks on the water toward the scene of our sinking, offering us questions that still the waves crashing on our heads. With the current under his feet, he experiences with us the current's strength without being submerged. He feels the mighty pull and swift movements that threaten to take everyone he loves far from him. But we must remember—the current is *under* his feet in submission to his authority.

He will stop at nothing. He's the only One who can rescue. He commands that the waves hush and the breakers still so his voice can be heard above the rushing din and chaos of our times and the times of every wave of humanity. He is saying something, something crucial, it turns out, for our rescue. If we lean in and listen very closely, we can hear something with waterlogged ears over the crying wind. We can hear what it is that proceeds from the curious mouth of God.

We hear questions—many, many questions.

"Where is your faith?" he asks each one of us—literally. Where? Where has our ability to trust wandered?

I'm afraid it's been swept out to sea.

Jesus wants to recover our lost trust, and he chooses questions in service of this recovery. We have an Inquisitive Christ, and his questions are a matter of life and death.

FOR CONTEMPLATION AND DISCUSSION

Lectio Divina Exercise:

Place yourself in the boat with Peter and the disciples. What are you thinking as you push off with a stomach full of miraculous abundance? Watch the sun sink and the clouds gather. Imagine the rising sensation that things are out of your control in this boat. At the height of your fear, you see Jesus walking on the water. What does this gravity-defiance look like? Do you want to go to him, or do you want to stay in the boat? What happens if you dare step into the sea with Peter? What does the water feel like as you lose faith? Look up as you see his face above the water, rescuing you from being sucked down by the current.

For Reflection:

1. Think back to your formative years. How did those in power reinforce the message of mistrust?
2. We all experience slight moments like Macy's. What are some of yours?
3. What are your thoughts about similarities between first-century Jews and our present culture?
4. Looking ahead to Jesus's rescue strategy, why do you think he asks questions? What is it about questions that speaks to the human heart?
5. What is your answer to Jesus's question: *"Where is your faith?"*

CHAPTER TWO

"Do You Not Yet Understand?"

Recognizing the Soul's Need for Questions

"Why do you confuse the issue?
Why do you talk without knowing what you're talking about? . . .
Let me ask the questions. You give the answers."

—Yahweh,
Job 38:2; 42:4

It is better to debate a question without settling it
than to settle a question without debating it.

—Joseph Joubert,
The Notebooks of Joseph Joubert, 1883

In the beginning, God asked no questions.

No veil he wore, God-in-Three laughed intimacy and roared wonder, never hiding his face from loving companions. The knowing union gathered conversation as flowers, pistils open to sunlight.

Father, Son, and Spirit, in spinning unanimity of inspired will, purposed as One to create something good. *Very* good. The Father spoke. The Son wore the Father's Word like a perfectly tailored suit. The Spirit brooded over the deep in divine aviation.

Land and sea locked arms, never resisting the gracious boundaries instructed them. Flora and fauna played on the surface of anything that would hold still. Fish and fowl spun in lively arcs across the canvases of blue and green. Legs prospered—creatures with legs that could jump, gallop, and climb tested every shining possibility of movement.

Man. Woman. The same and yet not.

Fresh from the earth, the baptism of dust sprinkled from their hair. Breathing deep into their lungs, they still tasted God's life-sparking kiss on their lips. The earliest vision their eyes beheld was not one another. Upon humanity's awakening, they first saw the glad smile of God.

As the sun waned pinkish light over Eden's treetops, they walked, the two with the Three, deep in conversation. They spoke to one another with full-faced openness. This sacred honeymoon, replete in delight, savored each moment of new discovery.

There was wonder. There was discovery. Still, there were no questions—not in the mouth, nor in the heart. The man and the woman drank great draughts of heaven revealed. They romped among God and the illumined playground of creation. They were content, as a lover is content in the beloved's arms.

It did not last.

The primordial question in all recorded history crept serpentine onto the happy scene. The first uncertainty uttered into our emerald world, glittering with fresh existence. The question was birthed with rasping breath, the breath that clouded vaporous confusion into the face of beautiful Eve. He opened his pungent mouth, all creation watching in distress.

"Did God actually say," the serpent tickled into the fair maiden's auricle, "'You shall not eat of any tree in the garden'?" (Genesis 3:1, ESV).

The beauty had never been questioned before. Only the welcoming certainties of an approachable God had touched her ear. The One who treaded in evening's coolness summoned no doubt.

With the question, hesitation came rushing into the heart of Eve. Misgivings entered. The question cast smoky silhouettes on the goodness of God-with-Us.

She looked around her at all the trees, burdened with glistening crop. She *had* eaten of the trees. She had done so in his presence. God would often choose for them the very best fruit to satisfy his hungry children. Their meals with him were a laden table of varied tastes.

All at once, she wondered if her feasting had indeed been *good*.

As she wondered, she saw the serpent's eyes float to a fixed point over her shoulder. She turned to see what caught his unblinking gaze. It was the One Forbidden Tree. The beast's uttered question rapidly spawned others in Eve's breast. She found herself standing next to the one tree. Caressing its silver bark, she looked upon it as she'd never looked at Adam, lusting after its secrets.

She plucked. She tasted. She watched as her quiet husband did the same.

How could she describe what she now saw? In a fantastic flash, the well-lit world around her swooned into dark shadow. She saw the naked body of the man. He saw hers. Their faces burned red, hands hurrying to cover what God had given and blessed. She saw before her not a lithe serpent but some dark creature, sick and rotting with evil malcontent.

The two now belonged to the question of Genesis 3. The question had bought their souls.

QUESTIONS: A BRIEF HISTORY

We all belong to the question. It haunts us.

It possesses us, pressing us toward what we will never achieve: complete knowledge. We crave total eradication of doubt, so we work to force subjugation of all questions to that aim. Questions are wolves—powerful, hungry, wild things. We seek to domesticate them like the family dog.

We sense the danger of questions. We've tasted our submission to them, and, like the Tower of Babel, we try to mold them into building blocks back to paradise.

No one knew how to do this better than Socrates. After staying long in the shadows, he brought questions into the public square and handed them a megaphone. Socrates made questions the property of the learned elite.

Most modern researchers agree that this ancient educator was something of an enigma, in both philosophy and appearance. Although an Athenian and an academic, he grew long locks like the Spartan soldier. He wore the rumpled, sweaty clothes in which he slept. According to *The Stanford Encyclopedia of Philosophy*, historians have described him as "profoundly ugly, resembling a satyr more than a man."[1] They continue,

> He had wide-set, bulging eyes that darted sideways and enabled him, like a crab, to see not only what was straight ahead, but what was beside him as well; a flat, upturned nose with flaring nostrils; and large fleshy lips like an ass. Socrates went about barefoot and unwashing, carrying a stick.[2]

Despite this, Socrates is given a seat of honor in the philosophic pantheon. In the brilliant culture of ancient Greece, a culture that worshipped the pursuit of knowledge, he shocked the entire establishment, flipping current scholastic methodology on its Grecian head.

Instead of telling students what to think, he showed them how. He did this by asking questions—public questions—to the complete shock of the intellectual elite. Socrates's new method emphasized the art of rhetoric, applauding critical thinking within debate. He began with a broad inquiry and then, like a master fly fisherman, gradually reeled in the mind with an ever-tightening line of questions.

Socrates, a contemporary of Old Testament Nehemiah, was among the first to teach the world how to bridle the question to the service of man.

His method wasn't warm. Debra Nails writes, "He was known for confusing, stinging and stunning his conversation partners into the unpleasant experience of realizing their own ignorance."[3] The questions of Socrates were weapons, weapons that drew blood.

Despite this, the Socratic method has taught students of all ages to make friends with the question. In the fourth grade, I asked my teacher how to spell the word "ridiculous." Mrs. Drake simply pointed to the thick, green dictionary on her bookshelf. I groaned inwardly, thinking how much easier it would be for her to just tell me the right answer. I even muttered under my breath, "This is *ridiculous*," as I hauled the book over to my desk.

It took awhile to find. I scanned the "re-" pages for quite some time before I realized "ridiculous" would not be there. It took even longer to discover there was no letter "q" in the word at all. When my finger finally found it, there was a shrill sense of triumph. I copied the word into my fourth-grade essay, discussing Roald Dahl's villain Ms. Trunchbull in *Matilda*. I closed the book with satisfaction and marched it to my teacher's shelf.

"Did you find it?" she asked.

I told her I did.

"How *do* you spell 'ridiculous'?" she asked.

I spelled it aloud.

She smiled that knowing half smile, the one only fourth-grade teachers possess, and said, "Now you'll never forget."

And Mrs. Drake was right. That journey to the shelf and back, lugging the physical burden of enclosed knowledge, opening its musty pages—it all began with a very simple question. If she had acquiesced, the journey launched by the question would have ended. I can guarantee I would have misspelled "ridiculous" on the next essay—most likely with a "q." Years of experience had taught her that, and so Mrs. Drake allowed me to wrestle my own question until I could discover my own answer.

We dig deeper, we learn more when we are challenged to tame questions for our own benefit. This is what fallen humanity attempts: the conquest of all uncertainty. Socrates championed this quest. "I know you won't believe me," writes Socrates, "but the highest form of Human Excellence is to question oneself and others."

Socrates was right—we don't believe him. We still mistrust questions. We also mistrust answers. We remember from our first parents that questions are not tame. They need to be handled with caution and due respect.

Socrates discovered this with bitterness as he drank the sour hemlock. Accused of "corrupt[ing] the youth" of Athens, he was sentenced to death by poisoning.[4] His life ended in desperation, once again enslaved to the primordial question. The questions he once owned were now pointed like arrows toward his breast.

He, like Eve and Adam, lost his paradise.

The Genesis 3 question, the accusation against God's good intentions, is still wreaking havoc a billion times over each day.

THE STORY OF QUESTIONS

Questions are a constant force in a careening world. They contain raw power—power to harm, power to bless. They are the oxygen of dialogue, existing in each breath. A conversation with no questions becomes a stagnant pond. When we observe our daily language, we notice that questions are favored darlings in any interaction. Questions punctuate the air around us, fluttering into our conversations like moths to light. Questions are the threads that connect a disconnected society. They enter our lives as quiet reminders of humanity's imperfect knowledge.

The world is a crammed closet, filled with questions. We cannot open our doors without being dealt a blow from a toppled question.

Humanity is intimately linked to question, for good and for ill. It is in our earliest history, burned into our souls with permanent branding. There's something innate about our need to question and be questioned. We cannot survive without it. Think of all that exists because of the question. Any scientific discovery, any technological advancement, any relationship of depth has occurred because someone asked a question. Both the atomic bomb and the cure for smallpox hinged upon the reality of inquiry. The Internet exists because someone asked strategic questions.

Literature reflects our connection with inquiry. Plots are driven by the question mark, signaling narrative change like a new wind. Sometimes, the questions initiate positive change in the protagonist. In *The Hobbit*, Bilbo had rejected the dwarves' invitation to burglary and was sitting down to his second breakfast when Gandalf burst onto the scene.

"My dear fellow," said the Grey Pilgrim, "whenever *are* you going to come?"[5]

Victor Hugo applied questions in *Les Misérables* to introduce his protagonist to God. Found sleeping on a bench, the former convict is awakened by a curious old woman.

> "What are you doing there, my friend?"
> He replied harshly, and with anger in his tone: "You see, my good woman, I am going to sleep."
> "Upon the bench?" said she.
> The good woman touched the man's arm and pointed out to him on the other side of the square, a little low house beside the bishop's palace.
> "You have knocked at every door?" she asked.
> "Yes."
> "Have you knocked at that one there?"[6]

And with those questions, a lifelong prisoner was set free.

But not all stories have a happy ending.

In literature, the power of questions can be wielded for harm. Authors use them as weapons against their characters. Some stories ask destruction, questions triggering violence and hatred, fear and accusation. Some even elicit death. In *Romeo and Juliet*, Shakespeare cruelly allows his male protagonist to be tricked by his love's sleep. In believing her dead, Romeo drinks poison, intending to join her in undying love. When Juliet awakes, it is with questions of dread.

> What's here? A cup, closed in my true love's hand?
> Poison, I see, hath been his timeless end.—

O churl, drunk all, and left no friendly drop
To help me after?[7]

Cruel questions are the hands that press the dagger into youthful heart.

It is with story that we have tried to express what is planted deep in our own hearts—that questions matter. We are an inquisitive species, and inquiry is the lingua franca of humanity.

BEDTIME QUESTIONS

Parents understand this constant query, for our minutes and hours can be measured by questions asked and answered, ticking as fixed hands on a clock. My daughters are professional inquirers—particularly at bedtime. Their strategy has become predictable.

They each have a cup of water by their beds. They've gone through their stack of books. The room has dimmed and nightlights glow. I have sung a favorite lullaby. My husband, Jimmy, has prayed. They are snug under covers. We've kissed their foreheads, both cheeks, and the tips of their noses. We bless and remind them of our love. We turn to back away from their bunk beds—slowly, like tourists on an African safari, retreating from a pride of feeding lions. All is quiet as a praying church.

Here enters the question.

"Mom?" squeaks a tiny voice.

We don't answer, but we delay our departure for just a millisecond. That's all they need. They smell the hesitation and one of them pounces.

"I just have one question."

"No more questions," I answer, sounding like a politician.

"It's just one little question."

"No more."

"But I'll forget it if I don't ask it now."

"No. Ask me in the morning."

"Please?"

Jimmy or I will try to escape the mauling, leaving the other remorselessly behind to deal with our clever, disobedient daughter and her one little question. They know they've gotten us. One parent is still in the room, and that is what they wanted all along. I have to admit—their questions are *hilarious.*

"Can I have a turtle?"

"How come gum is sticky?"

"Does God ever have to sneeze?"

But sometimes, the questions are quite classic: "Why do I have to go to bed? I'm not tired."

It's almost worth the whole ordeal just to see what odd question they've concocted to prevent bedtime.

Regardless of their ingenuity, we have a hostage situation on our hands. Questions are the captors, brandished weapons held in the fists of little girls. We all find ourselves hostages to questions more often than we'd like, beginning with the one in the Garden.

"Did God actually say...?"

With his asking, Satan bullied us into reproaching God for holding out. This doubt is embedded in so many other questions. We don't always realize this. When Eve fell prey to the serpent's suggestion, her progeny became intricately connected to all damaging inquiries. We belong to him *and* his question.

All the snake's questions create distance between Creator and creature. They also erect barriers between ourselves and others. Implicit mistrust lingers in the air between us like the stench of rotten eggs. We can't go anywhere without it burning our eyes and choking us.

But Genesis 3 does not end with the serpent.

Before his fatal question, good questions were already flooding the good heart of God. The question mark—poised for rescue—poured forth from the mouth of the most brilliant mind in the universe. Before Satan, Someone else had inquiry at the ready.

The first question initiated the fall of all humankind. The

second, like a fierce warrior, exploded into the Garden, intent on the redemption of all that was lost.

THE SECOND QUESTION

They waited in the brush, dread sinking in their bellies with the sun. He looked not at her face but her feet. Those perfect feet, five digits each—perfectly able to walk, run, and leap for joy. Tears fell to the ground next to unshod toes. Eve's face remained hidden behind a lilac branch. In her despair, the fragrant flowers bloomed invisible to eyes and nose.

Would God come? They didn't know what they hoped. The hearts of male and female were infested with questions and doubt.

The evening slipped quietly above the trees. Early stars, usually singing, looked in silence upon darkening Eden. A soft, warm rain like tears melted into the supple ground. Eve wanted to reach out to her husband, to find his strong arm to still her trembling. But Adam's face was not for her—only his back, turned and covered in the curving foliage of the fig tree. She looked at his profile and knew him no longer.

The serpent, coiled and gleaming, stared at the woman from across the garden. His eyes were a violation, and she sensed that protection was needed against his ill intent.

All at once, footsteps trod the orchard path. They could feel the ground vibrate beneath their squatting frames. Instinct screamed at them to hide—to go lower, deeper. If they could have burrowed into the earth from whence they came like groundhogs, they would have wept in relief. But their hands were designed for cultivating and creating, for caressing. They were not diggers.

They heard his breath. They felt Presence. They cowered in fear, arms covering fragile skulls, symbolically protecting the newfound knowledge of good and evil.

He had come indeed.

How fickle their memory before the fruit! If they could but remember his affection, his laughter, his kind face—but the question had obscured everything but the tyranny of shame. They prepared for his hot wrath to fall on their heads.

The noise of all but the Breath stopped. Every animal, every flower, even the waves stilled before the Breath.

What happened next they could never predict. No gifted author could write such a plot twist. They expected anger. They deserved punishment.

What they got was God's question.

"Where are you?" he called out in their direction. They could hear the lament in his voice.

The Great Questioner had entered their disgrace. The face of God sought their own, and the face of God was wet with tears.

THE GOD-WHO-ASKS

Genesis 3 tells the world's most important story. In one epic chapter the whole Gospel dwells.

We're invited to witness a Triune Godhead, three distinct Beings integrated in intimate union. No questions are recorded between Father, Son, and Spirit. There were no hidden secrets between the Three. Their knowing of one another's hearts, minds, and wills was complete.

Likewise, when God invited Adam and Eve into this fellowship, there was unbroken intimacy, full disclosure between God and man. In this environment of rich knowing, the tree of the knowledge of good and evil stood irrelevant. Apart from the serpent, there was nothing the tree could offer that the humans lacked. What we as humans desired to know was *already* known.

We knew God himself.

Into an unblemished creation, the serpent's question introduced a distance, a canyon no fallen human could traverse. His question was a weapon aimed at the soul of innocence, and that soul was pierced. Disorder replaced stability. Mistrust of God with clenched talons gripped their hearts and the hearts of all their children. The original question of the universe tricked us into believing we didn't know enough, that we didn't have access to the critical knowledge we needed to survive. With Satan's suggestion, we drank the cloudy water of mistrust. We believed there was more than what was being offered.

Satan gloated in triumph, but in his evil glee, he forgot something crucial. He forgot that God, too, could question, but his would be different. His questions would never introduce chaos but always clarity. Into this wreckage of broken relationship and squandered knowing, God entered with asking.

The second question, asked by God of his children, offered to restore something lost with the first. It offered to restore our ability to know God. From this moment on, the questions of God pursue the fallen soul of man. The next three exchanges in Genesis 3 between God and leaf-covered humanity are questions.

"Who told you that you were naked?" (3:11, ESV).

"Have you eaten of the tree of which I commanded you not to eat?" (3:11, ESV).

"What is this that you have done?" (3:13, ESV).

Though mournful in tone, God's questions remain open, vulnerable even. They seek something worth finding. They seek the lost and broken heart of humankind.

"Where are you?" God asked (3:9).

God wasn't confused. He was not playing hide-and-seek with naughty children. He didn't ask because he didn't know. He knew. He knows still.

We can be certain that God always knows where we are. Psalm 139 is a song spilling over to God's eyes that always see our location—both physical and spiritual.

You know when I leave and when I get back;
I'm never out of your sight...
Is there anyplace I can go to avoid your Spirit?

To be out of your sight?
If I climb to the sky, you're there!
If I go underground, you're there!
If I flew on morning's wings
to the far western horizon,
You'd find me in a minute—
you're already there waiting!
Then I said to myself,
"Oh, he even sees me in the dark!"

Psalm 139:3, 7–11

He knows exactly where we are at all times. He asked the first couple and continues to ask us because he intends to do something vital in the asking.

It is *we* who no longer know where we are. We are adrift, and all we see around us is an endless sea of doubt. We look around and haven't a clue as to our whereabouts, our belonging.

His question is the first step back into the holy knowing we were given from the start.

From Genesis 4 to Revelation 21, the whole of scripture presents a God who asks. God questions Cain, the enraged and murdering son of Adam, *"Why are you angry, and why has your face fallen?"* (Genesis 4:6, ESV).

To Jacob, *"What's your name?"* (Genesis 32:27).

With Job, God can't stop asking questions. It goes on for chapters.

He asks Moses *"And who do you think made the human mouth? And who makes some mute, some deaf, some sighted, some blind? Isn't it I, GOD?"* in Exodus (4:11).

In the famous encounter with King Solomon, one with which Socrates himself was probably familiar, God asks Israel's young king: *"What can I give you?"* (1 Kings 3:5).

From the great throne room of heaven, he poses a question to Isaiah: *"Whom shall I send? Who will go for us?"* (Isaiah 6:8).

To Jonah, God asks the question: *"What do you have to be angry about?"* (Jonah 4:4).

Then gradually, we notice that this curious God of ours has gone quiet. For four hundred years, the questions are silenced, and we are left waiting and wondering, praying for rescue.

THE SAVIOR-WHO-ASKS

Suddenly breaking a four-hundred-year hush with angelic concerts and royal pilgrims, questions burst back onto the scene with a crying baby. The advent of Jesus introduces a young-yet-ageless rabbi who won't stop asking.

Into the breathless void, the Serpent-Crusher of Genesis 3 wraps himself in coverings much like Adam and Eve—only his covering is the skin and bone of humanity, and he has no shame to hide. The Son of the God-Who-Asks moved into this warped garden to free us from the tyranny of doubt and questions, and his method is unexpected. We belong to the enemy's question. Our hearts are held captive to the mistrust of God.

He frees us from the one fatal question with *hundreds* of questions—Gospel questions.

Christ's first conversation in scripture is as pre-teen God. Like all teenagers, he is full of questions for his worried parents, parents who'd spent the better part of two days searching for their missing son.

> *"Why were you looking for me? Didn't you know that I had to be here, dealing with the things of my Father?"*
>
> Luke 2:49

This first question launches a life of asking. He asks more than three hundred questions, recorded by four unique authors. Jesus was never tricked by the serpent's question. He lives and breathes full trust in God. It is with this perfect trust and his asking that he redeems the effects of the fall, beginning with the heart of it: the question.

His first time speaking with John's disciples, Jesus introduces himself with a question. He questions the Pharisees and Temple priests. He questions the governing officials. He questions the leper, the beggar, the prostitute. He asks questions from the agony of the Cross. He even asks questions post-Resurrection— many times.

Jesus is still asking questions today. He loves questions, and with that love, we are now released. Our Liberator is the Inquisitive Christ.

Questions always lead us somewhere. Either they lead to mistrust and doubt, or they lead us to the source of truth. Our mistrust doesn't frighten Jesus. He not only rescues us from doubt, but he also engages with us *in* it. He uses questions as instruments—for our healing and for his glory.

Questions are meant to be sifted and measured against what truly owns our hearts. His questions are always meant to uncover what we've tried to hide with our own fig leaves. He understands that questions are painful, but he also knows what questions do for us. A statement of fact immediately forces us to defend our position. Lectures encourage a hasty stance. Internally, we feel pressured to either agree or disagree with what we've been told.

A question, however, playfully disarms. Even the Sermon on the Mount, the most famous of Jesus's "lectures," is peppered with questions designed for one purpose: to invite us into our own souls. For that is what his question does—it invites. It invites the truth of our hearts' reality to be told.

His question washes over our souls like a spring rain, cleansing the palate of both mind and heart to receive truth. In pursuit of our fearful hearts, Jesus gently sneaks past our natural defenses and probes into our depths. He craves what he designed— intimacy with a whole and holy heart.

He is the God of conversational intimacy. He asks because he wants to sit with us and talk. He uses the question to begin a conversation, eager to hear what we communicate to him from our hearts. Often, one question gives birth to others, and the conversation continues to the delight of both God and man.

Jesus befriends and welcomes the question, and he invites us to do the same. He doesn't invite as Socrates invited—for questions to harm or be manipulated in selfish use. He invites as One who has made all questions safe under his kingly authority. With God's pursuit of the heart of man, questions are now under submission to the One-Who-Asks like the seawater forever under his feet.

Jesus is asking a simple question: *"Do you not yet understand?"* (Mark 8:21, ESV).

He offers us the awareness we need regarding his intentions. After years of fearing his questions, we finally begin to understand that he uses them with everyone he loves. The road to salvation is paved with questions. It is trod by the Savior-Who-Asks.

THE RESURRECTION QUESTION

In the triumph of early light, the hillcrests glowed wet with gold. The bodies of the entombed dead were shut within the rocks. A woman cried quiet tears for her missing Lord. The mouth of the cave yawned in mockery, its emptiness a cruel joke.

Where was his body? Why was the tomb empty?

Questions buzzed about her face like flies, stinging with their doubt.

The perfumed oils she carried weighed heavy in weak hands. She sat down on a rock to think, her back to the open grave, and dropped the vials with a thud in the grass. She tried to make sense of the questions. She tried to answer the questions.

She was choking on the questions.

Before he had come, she had armed herself with brittle inquiry, using it as a steel breastplate to cover a heart long bloodied by the world of greed. After, however—after that first moment he strode into her life, giving her the gifts of freedom and innocence without demanding payment—questions had changed. He taught her to give him the daggered doubt lodged in her soul.

He taught her to love *his* questions.

But he was gone now. All of those gifts went away with his stolen body.

Movement entered the periphery of vision. She strained to see who it was, but it was the way the light fell on the Man's face. She did not know him.

He moved closer, startling the mourning woman with a question.

"Woman, why do you weep?"

John 20:15

She'd never heard a more foolish question in all her life.

But his question was not foolish. His question was laughter. His question was the arrival of April after a lifelong winter. By asking her why she wept, he returned Mary to the place of Eve. He returned her to the tears of all humanity. He bid her look one final time upon the question that scarred and scorched a perfect earth with perfect creatures.

And with the rising of the sun, he exploded that question into a million fragments.

The first question of a Resurrected God destroyed the curse of the original question forever. This is the Resurrection power of the God-Who-Asks.

It is with asking that he introduces himself to us. It is with asking that he invites us to draw closer. God's open invitation to know him stands before us. He wants us to understand why he asks us questions. In this understanding, we can enter his asking without fear.

The questions that Jesus asked in the Gospels are for us. They speak into the chaotic, world-weary culture in which we live. They were relevant when first asked. They are still relevant today, and they will stay relevant until questions are no longer necessary.

We can trust the questions of Jesus, and we can trust the Questioner. As we hear the Gospel questions, Jesus is inviting us to begin the journey back to knowing him, back to the Garden.

We only need the courage to answer "yes."

FOR CONTEMPLATION AND DISCUSSION

Lectio Divina Exercise:

Enter into the perfect Garden of Genesis 3. What do you see as you look around? What is it like to walk and talk with the Trinity? Watch as the serpent enters, introducing the first question. Feel the weight of what he suggests. How do you respond? Once the fruit is eaten, how does the world around you change? How do you change? In what manner do you anticipate God's arrival into the Garden? What does his face look like as he asks, "*Where are you?*" What rises up in response to his question?

For Reflection:

1. Look at the list of Jesus's questions in the Appendix. Do any of his questions stand out to you? Why do you think so? Journal your experience as you sit with this question.
2. Where is the fatal question still at work in your life? What questions linger in your heart that encourage you to mistrust God?
3. What are your thoughts about the scene in Genesis 3? What do you think Adam and Eve experienced between the asking of the first and second questions?
4. Why do you think Jesus asked questions?
5. What is your answer to Jesus's question: "*Do you not yet understand?*"

PART II:

PUSHING AGAINST
THE NATURAL

CHAPTER THREE

"Why Are You Sleeping?"

Struggling with Spiritual Narcolepsy

"Our friend has fallen asleep. I'm going to wake him up."
—Jesus Christ,
John 11:11

You know you're in love when you can't fall asleep
because reality is finally better than your dreams.

—Dr. Seuss

There's something so unnatural when the hero of the story falls asleep in the middle of the conflict. So many of the great tales include the allegory of slumbering villainy—the poppy scene in *The Wizard of Oz*, the sleeping nobles at table in *The Voyage of the Dawn Treader*, and, of course, the prick of the spindle in *Sleeping Beauty*. The protagonist needs to fight the battle, to devise a game-changing strategy, but instead, the hero gets tricked into sleep. From early youth, children are taught by these tales the dangers of premature and prolonged slumber. We learn from these common tales that if we are not on our guard, we, too, can fall prey to the sleep that descends in an instant.

As a small child, I was drawn to Washington Irving's classic story "Rip Van Winkle." I had an older edition, oversized watercolor illustrations weaving the tale more vividly than words. Rip Van Winkle slept and slept, lying exposed and vulnerable to the elements and changes of time. He stayed as dormant as a tree in perpetual winter, uncaring that the American Revolution was being fought in the hills below him. I remember wishing I could reach into those pages and wake Rip, ending the dreadful nightmare of untimely sleep.

The most climactic moment in the reading came when I turned to the painting of a freshly woken Rip Van Winkle. In twenty years' time, he had become a confused old man, wild-eyed with a long, scraggly beard, nesting with squirrels. The imagery of his physical change during hibernation burned into my developing mind. I was both fascinated and horrified by the idea of a man who could fall asleep—not for a night, but decades.

I would ask for this story often, inviting it to disrupt something in my childlike common sense that knew a man should not sleep when he's supposed to be awake. In my impressionable imagination, I wondered if his fate could be real. My parents had great difficulty tucking me in for bed after reading that story. Eventually, they stopped allowing "Rip Van Winkle" before bedtime. But still, I was left wondering—was it possible to live an entire adult life asleep like Rip Van Winkle or Briar Rose? Could that happen to me?

Unfortunately, his fate wasn't as fictional as I had hoped. It is all too common to sleep through the important moments in life.

Proverbs 24 tells its own version of "Rip Van Winkle," and it does not have a happy ending:

> I passed by the field of a sluggard,
> by the vineyard of a man lacking sense,
> and behold, it was all overgrown with thorns;
> the ground was covered with nettles,
> and its stone wall was broken down.
> Then I saw and considered it;
> I looked and received instruction.
> A little sleep, a little slumber,
> a little folding of the hands to rest,
> and poverty will come upon you like a robber,
> and want like an armed man.
>
> Proverbs 24:30–34 (ESV)

This is the story of Rip Van Winkle. This is our story as well.

A STATE OF TORPOR

We are a population that struggles to stay awake. The Narco-lepsy Network estimates that this sleep disorder affects one in every 2,000 people in the United States.[1] Likewise, according to the American Sleep Association, 37.9 percent of adults have admitted to "*unintentionally* falling asleep" during meals, at work, driving their cars.[2]

Our culture is asleep at the wheel, both literally and figuratively.

This epidemic goes far beyond the physical, however. While our schedules and calendars have become busier, our interior lives have slowed to a crawl, slothlike and sluggish in our ability to stay alert. We're lethargic, lacking physical vitality. Sucking down Starbucks like gasoline, we are a tired, wired people.

Our physical fatigue stems from an exhaustion of the soul, the burden of striving we carry day after day. It plagues our hearts as acutely as it does our bodies. We find ourselves coasting through the day, not really present, not finding much joy. We lack energy for worship or talking with God. Problems and struggles look really dark and really ugly, hopeless even. In our striving, all we want is to go to the places that bring relief and a little bit of happiness, so we watch ourselves practice socially acceptable idolatry.

We can all feel it—that moment at the end of a long and tiring day in which we can't remember being conscious. The details are nothing but a blur. We wonder where we've been all day, and why we can't recall the beauty or pain in the midst of our daily grind.

This struggle to stay awake is the portrait of the soul. It represents the danger that is present on the level of spiritual reality. Why can't we stop sleeping through our moments?

We have separated from the source of life, and in doing so, we have fallen asleep on God.

Paul writes,

But make sure that you don't get so absorbed and exhausted in taking care of all your day-by-day obligations that you lose track of the time and doze off, oblivious to God. The night is about over, dawn is about to break. Be up and awake to what God is doing!

Romans 13:11

The night is over, Paul states, but to us it feels like the night is never-ending.

According to A *Dictionary of Zoology*, the animal kingdom has a term for this: torpor. This is the state of an animal that does not have the necessary resources available for survival, so physical processes begin to slow. The body temperature drops. The metabolism drops. Everything simply slows down. The only thing left for the creature is to drift ever so calmly into prolonged sleep.[3]

This state of torpor describes our spiritual lives.

As followers of Jesus, we aren't taking in the nourishment and rest for which we were designed. We lack energy and vitality. We lack life. In this void, we see hibernation as a better option than the hard work it takes to wrestle with and sincerely question our lack.

We are tired. We're tired of being tired. We need to return to the garden of the Gospels, for it is there we'll find Jesus, awake and asking us a question.

ASLEEP IN THE GARDEN

The night was a heavy cloak, touching every part of the disciples' exposed skin with an electric current of fear. The moon revealed only the shadowy movements of branches against an inked sky. The darkness was a feature of his face, one they'd never seen present before. Although the air was cool, there were clusters of sweat colliding on his forehead and beard. His neck was strained, his shrouded jaw was set tight. His eyes—the eyes that had always revealed peace, authority, passion—now showed something unfamiliar, something disturbing and desperate. It frightened them.

He addressed the group: "*Kathisate*"—*Sit here.*[4] He motioned to the grove of olive trees at the entrance of the garden. They sat, watching his every move. His eyes looked beyond them to something only he could see in the thickness of night.

"*I must pray,*" he murmured as if to himself.

He began to walk away but turned back. With gestures that conveyed impulse, he looked to Peter, then to the brothers—without words, they knew they were to follow him farther into the night, into a dark corner of the olive grove where they did not wish to go. They didn't want to see what would happen next.

They turned the corner behind a low stone wall, a thicket of shrubs and trees shielding the others from their sight. It was here, behind this wall, that God dropped to his knees, holding his stomach and groaning like a delivering heifer. The brothers took a step back without knowing they did. Peter knelt beside Jesus, concerned—"Rabboni?"

Jesus looked at Peter, the tears mingling with rouged sweat that beaded like pox on his brow. Jesus groaned again, and Peter dropped his eyes. With every fragment of his being, he wanted Jesus to stop. He wanted to take his Teacher by the shoulders and command him to snap out of it. To behave like the *Mashiach.*

But Jesus understood what Peter couldn't. Peter couldn't grasp that Jesus was *being* God—and that God was suffering to the point of death.

"*Meinate,*" Jesus whispered.[5] *Don't leave me. Be with me.*

"Of course, Rabboni," Peter returned, shaking in his fear.

Taking Peter's rocklike frame with one hand and the stone wall with the other, Jesus staggered to his feet and walked a few slow paces into the ever-gathering dark.

Peter, still on his knees, sat down and leaned his back and head against the rough wall. His hand rested on the hilt of his sheathed dagger. The Sons of Thunder joined him, one whispering to the other, "What was that about?" Their bewildered companion with large eyes shook his head in unknowing.

For a while, the three tried to watch for Jesus's return—and for a while, they did.

But one by one their waiting soured, and one by one, they closed their eyes to Jesus in sleep.

WHY ARE YOU SLEEPING?

This narrative of Jesus's last moments with his disciples is designed to steal our breath. The vulnerability of Jesus is piercing. It's confusing. This is God, is it not? His unabashed need comes across like a sucker punch in the gut. What can we do with a Jesus who seems—*stressed?* Desperate? Despairing?

This makes me profoundly uncomfortable. My first reaction is to minimize the theological awkwardness. However, before we find a way to cover the rawness of Jesus's behavior, we must consider the strong language conveyed by the Greek vocabulary.

We are told in Mark 14:33 that the look on the face of Jesus conveyed the state of being "thrown into a terror," from the Greek *ekthambeō* (ek-tham-beh´-o).[6] He was anguished, agonized to such a degree that the historical account includes details of a medical condition known as hematidrosis. Luke, both a man of science and a physician, indicated that Jesus was under such tremendous emotional and physical duress, he was literally sweating blood.

In the same verse, Jesus again verbalized to his friends that his state of being was *adēmoneō* (ad-ay-mon-eh´-o)—one of "immense distress, anguish, heaviness."[7] Of the three Greek verbs that convey the condition of depression, the NAS *New Testament Greek Lexicon* indicates that this verb bears the most weight.[8] On this night, on his knees before the Father, Jesus was depressed.

He tells his alarmed disciples that the reality of his divine soul is one of exceeding sorrow, from the adjective *perilupos* (per-il´-oo-pos).[9] With incredible candor, he shares with Peter, James, and John that his soul is *"very sorrowful, even unto death"* (Matthew 26:38, ESV).

Thrown into a terror. Immense distress. Heavy depression. Exceeding sorrow, *"even unto death."* It's almost as if the Word-Made-Flesh himself can't find the right words to express his depth of grief. The English translations can hardly keep up with the intensity of these words.

Matthew records that Jesus fell to the earth, his face pressed into the dirt, transparent in his need for the courage and strength to do the will of his Father.

This was unusual for this Man, and the oddness of the situation called for unequaled attention from his closest friends. The disciples had never encountered *this* Jesus. The Son of Man was many things before them—playful, clever, kind. He could handle a whip, the Pharisees, and the politicians. He could weep without shame. But *this* Jesus—this was new, a part of him they had not yet seen. In a moment of holy mystery, he needed them: their companionship in this terrible garden, their witness to his turmoil and vulnerability and incomprehensible suffering. This bleeding, prostrate Jesus was shocking. He was utterly unfamiliar to his best friends.

You'd think they'd stay awake. Wide awake—but they don't.

"When he came back to his disciples, he found them sound asleep" (Matthew 26:40).

Matthew pens these words, a haunting quality echoing in their simplicity. How long was Jesus praying? Thirty minutes? Fifteen? Five?

How long did they wait?

Written into three out of the four Gospel narratives, this succinct commentary offers us something profound. The apostles made sure their failure during Jesus's time of need would live forever in the annals of history. I can sense the writer, as he pens his account, wincing with unspeakable sorrow that he fell asleep in his Friend's dire need.

Jesus, hands and face wet from wiping the tears that surely poured out, staggered to the three, intoxicated with great sorrow. He finds them—not wide-eyed with fear and concern, but propped against tree trunks and walls, dozing through the cataclysmic clash of spiritual powers in the unseen world. Jesus found the disciples to whom he would entrust the Kingdom Among Us asleep while he was sweating blood.

The narrative holds its breath, inviting us to watch as Jesus bends down and gently shakes Peter, James, and John awake. Are they startled by the look on his face, trying to make sense of what's happening in the fringes of wakefulness? Do they even remember his request?

"*Don't leave me*," he had implored. But they did. They abandoned the Son of God in sleep.

"He found them asleep." I'm not sure there is any other verse in scripture that affects me quite like this one. I intimately know this failure, this abandonment of God. Jesus finds me sleeping so often.

It's such a simple request, really, to remain awake with Jesus, but there's almost none more difficult to honor.

They cannot avoid the question that Jesus asks:

"*Could you not watch for me one brief hour?*"

(Matthew 26:40, ESV)

I wish the Gospels had recorded their responses to Jesus. Did they try to make excuses? Did they apologize? Did they say nothing, their curly heads hanging with shame and regret?

Like them, we cannot avoid his pressing question. I want to know what to tell him. What can we possibly say in our defense? What *can* be said in answer to the grieving Jesus, the One who simply wants our company as we wait together for the Father's will to unfold?

CHOOSING NOT TO WAIT

I am no longer mad at my husband, Jimmy. I will begin my story here.

On this particular night, however—this long, brutal, intense night, I was very mad. Livid. Unreasonably enraged. What could cause such a response from a God-fearing woman who loves her husband?

Labor.

Laboring with our first child eighteen hours. Laboring through the night in an intimidating hospital room, sterile tools gleaming in the halogen light. Laboring to birth a baby with a fading husband by my side.

To me, it was obvious that his role was to stay constantly vigilant for ice chips and soothing music, anticipating all irrational whimsy. He was to be by my side, taking the brunt of my ranting and grunts and vomiting. He could let me crush the bones of his sweaty hand while I was sucked once again into the swirling vortex of the inexplicable sensation that is labor. He could let me do all the talking, yelling whatever wicked thing popped into my head.

He could stay with me in it for the long haul, and he did. He did all these things for me and more. He was my champion, my birth coach, my hero.

Even heroes, however, need to sleep.

With a labor that began at seven a.m. and was still far from over by the next morning's wee hours, we were both beyond our personal threshold of exhaustion. In between the exciting moments, Jimmy would naturally drift off to sleep.

He is a very heavy sleeper.

I think back to that night over a decade ago, remembering how extreme I was, shaking him and squeezing his face, yelling his name. He struggled to wake up and rejoin me coherently. This first-time father was grappling with the need for sleep and the desire to stay awake, just like the disciples. I wanted his companionship in a lonely and fearful moment. All he could respond with was desperately fighting the battle to stay present with me in it, and that was proving difficult.

Jesus is asking something similar of us.

He invites us to engage in some labor process with him. He offers us the chance to participate with him in the birth of our own healing, transformation, and wholeness. We'd rather sleep, however, than stay present.

We choose not to engage with Jesus where he is at work in our lives. It's much easier.

This narcolepsy of soul prompts us to ignore his request: *Stay with me.* He asks us to wait with him in the dark, and we choose not to. It's too painful. It's too frightening. It's too hard. We'd rather engage *anywhere* else. We find it better to be distracted by whatever brings us relief and anesthetizes us. Or sometimes, like the disciples, we are overcome with the suffering that is waiting with uncertain outcomes and simply pass out. In his account, Luke writes that Jesus went back to find the disciples asleep, "drugged by grief" (Luke 22:45).

Waiting is so painful. A good friend told me that the waiting process *feels* like abandonment. After a while—perhaps an "hour"—don't we just want to fall asleep to bypass the fury and helplessness of waiting with God?

Falling asleep looks so different for each of us. We are all tempted to numb ourselves rather than feel the suffering in waiting for something we need. We want to wait with Jesus, but far too often, the stress and strain of having to wait both *with* him and *upon* him cause us to slip back into a fitful sleep. This is not a nourishing sleep but the tossing, erratic sleep of those who aren't at rest.

Falling asleep when Jesus asks us to wait with him is among the most painful of spiritual failures. It's blowing it and blowing him off in the worst way.

THE FAILURE OF SLEEP

When our Macy was six months old, she received a most unexpected diagnosis. I had taken her for a routine checkup with her physician, and I watched with mounting alarm as the doctor ordered unfamiliar tests, asking me unusual questions about the development of our happy baby. She hesitated before saying that our daughter might have brain disabilities. She ordered further testing, made a referral to a pediatric specialist, and promised to call me as soon as the results returned.

For one week, we had to wait. We waited for test results to return. We waited for life to stop spinning like a chaotic top. We waited. And waited.

I sat by our daughter's crib for hours at night, watching her sleep, wondering what her life would be like with this diagnosis. I wondered what our lives as her parents would be like. I watched so many dreams I'd had for a healthy child slip away in an unfair reality. I was sick with fear, both named and unnamed. I was angry with God. Yet in the midst of all of this, I heard his invitation as clearly as the disciples had that night in the garden:

Meinate. Stay with me. Wait with me.

I couldn't. For that one week of hellish waiting, I tried absolutely everything to sleep through the uncertainty.

And I was successful.

I slept by inviting fear and worry to consume me, rejecting God's invitation to *stay* with him. I slept by binge-watching really sad movies. I slept by withdrawing, pushing away my husband. I slept by embracing with abandon the multitude of petty vices that promised me just a little relief. I didn't want to stay awake, and I didn't want to stay and wait with God.

All I wanted was to sleep through the pain.

When the week ended, and the test results came back conclusively negative for any form of brain abnormality, we wept. We wept with joy. We wept with utter relief. We wept with exhaustion. And I know that my tears were also tears of shame and regret.

I had fallen asleep when I could have stayed awake to see the glory of God come for me.

Without heaping shame, Jesus gently asked his question as only he can:

"Why are you sleeping? Could you not wait with me for one hour?"

EXHAUSTED DISCIPLES

This question lingered then and lingers still. This question asks something of us that's crucial to our lives with God. Jesus stays with this question, three times in three accounts.

He asked me. I heard him ask me once, and when I didn't answer, he asked again. Frankly, I thought it was a ridiculous question. Therefore, I responded to him out of self-defense and impatience. My internal censor couldn't stop the words from leaping up from a bitter throat and out a bitter mouth: "Why am I sleeping? Because I'm overwhelmed. Because I'm tired of waiting and watching with you for things to happen.

"Because I'm exhausted."

As I watched myself react to his question in this manner, something in me finally woke up. This question, like all his questions, is not ridiculous, no matter how many times it's asked. The question *is* fresh. It's asked strategically by a strategic God. It never stales, and it needs to be asked until we truly wrestle with our spiritual narcolepsy in life with God.

Jesus is insistent. He wants to know, and he won't relent.

As so often happens with Jesus's pursuit of our hearts, one question often leads to an awakening. It also leads to further inquiry. His next words followed logically:

"Why are you so exhausted?"

It's a good question, an important one. As his disciples, have we thought carefully about our answer? I know that when I experience this exhaustion that touches soul first, then creeps into my body, it's because of one, simple thing: I'm striving.

Somewhere, somehow, I have come to a quiet decision in my soul that I must make life work for myself. If good things are created for me, then it's because *I* will create them. If bad things are to be prevented, then it's because *I* will prevent them. I will push forward in my career, building bigger and better barns for myself. I will give my daughters a thoroughly enriching childhood. I will keep the romance alive in my marriage. I will make it all happen, because it is all up to me.

By default, we likewise teach the next generation to be striving narcoleptics like the one before. When we look around, we see evidence of an epidemic, the disease of drained and weary sleepwalkers, and yet we seem to keep straining against our exhaustion, grasping for more and more.

This is, of course, striving. It's a subtle and twisted agreement with the enemy. It is sin. And it is *exhausting*.

That word, "exhausted," is one we hear constantly. It comes from the Latin *ex*, "out," and *haurire*, "to draw (drain water)."[10] Exhaustion is a wringing-out of the soul, a draining of a vital source of life and refreshment. We are a wrung-out, exhausted people—exhausted families with exhausted marriages, children, and schedules. We experience stress more regularly than peace. When we are exhausted in this way, we lay heads on the pillow at night, and sometimes it's the first time that day we feel happy.

That is troubling.

There's a relief in finally crawling into bed and flipping the switch on exhaustion, a night's respite from our chronic fatigue that plagues both body and mind. We sense that our physical lives are being taxed, not working at their optimum. The constant tiredness begins to cause fatigue-induced physical symptoms and even illnesses. We also sense that our mental processes and decision-making are impaired. Our brains just don't work quite right when we're exhausted.

Lest we forget, sleep is good. We work hard during our days and want to enjoy a night of rest. Our bodies and souls were designed to enter into the cyclical rhythm of slumber and wakefulness. This rest is a gift from God. The scriptures teach us that God gives restorative sleep to his people. It's necessary and healthy. This gift is offered in generous abundance to us each and every day.

The exhaustion we carry, however, is bigger than simply needing a good night's sleep. When we awake to find we haven't escaped our waiting exhaustion, it's almost too much to bear. We need rest. We can feel it, and that feeling goes really deep.

When we're tired day after day, we have a tired life. We need to be woken up from this vicious cycle of restless sleep and obsessive striving.

Once again, we need the God-Who-Awakens.

AWAKENING TO COMPLEXITY

We are left with the questions: What can be done? What does Jesus do with our consistent inability to stay awake with him? What does he do when he finds us sleeping?

How we answer these questions is very important.

It is important because it exposes our belief about how Jesus deals with our failure.

Once again, let's put ourselves in the garden of Gethsemane. For a moment, we experience Jesus's hand on our shoulders, inviting us to awaken. When we find ourselves awake once again, how would we describe his face? Is he annoyed? Irate? Or maybe he just turns his back and walks away. When I put myself in Gethsemane, I expect him to be disgusted, and simply quit wasting his time and energy on me. I expect him to be exactly like I was with Jimmy in that hospital—frustrated and fed up.

We all anticipate his response, and what we anticipate tells us a lot about our practical theology.

In Mark's account of this question, Simon Peter is singled out by name. He's always able to provide an example of how *not* to do something. He was always unpredictable, saying the right thing—then the wrong thing. He would fight and argue when he should have been at peace, and sleep when he should have been in prayer. He never seemed to know what the moment required.

Neither do we. Jesus's response in Mark 14 to both Peter and us speaks to this mixed bag of our souls. In this case, Jesus wants to teach us something about the complexity of our natures.

"*Simon, are you asleep?*" he asked, knowing the answer already. "*Don't be naïve,*" Jesus warned Peter. "*Part of you is eager, ready for anything in God. But another part is as lazy as an old dog sleeping by the fire*" (Mark 14:38).

Ready for anything in God. Lazy as an old dog by the fire. Jesus's words dissect the warring sides of each of us, and with a surgeon's precision.

As a good friend often reminds me, we are all complex beings. We are not just one thing. That's obvious but often forgotten.

When we feel we're doing well, then we see ourselves as people who are doing well and only ever do well. We are perpetually awake, never to fall asleep on God again. All that can change, however, with one thought, one word, one action, one nap.

It's not helpful for us to live in ignorance of who we truly are. We are often afraid to own our complexity. It's much easier to call ourselves good or bad. It's much messier to try to hold love for God *and* self-centeredness, as we often do. It's much tidier to have a label and a name.

We defy labels. We are both ready disciples and lazy dogs.

Jesus handles our failure with the mercy of truth. He names something important and then invites us to return to a place of receiving our complexity like children. He wants this because it's naïve not to. We are complex, whether we want to be or not. I think of my children, who are utterly unafraid of their complexity. I will often ask how their day was and the answer sounds like this: "It was the best day ever, but also not so good."

They will say this without seeing anything odd. They don't realize that in the adult world, that answer sounds completely irrational, incongruent. Not to them. They can be happy and sad at once. They can need me and want their independence. They can be wildly tired and tiredly wild. It just works with children.

The Peter in me wonders if my complexity is just too much for Jesus. I wait for him to get frustrated, tired of my shenanigans and inconsistencies, and walk out of the room. We are believers who sleep. We are sleepers who want God. We are both, and in both, we are unwilling to believe that we're beloved.

What Jesus saw in Peter he sees in us. The God-Who-Awakens

looks into the depths of our hearts and knows there is a battle being waged in each moment, each breath. He sees our love for him. He sees that we, like Peter, are eager, passionate even, for him. He sees that we have tasted his goodness and want more: more life, more Kingdom, more God. He sees and knows that our hearts search out his heart as a child holds her arms out to be held.

It is in this way that we must behave like children who never want to go to bed.

One of the first steps to waking up is to own the fact of both our readiness and our laziness—and not expect Jesus to give up on us. We can come to him with our complexity and be assured he won't turn away.

When we allow our complexity to be true, we are present. We are awake.

The most amazing paradox of it all is that we are not alone in bearing complexity. Jesus is complex, too. In fact, he is the Complex One, and as such, we bear the *imago Dei* of this complex God. He holds justice in one hand and mercy with the other. Both love and wrath are within him, sorrow and joy remain true to his holy being. He has been complex since before the dawn of time. Even the mystery of the Trinity speaks to one God and three personalities. He is not just one label, and he never has been. He understands our complexity, and it doesn't deter him.

His response to our shared complexity is a hilarious irony. His response is to give us a new kind of sleep.

His response is to give us *rest*.

HOLY SLEEP

In the conclusion of C. S. Lewis's story *The Magician's Nephew*, there's an interesting scene between Aslan and the wicked Uncle Andrew. This self-consumed, small man has been induced to hysterics by the raw beauty of newly created Narnia. He simply cannot handle the power of creative energy and life. Taking pity on him, his nephew Digory requests that Aslan do something to help the poor chap, little deserving as he may be. This is Aslan's response:

> "I cannot comfort him; he has made himself unable to hear my voice. If I spoke to him, he would hear only growlings and roarings. Oh, Adam's sons, how cleverly you defend yourselves against all that might do you good! *But I will give him the only gift he is still able to receive.*" He bowed his great head rather sadly, and breathed into the Magician's terrified face. "Sleep," he said. "Sleep and be separated for some few hours from all the torments you have devised for yourself."[11]

Aslan understands that Uncle Andrew cannot receive him. When he sees Aslan, all he can see is a ferocious, wild beast. This is sometimes how we see God. How can the Lion of Judah be trusted? How can he be anything but a ravenous brute, eager to devour us because of our failure to stay faithful?

He has seen the chronic soul fatigue we carry. He sees that we are feeble and tired and made of dust. He sees that we want what's easiest and most comfortable. He sees that we'll turn from him again and again, falling asleep at the worst possible moments. He sees and knows that we will abandon him, ignore him, reject him without our even realizing it. We are like the unwise virgins, sleeping through our long-awaited wedding: "The bridegroom didn't show up when they expected him, and they all fell asleep" (Matthew 25:5). He doesn't do what we think he's going to do, when we think he ought to do it. We curl up and go to sleep when the adventure with him is just beginning.

The Lion of Judah sees, and he has compassion on what he sees. Instead of wrath, he gives us the divine gift of a new kind of sleep, simply to show us that when we reawaken, we are still intact. We are still loved.

The Gospel is that he has made us good *in the midst* of our sleep. He wants to show us that he's remained a loving God while we've been caught in our torpor. When we could do nothing for ourselves but habitually hibernate from the Kingdom, Jesus was sent from the heart of God to wake us.

He tells us this story again and again throughout scripture. When Adam could find no other breathing, warm-blooded creature to love, "God put the Man into a deep sleep" (Genesis 2:21). It is into this deep, God-inspired sleep that he brings forth the promise of union and life. Adam could have tried in all his newly formed capacity to make life work with a grizzly or swallowtail. He could have begun striving.

God intervened.

Likewise, when I AM, the unknown Desert God, calls Abram into a wildly unpredictable journey, he entrances the dusty pilgrim, proving his abundant ability to take the entire weight of the promise-keeping. "As the sun went down a deep sleep overcame Abram and then a sense of dread, dark and heavy" (Genesis 15:12). It is into this deep, God-inspired sleep that God enacts a covenant relationship with Abram. He knew Abram would never be able to uphold covenant.

Knowing this, God still intervened.

In the garden of Gethsemane, Jesus knew his closest friends would falter. He knew they would fail him. He knew they would close their eyes in a torpor so strong that only God could wake them.

And yet, Jesus still intervened. He walked that dark road to the Cross while we were yet sleeping.

That is the Gospel.

We all inherently know that we, too, will fail Jesus. We will fall asleep. Like Adam, we cannot bring forth life. Like Abram, we cannot keep our end of the covenant. Like the disciples, we cannot save ourselves from the fate we deserve: eternal sleep.

Jesus speaks into this and reminds us while we're yet sleeping: *Even when you fall asleep, forgetting my love for a time, I still have you.*

In an ironic reversal described in Matthew 8, we find Someone else sleeping—and this time, it's Jesus himself. The disciples are struggling with ropes and sails and oars, bailing buckets of water from their leaking craft. They have the God-Who-Awakens in the boat, and they can't wake him up. They are running from bow to stern, scurrying like ants, trying to save themselves. In other words, they are striving.

What is Jesus doing? He is sleeping the deep, life-giving sleep of the unexhausted. He is perfectly untroubled in the midst of the storm. That is not how we usually operate.

The lads look over and see this marvel. His disciples scream Jesus's question back at him in the middle of gale-force winds and turbulent seas. In panicked frustration, they bellow like angered cows at the Son of God: "JESUS! Why are you sleeping? WAKE UP! Don't you care if we die?"

Jesus does indeed wake up, rubbing the sleep from his eyes. Now it's his turn to marvel, but sadly, the astonishment is caused by their lack of understanding. After all this time, they still don't trust him. They're still striving. They're in a state of advanced torpor.

Not Jesus. Jesus *could* sleep because he knew that the Father had them, all of them. He lived the words of the psalmist:

In peace I will lie down and sleep, for you alone, LORD,
make me dwell in safety.

Psalm 4:8 (ESV)

Jesus didn't have to live an exhausted life, trying to keep himself out of trouble and in prosperity. Because he knew God's care, striving was unnecessary. He wants us to partake in this same experiential knowledge, this abundant rest of God.

THE GOD-WHO-AWAKENS

Jesus doesn't rescue and redeem us so we can live the rest of our tiresome lives on our own, taking care of ourselves.

He invites us to enter into a life free of exhaustion, a life that has no room for striving. He invites us, again and again without fail, to awaken. He invites us to live fully present, fully at rest.

In the boat, his body may have been asleep, but his soul never fell asleep on his Father. He never falls asleep on us. Jesus took on the consequences of our torpor—the alienation, the loneliness in the garden, so we would never need to.

He is not under the control of our unholy sleep. He is never a "lazy dog by the fire." His soul is always fully awake, fully alive, ready for anything with God. He never separates from the oneness that is constantly offered to him—and to us.

> He won't let you stumble,
> your Guardian God won't fall asleep.
> Not on your life!
> Israel's Guardian will never doze or sleep.
> God's your Guardian,
> right at your side to protect you.
>
> Psalm 121:3–5

This is a life that knows it's cared for by the Living, Breathing God-Who-Awakens.

We will fall asleep. It's what we humans do. The question is—for how long? How long will our slumber last?

Again, and again, his Spirit gently wakens us and invites us to shake off the exhaustion and numbness and indifference of our souls, taking our place once more with Jesus in the garden—watching, waiting, talking with our Father.

As he intimately views our weaknesses, our complexities, our failures, we expect his disgust. We expect him to leave when we desperately want him to *meinate*—stay. But, of course, he doesn't leave. He never has. He never will. He's never shown me his back.

It's all face with Jesus, fierce eyes filled with delight and fiery love.

He shows me, once again, that he wants me to trust that whether I'm asleep or awake with him, he'll never leave. He loves us, in the complexity, in the struggle, in the sin. He even loves us in the sleeping. He loves us because he loves us.

His invitation for us to awaken is limitless:

> Awake, O sleeper,
> and arise from the dead,
> and Christ will shine on you.
>
> Ephesians 5:14 (ESV)

He'll never, ever stop asking his question.

Don't be naïve, he reminds us as he gently shakes us awake. Naïveté is not a blessed state of mind. He wants us to be wise— childlike and wise. We are not black-and-white creatures. We are a mixed bag of redemption and ulterior motives, both ready for God and like sleeping dogs. When we can see this and hold the complexity of our souls, he invites us to bring it all to him. He will hold it with us.

The next time we find ourselves overcome with exhaustion, we know that Jesus is beckoning with his questions. It may be a call to lay down our anxious striving. It may be a time to receive his holy sleep, the gift of an untroubled Jesus in a rocking boat.

The Risen God is awake. He will never slumber the torpid sleep that is deaf to our cries. He is ever watchful in the wait with us.

> I pray to GOD—my life a prayer—
> and wait for what he'll say and do.
> My life's on the line before God, my Lord,
> waiting and watching till morning,
> waiting and watching till morning.
>
> Psalm 130:5–6

FOR CONTEMPLATION AND DISCUSSION

Lectio Divina Exercise:

Enter into the garden of Gethsemane with Jesus and his disciples. What does the mood of the night feel like? What do you see in the face of Jesus as he asks his friends: *"Meinate—Stay with me?"* Feel the intimacy in his request. How do you respond? Imagine falling asleep and being woken by an anguished Jesus. How do you handle your inability to stay awake and wait with Jesus? What does his face look like as he asks, *"Why are you sleeping?"* What rises up in response to his question?

For Reflection:

1. For one day, pay attention to your level of exhaustion. Do you awake in the morning refreshed? Do you move through the day with energy and vitality? How do you feel as you anticipate going to bed? Listen to the message your body is telling you. Invite the God-Who-Awakens to speak into this place. Journal what you hear from him.

2. Where is God asking you to *meinate*—stay with him? Where is the greatest temptation in your life to fall asleep on God?

3. What are your thoughts about the Jesus you encounter in the garden of Gethsemane? Does his emotional state or request make you uncomfortable?

4. How do you view your own complexity? How would you describe its presence in your life with God?

5. What is your answer to Jesus's question: *"Why are you sleeping?"*

CHAPTER FOUR

"What Do You Want Me to Do for You?"

Pursuing the Nature of True Desire

You can't always get what you want.

> —The Rolling Stones,
> "You Can't Always Get What You Want"

Practically everything that goes on in the world—
wanting your own way, wanting everything for yourself, wanting
*   to appear important—*
has nothing to do with the Father. It just isolates you from him.
The world and all its wanting, wanting, wanting is on the
*   way out.*

> —The Apostle John,
> 1 John 2:16

His world was dark, chaotic. Life happened in the space of upright humanity, three feet above where he sat. Though he was not lame, he chose to stay low. He communed with the creatures of his level, the flea-ridden street dogs that came to lick his face and hands. They hungered for breadcrumbs and salt the same way he hungered. Like the strays, he begged for food and kindness. He found little.

He'd been rendered sightless as a small child, stricken with a sickness that stole his ability to navigate the spinning world. His parents mourned their son's darkened state. When they died soon after, so did any chance he had in a society moving too fast to notice one small boy, lost in premature nightfall.

There was no protector. There was no advocate. There was no place but the curb for an orphan without eyes.

The blind boy lived hard years, becoming older, weathered before his time. He grew to manhood on the street, the length of his hair and beard marking the passage from child to adult. He staggered the same stretch of street just outside Jericho he'd lived since boyhood. There, he badgered busy travelers for small mercies.

Little else about him changed.

The boy begged, and so did the man. The boy starved, and so did the man. The boy knew cold loneliness, and so did the man, only the cold had spread like an oil slick on the surface of his soul.

He played the fool to survive. As people passed his spot in the dirt, he would bellow for mercy, just a scrap, until he was hoarse. People laughed. Sometimes he'd feel the cold thud of a coin and stop shouting. Mostly, he screamed until those walking had long passed. He knew he was filthy. He knew he was unwelcomed in the seeing world, but the drive to live was strong. He'd left his broken pride long ago in the ashes of a forgotten life. He clung to something, an unnamed fraying thread that willed him to keep breathing, keep prostrating himself before the Jericho seeing.

It wasn't hope. He wouldn't dare call it hope—it was more like desperate desire.

It was a desperation that one day, he'd see the colors he was meant to see, the colors he remembered from his youth. He hated the dark fiercely. It was his prison, and he ached for release. He was recklessly in love with the light. He dreamed in sunlit color, loath to wake again to the tragedy of his black world.

He recalled in his mind the way the sun's rays shone between the needles of the cedar grove, the silvered rainbow of fish scales in the river, the scarlet flush of pomegranates, and the crimson flesh of figs. He could see the tanned skin of his mother's hands, the wrinkled brown of his father's cheeks. All these he remembered with the blurry vision of a mind long wrecked.

He wanted to see again more than he wanted to eat, more than he wanted safe shelter. And yet, his useless eyes stared into the world, unseeing and unseen.

One winter day, word of strange happenings reached the crossroads of Jericho from the lofty heights of Jerusalem. Those riddled with disease were healed without a physician, without medication. Maimed Jews, tortured Jews, crippled Jews were made whole with an utterance. Free bread was distributed without a day's labor or a day's begging.

And the name *Jesus the Nazarene* was spoken with each retelling.

Most said his name like a question. Some spoke of him with a whisper. Others spat his name as profanity. Invisible to all the seeing eyes around him, the blind man listened intently to the tales being told over his matted head. One market day, he heard two vendors discuss how on the very steps of the Temple itself, Jesus the Nazarene had healed a man born blind. No doctor had ever cured such a congenital disease—but the Nazarene had.

This is when the blind man's heart began pumping oxygen to desire's small flame.

But how could he ever get to the Temple? Who would take him? Who would help? He could never travel the crooked road to Jerusalem alone. The fifteen miles that lay between him and the Nazarene might as well have been fifteen hundred. He did not despair, for he'd also heard this was an itinerant man. The Rabbi was like himself—a man with no home. Maybe this Nazarene would make the trek to Jericho. Maybe Jesus would perform another miracle. It was said that he had mercy in spades. Maybe the mercy of Jesus would fall by the wayside, and he could have a scrap for himself. Wasn't it true that just a crumb of the mercy of God could make a difference for a man like him? Too many maybes to count, and yet he continued to let his desire unfurl like new leaves before the sun.

He was sick with desire, clinging to the dying sparks of wanting something he couldn't have. There was so much pain in wanting. The months that passed as he waited seemed to him the worst he'd lived. Desire awake was painful to hold.

It all happened without warning. The city buzzed like a hive with unexpected news.

The Nazarene was on his way.

A procession of followers trickled into the city ahead of him, full of story and eagerness to spread the unbelievable tales. The bored and jaded of Jericho thronged the narrow street, jostling for the best position to see this miracle-man pass by their shops and stalls. They wanted a spectacle. It's what drove them, the Jews and Roman squatters, to line the road, waiting for this new parade to arrive. They were ready to see a miracle, but they didn't want to be changed.

As the crowd pressed together, the blind man was pushed and trampled under the feet of his neighbors. He knew he was invisible to them, and he hated his ability to be unseen.

He imagined the Nazarene within reach but not being able to get to him. It was the darkest of his dreams. Rage churned in his gut. He was desperate.

It was in this desperation that he realized what he wanted more than his sight. His desire was not to see, but to *be seen*. He wanted the eyes of the Nazarene to see his situation. He didn't want invisibility one more day. He wanted those eyes to behold his desire. The ability to want something within his grasp flooded the man. In anguish, he shouted with all the power his lungs contained. It was the shriek of a creature in travail.

"Jesus! Son of David!" he bawled, a man wild with desire. "SEE ME!"

The blind man's howl pierced the din of the thronging crowd. They'd heard him before; they'd heard him their whole lives— but never like this. His pitch was otherworldly. He was panting and sweating. And as it continued, their curiosity turned to annoyance, then to anger. One man shoved his way to him and spat into the upturned face of the blind beggar, "Shut up, you twit!"

But the blind man would not be silenced. His desire would not be silenced.

"I said, 'Shut up!'" The prostrate man couldn't see it, but he could feel it coming. With the back of his hand, the angry man sent him sprawling into the building behind. It was not the first time he'd been hit. A few others, too, took up the abuse of the man. Most of the crowd just looked away, not wanting to see the ugly scene at their feet.

The blind man lay there, dizzied by blows. He was curled into a ball, his knees pressing into his chest. Silently, the instinct to protect himself surged stronger than any other. He felt the warmth of blood trickling down the back of his scalp. Slowly, he straightened. Holding the wall, he struggled to his feet, panting with adrenaline and pain.

For a brief moment, he thought about giving up.

In that flickering decision, the hungriest part of his soul would not be cowed into silence—the part that *wanted*, the part that *desired*. This part chugged breath into his lungs, and he heard himself baying, over and over, like a hound on the hunt: "Jesus! Son of David! Mercy, have mercy on me!" (Luke 18:38, ESV).

Mercy. As the men around him shoved him down, his face in the mud, he screamed out, "I want some mercy of my own."

The crowd hushed as Jesus the Nazarene stopped midstride. He spoke.

"Bring him to me."

He said it with such authority. There was no question of who he meant. No one dared disobey. The man felt two powerful arms pull him to his feet and lead him between bodies over the smoothed dirt of the street. He stopped. He could sense eyes beholding him. Hundreds of unfriendly eyes, seeing his filth, his wildness, the rawness of his desire. He knew he must be in the Nazarene's presence, and he felt those eyes, too. He held his breath; was the Nazarene disgusted by what he saw, too?

"What do you want me to do for you?" the Voice asked (Luke 18:41, ESV).

His question lingered in the space between them. This blind

son of Israel wanted to be seen, and he was. He'd been given what he wanted. This knowledge broke something loose in him, and for the first time, he felt the freedom in desire bubbling like a spring from within. With tears streaming into his beard and blood oozing down his neck, he spoke.

"I want—" he said, gasping, his hoarse throat choked with desire. "I want to see again."

There was a holy pause, the profound silence of a soul at rest. In that silent moment, the unblinking eye in his mind finally closed. The fine-tuned ears were filled with the sound of inhale and exhale.

Jesus nodded his head. He smiled. None of this the blind man could see.

The Voice leaned in close, his breath warm on the unseeing face.

"Then let it be done."

Instantly, the world exploded with reams of eager light and untamed color. Like the first dawn of creation, this man was stepping into a new world, a fresh world with the glittering dew of life winking from every surface. The first image his new eyes settled on was the smiling face of the Nazarene.

What once was blind now beheld. He'd gotten what he'd craved. The mercy of God was given freely, and he found what his soul truly desired.

He'd found it in the question of Jesus the Nazarene.

A DIRTY WORD

"What do you want?" Why does such a simple question catch us off-guard?

This question contains extraordinary complexity, because it is not—nor will it ever be—rhetorical. It is no surface inquiry. It is not abstract. This is a question of bone and blood, demanding a tangible response. Jesus wants to know what we spend our minutes and dollars looking for, our weekends and downtimes.

This question is intensely individual. There is no neutrality when it comes to want. No one else can answer this in my stead. It makes us uncomfortable that we cannot give a universal answer, something in the generic tones of gray. It can make us angry, as it requires a personal reckoning at inconvenient times. We're designed to know what desires are lodged in us, but many of us have locked away wanting so deep and for so long that it may never see the light.

Do we know what we truly want?

"Desire" has become a dirty word in Christendom. We equate desire with lust, and lust with deviance. In a culture that is fiercely committed to excess and wanton hedonism, Christians have been turned off to want. We see despicable, over-the-top displays of lust on every website and television channel. We're exposed to the fallout of broken desire in our own homes and hearts. As he watched the world crumble at his feet, the Old Testament prophet Jeremiah questioned, "The heart is deceitful above all things, and desperately sick; who can understand it?" (Jeremiah 17:9, ESV).

I think *we* can.

We get it. We get the heart's deceit, because we see it every day. As the sanctified Bride, we're sick with what we see.

We don't want to want the way the world wants.

There's a reason that many equate words like "desire," "lust," and "want" with sexuality. These words, though abstract, become palpable reminders of something intimate, something deeply private. Desire, like sex, requires a nakedness of soul that disrupts the status quo. Like the blind man, we find that our raw desire is unwanted, so we dig a ditch and bury the desire that throbs in our chests.

To desire is to risk, because desire makes no promises. Desire exposes the cankers of the soul. Desire reveals the hidden man. And we hate that—all of it. But still, *something* presses us to dig up what would be easier to keep buried. That something is the relentless question of Jesus.

Our response is to ask Jesus to please be quiet. We're trying very hard to be good, and wanting only gets in the way of goodness. The complexity and power of desire can frighten us into shunning it. Suffocated desire, however, will not stay hidden long. It demands to be seen. One way or another, what we've stifled will one day leak.

With a need to separate, the church has swung hard the pendulum to the opposing extreme. Unfortunately, when we remove desire from the church, we also remove God.

DRIVEN MAD WITH DESIRE

What is desire? Isn't it simply wanting what we don't have? Isn't it nothing more than a very un-Christian lack of contentment? We want the things that we want, and we want those things *now*. We want to possess them, to hold them in the grip of our own two hands. When we finally get what we want, and it doesn't satisfy what's insatiable inside us, we just find something else to want.

With broken desire, we seek to become gods. If we can satisfy and fulfill the deepest longings of our souls, then we have no need for Jesus. We become self-sufficient creatures. And we *want* to be. Who among us wants to wait on the good will and pleasure of another Being before we can quench the thirst of desire in us? Who among us has the blind man's courage to expose what's most vulnerable? Who among us can stomach being seen and known, warts and all?

There aren't many.

We observe within ourselves that perverted desire leads to idolatry. The worship of want compels us to pursue our desires with an unhealthy abandon, a surrendering of our will to whatever this god of the stomach will offer us. It was desire that caused the fall of a third of the angelic host. It was also desire that triggered all of humanity's descent into sin. Perhaps desire is nothing more than an aberration from original design. Perhaps it's time we name it according to its nature.

Or perhaps to know the heart's desire is to get to the core of *imago Dei*.

In the New Testament, the concept of desire is quite complex. The diversity of the Greek conveys very different intentions. One term is *epithumeō* (ep-ee-thoo-meh´-o). *Epithumeō* conveys passion. It expresses single-minded intentionality. It is raw, vocal. It *almost* sounds like the blind man—except that this is not the word used by Jesus in his question.

This verb reads well on paper, but its outward appeal hides a sinister nature within.

This is a word that denotes the idolatry of desire and is used almost exclusively as a negative in New Testament terminology. The noun-root of *epithumeō* (the *thumos*, or mind) shows a manic fixation on the object of one's desire. It's an obsessive turning toward lust.[1] This is Frankenstein desire, an unhealthy loss of control in wanting. The tenth command in Exodus 20 (LXX) uses *epithumeō* for the prohibition to covet. James, the brother of Christ, also uses this verb in his epistle:

You *want* your own way, and fight for it deep inside yourselves. You *lust* for what you don't have and are willing to kill to get it. You *want* what isn't yours and will risk violence to get your hands on it.

> James 4:2, emphasis mine

In the Sermon on the Mount, Jesus warns us that *epithumeō* has the capacity to disease us from the inside out: "*Your heart can be corrupted by* epithumeō *even quicker than your body*" (Matthew 5:28).

The world has watched in horror as this corruption of desire has spread into every facet of society. Politics, athletics, and artistry have all been assaulted by radical lust. Great writers have captured this, the tragedy of *epithumeō*, in classic literature. Herman Melville depicted how bloodlust can possess a man's soul.

He shouted with a terrific, loud, animal sob, like that of a heart-stricken moose; "Aye, aye! it was that accursed white whale that razeed me!"...Then tossing both arms, with measureless imprecations he shouted out: "Aye, aye! and I'll chase him round Good Hope, and round the Horn, and round the Norway Maelstrom, and round perdition's flames before I give him up."[2]

Epithumeō drove Captain Ahab mad with the desire to hunt and kill the white whale. It is also featured in Lewis's Narnian tales. Edmund Pevensie, a boy vulnerable to jealousy and greed, betrayed his sisters and brother for just one more taste of Turkish delight, for "anyone who had once tasted it would want more and more of it, and would even, if they were allowed, go on eating it till they killed themselves."[3]

Edmund's *epithumeō* incited war against Narnia and the death of Aslan upon the stone table. But perhaps there is no better picture of *epithumeō* in literature than Tolkien's portrait of the creature Gollum. Sméagol's hobbitlike nature degenerated into the hacking, murderous villain by green-eyed greed for his Precious.

Gollum, dancing like a mad thing, held aloft the ring, a finger still thrust within its circle. "Precious, precious, precious!" Gollum cried. "My Precious! O my Precious!" And with that, even as his eyes were lifted up to gloat on his prize, he stepped too far, toppled, wavered for a moment on the brink, and then with a shriek he fell. Out of the depths came his last wail precious, and he was gone.[4]

All of humanity has our white whale, our own personal Precious. Every human heart is ready to consume the Turkish delight until it kills us.

IN THE BEGINNING

What we too often forget is the *stomach's* wants are not always the *heart's* desires. We want to continue to play in mud puddles, but our deeper longings are not fooled. Counterfeit desire never satisfies what the soul truly craves. The Nazarene invites us, as Lewis's *The Weight of Glory* describes, to "a holiday at the sea." He wants to help us feel at home there. But our fragmented half-hearts choose to sit out on playing with Jesus and experiencing the adventure of desiring with God.

We often want things from a striving, selfish, anxious place. There's an obsession in that wanting that doesn't fit my soul's true design. Desire itself is not evil. It's not unbiblical. It was not designed by God to endanger us. What can become dangerous, however, is the voracious appetite that degrades healthy desire.

It *was* desire that waged war on heaven's gates and spiraled the earth into chaotic descent. What lust has wrought is inconceivably tragic, and we must weep over this tragedy in the quiet of our souls. But lust isn't the end of desire's story—or ours.

The god of the stomach does not own desire.

Desire arrived long before the fall. Indeed, desire existed earlier than the ticking of time. Before world history ever began, before a single creation, desire danced in Triune fellowship. Lacking nothing, Father, Son, and Spirit still mysteriously lacked *something*. In impossible tandem, the Godhead held full perfection in one hand, holy discontent in the other. A deeper intimacy was craved. A wider circle was desirable. It was desire that spoke a world where there was void. It was desire that brought the woman to man. It was desire that brought man to God.

It is desire that continues to bring man to God.

WHERE ARE YOU STAYING?

Four boys traveled south from Galilee in the quest of all youth—for significance, justice, belonging. They'd tired of the staleness of the synagogue, and they were hungry for something fresh from a God too long silent. They'd heard of a wild man in the deep south, a river prophet who was wading in proclamations along the Jordan. Making the arduous journey, they bypassed the Temple on their starboard side and headed straight for the wilderness, telling jokes and behaving like bachelors along the way.

They liked wild John immediately. He was what they'd been looking for—*almost*. John was John, but even he deflected their eagerness to put their hopes in his soggy hands.

They didn't want to go home. They didn't want to give up, so they stayed, keeping their eyes open. One day, the Baptizer pointed to Jesus, and two of the four followed. They kept a little distance, unsure of whether John was right or if he was just trying to get rid of them.

Jesus knew they loitered behind him. They skulked like spies in a second-rate movie. He walked slower; they slowed, too. They were just getting up the nerve to call his name when one of them tripped on a rock onto the jagged shore, catching the fall with his face. The other cursed in Aramaic. The one covered in sand cursed back, blood dripping from his nose. They both remained unaware that Jesus had turned around and was watching. He retraced his steps to where they'd stopped. Extending his hand, he helped the fallen youth to his feet.

"Hello, *lads*," he said. In my mind, Jesus sounds Irish. "*What are you looking for?*"

John's text makes it clear to his readers: They had no idea how to answer this question.

Perhaps they were looking for what many Jews were looking for at the time of Christ's incarnation—something to satisfy their sense of national justice. They'd been oppressed by foreign dictation for too long. They'd waited for God to speak for far too long. They wanted the Kingdom of God to descend among his people. They were looking for the One they'd been promised.

They were staring right at him.

All these thoughts coursed through their heads. But in that moment, they articulated nothing. Jesus watched their fumbling with compassion. He saw the mental process, the racking of their brains for the right answer. What eventually spilled out was the awkwardness of untested youth: "Uh, Rabbi—where are you staying?"

Like a favorite older brother, Jesus didn't laugh at their immaturity. He smiled, a smile that showed the boys a row of crooked teeth, a smile that instantly put them at ease.

"*Come and see*" was all he said. He turned, walking toward an unseen destination.

They were left standing there, uncertain, unaware of the eternal weight of this moment. Without looking at what the other would do, the young man with a bloody nose yelled out, "Wait up—we're coming!" The two jogged the beach to catch the Rabbi on the move.

"*What are you looking for?*" Like Jesus's young friends, we want to fill that uncomfortable space between question and answer too quickly. In our haste, we rush to respond. But sometimes that first answer isn't the right one, so Jesus asks again. He wants us to know where our souls rove, day and night unending. If we cannot answer this question on a level deeper than "*Where are you staying?*" (John 1:39, ESV), let's stop and ask God why.

"Come," he invites. "*Come and see.*"

John ends the narrative with tongue-in-cheek brevity. "They came, saw where he was living, and ended up staying with him for the day" (John 1:39). In its sparseness, John's commentary shows an element of surprise. The boys are surprised to find they feel comfortable to stay with Jesus in their desire.

NINJAS AND COOKIES

Epithumeō doesn't have the last word in the New Testament. In the original Greek, there exists a richer, dark-roast term for desire that makes *epithumeō* taste vanilla. Throughout the scriptures, another word is unyielding, whispering the true nature of God-ordained desire. This verb is *thelō* (thel´-o), a marriage of both the heart and the mind. *Thelō* indicates a desire that is under obedience to the will. This word is classified as a Hebraism, alluding to something in which we take great delight.[5]

Like *epithumeō*, *thelō* is active. It has power. It refuses to be forgotten. But unlike *epithumeō*, it is not obsessive. It is passion under submission.

This kind of desire is associated with a disciplined delight. It's a desire that is deep, but not one that takes possession of all that one is. This is the word that Jesus used to question the blind man, and this is the word that he uses while asking us. This is the desire found in the deep moonlight of the garden of Gethsemane, where Jesus cried from the depths of his soul to his Father—"*Not what I want, but what do you want?*" (Mark 14:26).

Jesus can ask us what we want. He's the only One who has the *right* to ask it and have us lay all bare. He has this authority because he is the only One who has held *thelō* without the corruption of *epithumeō*. He's the only One who has desired without sin. He is the only One who has allowed desire to flood his soul and then given it in fullness to his Father.

Jesus teaches us how to desire. He is Rabbi in the school of want.

He begins his lessons by asking us the question, a question that unravels us until he gets to the center of the one he loves. "*What do you want?*"

Children have no difficulty with Jesus's question. Even when the answer is preposterous and impossible, children are unashamed in the vocalization of their wanting. Our daughter Macy wants to be a ninja. She wants it with the dogged wanting of a beagle on the scent. She practices martial arts in the basement every day. She faithfully attends her dojo classes with Sensei Bruce. She has genuine and deep *thelō*—not just to be good at karate, but to one day become a ninja. I've tried to explain to her that I don't think *ninja* is a profession.

"That doesn't matter, Mom," she says. "I still want it." And just because it doesn't seem realistic, she won't stop wanting it.

But as adults, we treat desire like the bubonic plague. We find the act of desiring too painful, because who among us gets what we truly want? Many of us don't acknowledge its presence in our lives at all. If we do recognize our desires, it's with a forlorn sigh, and then we carefully tuck it away with the Christmas ornaments to gather dust until it's time again. There aren't a lot of ninjas running the streets. Like Macy, we sense the improbable nature of desire's outcome.

Desire—*authentic* desire—hurts. It's at the blind-man level of our souls. It's difficult to define, impossible to fulfill. Most of us just give up and go after the lesser desires that are easier to achieve. We allow *epithumeō* once again to take the reins.

We end up wanting what *we* can achieve. The third cookie. The third episode of *The Office*. The three-hundredth dollar on the hobby we stopped really enjoying months ago. The sexual titillation, the sports fanaticism, the ministry overcommitment— we can't seem to get enough to slake the terrible thirst. We indulge and scrape and knock together something that *seems* like fulfillment of desire when it's really just the engorgement of the hungry gut. I don't truly desire that third cookie, but I'm hungry for something else, something far sweeter and more satisfying.

But it's the cookie that's within reach.

WHAT DO I WANT?

Answering Jesus, really answering, is daunting. Telling anyone, especially God, what we want is scary. Even if we can name it, speaking it requires vulnerability. We often evade what we're truly looking for, fearing we may never find what we seek. When we name something, it begins to have weight. It becomes real. We're scared of the realness, so we reject our ninja desires for more cookies, naming something lesser, something that feels more attainable than what our souls truly crave. If our desires are named and real, it's all the more painful when we don't obtain them.

Jesus knows this. He looks into my face as he looked to the ruddy faces of two fishing buddies and draws a little closer. Jesus welcomes our need to follow at a distance, watching to see if he is capable of satisfying our hearts' anguished ache.

The Gospel takes these *epithumeō* desires and employs them for holy use, for they speak to us about what's deeper than the gut. Though veiled by grime and dirt, our lusts and idolatries and cookies reveal the seedlings of true desire. He asks as we stand before him, unhindered by our darkened state, unrestricted by our shameful blindness—"*What do you want?*"

Here goes.

What rises in me is manifold, complex: My family. West Coast Ireland. Writing. Celtic disciplines of silence and solitude. Adventure. Hearing my Father. Play. Healing. Pursuing the hearts of others. Beauty. I know it goes even deeper.

I want excitement. Boredom feels like death.

I want safety. I want to feel comfortable and secure.

I want love. I hunger to be pursued for who I am.

I want an anesthetic to numb any pain that hurts me.

I want fulfillment and purpose, something to drive away the empty pit in my soul.

And like the blind man, I want to be seen. Seen deeply.

When I look for any of these desires apart from Jesus, I will never find them. I know this is true. I've experienced this truth unnumbered times. I have devoted my life to the pursuit of these wants in the past, and in so doing, I have lost them.

However, I am learning that when I pursue the One who made desire, the One who called it *good*, all these desires begin pursuing *me*. The things I most deeply crave chase after me until I'm good and caught.

> I'm asking God for *one thing,*
> *only one thing:*
> To live with him in his house
> my whole life long.
> I'll contemplate his beauty;
> I'll study at his feet.
>
> Psalm 27:4, emphasis mine

Desiring God is the only *epithumeō* we are allowed. No other desires have permission to possess us.

A RETURN TO DESIRE

Jesus addresses the deeper desires of our souls. He gave them to us, and only he can fulfill them. Authentic desire, desire coming alive, is the evidence of a surrendered life.

God is calling us to a place of holy discontent. He wants us to want. He desires us to desire. He is desperate that we would ache, from the pit of our souls, for more of him. He rejoices in this want, this dissatisfaction with what we have of him. Jesus is waiting, ready to be the answer to the insatiable hunger of the soul. All that I'm looking for finds its end in him, the Desirable One.

In the end, all I really want is life. More life than what I am currently living. *He* is what I want. I just keep forgetting, so he keeps asking.

He asks because this is the most vulnerable place in which my heart and his can intersect. To know our mutual desires and hold them open—God and man—is a personal act of the deepest intimacy. It is in this place of desire that we can hear God speak most clearly to us, for it is with *thelō* desire he first spoke with man in the Garden.

It is in this place that he speaks with the blind man in me.

I look into the mirror of my soul and what it seeks, and I try not to loathe what I see. I am learning to give what's in there the space to simply exist. Unacknowledged needs and wants are still real; they're just hidden. In their hiddenness, they exert a fierce influence over my inner motivation and outward decisions. I invite all of this to Jesus's table, and I see that Jesus is here, sitting with me and all that I'm looking for. He's not shocked by my selfishness or insatiable need. He's truly delighted that I've invited *him* to come and see. I want him to touch all that I'm looking for and make it his, make it good.

He returns my desire to his design.

God gave first humanity a heart capable of good desires, and he blesses those desires with godly fulfillment. This is in his original design, and this original design is being redeemed in the Gospel. As his Son asks the question, he continues to present himself as the God of great desire.

We can get to the place where we are bold in our approach to wanting, because our wanting causes us no shame. We can be like the Greeks of John 12, making a beeline to Jesus, simply because he is our hearts' one desire.

"Sir, we want to see Jesus."

John 12:21

When we want from that place of redeemed wanting, it always boils down to this: Desire is relational at its core. The nature of true desire is a longing for more and a deeper relationship with the Creator of our souls.

WHAT DOES GOD WANT?

Jesus's question to me invites another: What is it that God wants? What is his desire? To ask this question of God conveys a longing for intimacy that pleases his heart like nothing else.

We hear his answer echo throughout eternity. In a display of holy discontentment, Jesus prays and asks his Father for *more* communion with us:

> "*Father, I want those you gave me*
> *to be with me, right where I am,*
> *so they can see my glory.*"
>
> John 17:24

As Yahweh proclaimed in Hosea 6:6, Jesus reclaimed in Matthew 9:13: "*I desire steadfast love and not sacrifice*" (ESV).

His heart is a clear pool. We can see all the way to the bottom.

He wants depth. He wants closeness. He wants conversational intimacy. He wants me. He wants us. Before the creation of the world, he longed for more of us. Like us, he also wants to be seen, and in seeing, to be loved. It's no coincidence that God and I want the same thing—to love and be loved, know and be known. In this vulnerable space, we become open to his entry, to his knowing.

This is the Gospel. God desires that we behold him as he truly is, in his glory. In another divine conspiracy, it's in mutual desire—ours and God's—we find our souls fulfilled beyond wildest expectations.

Divine *thelō*, the marriage of God's will with God's desire, is all throughout scripture. God's will *is* his good pleasure, his desire. He invites us to pray that his willing desires would be accomplished here on our fallen planet: "*Your kingdom come, your will be done*" (Matthew 6:10, ESV). The good desires of God long to fall like warm rain and be fulfilled in this earthly realm.

He invites each of us to enter the nature of true desire by

knowing his heart. This is the place where everything we've been looking for truly exists. It may defy our expectations. In fact, it *will* defy our expectations, because our expectations are simply too small.

VALIDATING DESIRE

Jesus offers more life than we could possibly hold, and still he keeps pouring it out. He replaces our petty desires with the larger-than-life Reality contained in his breast.

Our truest desires require a home, a safe place in which to take refuge. If we try to hold our desires alone or, far worse, bring them to fruition in our own talent, gifting, strength, and ability, we lose them. This is why he asks, "*What do you want me to do for you?*"

The psalmist pleads with the intensity of the blind man,

Open up before God, keep nothing back;
he'll do whatever needs to be done:
he'll validate your life in the clear light of day.

Psalm 37:5–6

He invites his children to desire, to dream, to open up the landscape of our hearts and breathe. That's how he created us— people fully awake, fully formed in all our desires. But we were never meant to carry the weight of them alone. We share them, and then we behold how the life and energy of God works within us and around us to a greater harvest.

We need restored hearts, hearts that are capable of true desire. We need hearts that are intrigued with this question of Jesus. We need hearts that are enlarged with the presence of the Inquisitive Christ.

He will do it. He will hold our desires better than even we can hold them. He's given them to us anyway. He will teach us how to hold them, that beautiful balance of deep satisfaction and holy discontentment. He has implanted his good will in each of us.

Let desire come without internal editing or harsh chastisement. Let desire "*come and see.*"

Let desire arise.

FOR CONTEMPLATION AND DISCUSSION

Lectio Divina Exercise:

Sit beside the blind man in the dirt. What does life without sight mean for you? Relate with this man a moment in his shame and desire. What does it feel like to be invisible? Feel the desperation at being muzzled in Jesus's presence. How do you respond? What do you do with your desire? Do you have the courage to shout out your deep need? Imagine being led through the crowd to Jesus. Hear as he asks you: "*What do you want me to do?*" What rises to the surface?

For Reflection:

1. What is your history with desire? What is your perspective on its legitimacy and role within the church?
2. Where do you see *epithumeō*, corrupted desire, in your own pursuit of the things you want? What are some lesser desires that replace what's most deep?
3. How would you describe *thelō*'s presence in your life? In the life of God?
4. How does it make you feel that what God desires is you? Do you see this as true? How do you experience this on a daily basis?
5. What is your answer to Jesus's question: "*What do you want?*"

CHAPTER FIVE

"Why Are You Trying to Kill Me?"

Demanding Guarantees from Jesus

*The chief priests and the teachers of the law began looking for a
way to destroy him, for they feared him.*
—Gospel of Mark,
11:18, ESV

*God is dead. God remains dead. And we have killed him...
Who will wipe this blood off us? What water is there for us to
clean ourselves?*
—Friedrich Nietzsche,
The Gay Science

Their story fills Gospel pages, demanding an audience, demanding the right to be seen and heard. Their intentions weigh heavy upon the space between words. With contrasting messages, public traps, and closed-door assassination plots, the Pharisees become some of the main characters in the drama that enfolds Jesus.

But the Pharisees were not always the antagonists of the story.

Their movement began like many good movements throughout history—with passion, determination, desire. They didn't want to live like everyone else, attending only to selfish need and personal comfort. They desired to be different, to stand apart. They wanted a holy separation. They were the original Protestants, Puritans, and Quakers combined.[1] In fact, the *Jewish*

Encyclopedia indicates the name "Pharisee" originates from the Hebrew root *perushim*—"to separate, detach."[2]

In the end, this is exactly what happened. They detached.

Their origins were heroic, the stuff of legend and lore. Like Ezra of old, they would return their neighbors to obedience. Little more than one hundred years before the birth of Christ, they faced the mountainous challenge of keeping holy a chosen race, the people of the Law, back into a life lived by the Law. A people long scattered, living out the rituals and customs of former captors and current tyrants. A people who'd grown accustomed to wandering, who were weary and tired and simply wanting to be left in peace to raise their crops, sheep, and children. From this people, a faithful remnant arose— stout-hearted, fiercely intentional, without compromise. They would *detach* from the people in order to lead the people. They would become the teachers, the wisest in the holy land, the keepers of God's righteous order according to the Law.

Their interpretation of God's commands was simple—simple and literal. God had said it, and they intended to obey it, no matter what. While they watched the Jewish culture around them sink deeper and further into Hellenistic assimilation, they were determined to illustrate that obedience was not only possible, but required.

They hailed the return of the Jewish nation-state and a Jewish king after the Maccabee revolution. The intertestamental time of self-rule should have been a continual celebration. The Hebrew people were once again under a Hebrew administration. After hundreds of years of wartime atrocities, kidnappings, and displacement, the Jews were finally in their homeland, governing themselves.

But it was not to be.

At the time of their formation and rise of influence, they suffered cruelly at the hands of their own Jewish king. Just as John the Baptist after them, the Pharisees spoke the truth regarding their king, Alexander Janneus. According to *The International Study Bible Encyclopedia*, they publicly accused him of breaking Levitical law. As a result, 800 Pharisees were crucified in a single day. As they were nailed, their wives and children were made to watch before being executed themselves, one by one, at the foot of each cross.[3]

Their allegiance to God's Law came with unfathomable cost.

As years mounted and generations passed, both their anger and their fear gained the velocity of a cresting tidal wave. With an ever-tightening noose, they discovered that obedience required more than what the Law provided. They found that in order to sustain rigorous law-keeping, more laws were necessary.

Yahweh, the great Law-Giver, had not given enough.

This oral tradition, known as the Mishna or "second law," gradually became of greater import to the Pharisees than the Law itself.[4] Believed to be spoken from the lips of God to Moses's ear, "these additions to the written law and interpretations of it had been given by Moses to the elders and by them had been transmitted orally down through the ages."[5] *Baker's Evangelical Dictionary of Biblical Theology* records, "The Pharisees...added regulations ('fences' or 'hedges') [that] were designed to prevent even coming close to breaking the Law."[6] These fences began covering larger and larger territories until the people found themselves trapped.

What often happens in religious service happened quickly to these separatists—what had at first compelled slowly corrupted. The love of Law, spoken of so poetically throughout Psalm 119, became the lust for law. They wanted to be like God, writing their own commands on the stony tablets of man's heart.

> The great defect of Pharisaism was that it made sin so purely external. An act was right or wrong according as some external condition was present or absent...A man did not break the Sabbath rest of his ass, though he rode on it, and hence didn't break the Sabbath law, but if he carried a switch with which to expedite the pace of the beast he was guilty, because he laid a burden on it.[7]

Would the beast have preferred the burden of a stick or a heavyset man? Logic was upended to protect their divine right to interpret Law as they chose. What was intended to add clarity introduced chaos. Spirit was replaced by letter, and they were blinded to both corporate and personal compromise. All of their self-written laws were designed to produce a guarantee that God would bless them in the manner they saw fit.

While the minutiae of jots and tittles were kept, the greatest command, wholehearted love, was neglected to rust with underuse. They despised the foreigner in their midst (Deuteronomy 10:19). They rejected the sick and diseased (Ezekiel 34:3–4). Their Sabbath became a chore, not a rest (Exodus 20:8–11). By the time the first Herod was crowned, the Pharisees numbered over five thousand strong.[8] This remnant of God, blessed to be a blessing, saw the time of Jesus's approach and hated every moment.

They could have been the welcome party that received the Messiah. Instead, these Law-enforcers were the jealous mob that sought his death.

HUNGRY FOR MASHIACH

At first, the Pharisees watched him. Perhaps some even remembered him as the precocious boy who had asked so many intelligent questions seventeen years earlier. They considered him—his origin, his words, his deeds. They discussed among themselves how this Nazarene was to be best handled. Some issued him strategic, public invitations to dinner (Luke 7:36–50). Others sought him in secret, at night (John 3:1–21). They compared him to their interpretations of what the Christ should be, and in their comparisons, Jesus fell short.

They couldn't allow Jesus to be God. Neither could they allow Jesus to be Jesus.

With the Roman destruction of their Temple in A.D. 70, they began a new quest, fueled with fresh rage, to flip the switch on foreign oppression. One hundred years after they nailed Jesus to the scourge of their own painful history, they were finally ready to crown God's Mashiach, a Messiah who would guarantee them their two deepest desires: the overthrow of the oppressive Roman governance and their own personal elevation of status in God's Kingdom-come-down. They urged the people to receive this Messiah, Shimon Bar-Kokhba,[9] named by the Pharisees as "Son of the Star": "There shall come a star out of Jacob" (Numbers 24:17, KJV).

But the Star of Jacob had already come, heavens ablaze with celestial bodies and a chorus of song. The Star of Jacob had also lived a perfect life, fulfilling the whole Law as no human ever could. This Star had taken from humanity all broken commands and ignored laws unto himself. The Star's light was quenched, but not for long, and not forever.

Like Jesus, Bar-Kokhba would not deliver to the Pharisees the guaranteed blessing they sought. He, too, died a horrible death, besieged and slaughtered by cruel Roman hands.

Before he was crucified, Jesus shocked the Pharisees with many questions, but one in particular startled them in its honesty. He asked it before a crowd, the shadow of the Temple falling on their backs.

"Why are you trying to kill me?"

John 7:19

They could not answer him then, but the answer was simple nonetheless. They were trying to kill him because obedience to the Law-Made-Flesh came with no guarantees.

This dangerous Mashiach had become uncaged.

IN PLAIN SIGHT

He was no stranger to hatred. He'd felt the sulfur-breath of the serpent on his feet since the dark angel's mind turned early to war. Incarnate Love could not be confused by hatred, nor would he be shamed by it. The Son of Heaven, keenly aware of the hearts of all men, knew hatred's presence without ever being conquered by its power. The curses of humanity fell upon him like acid rain from the fruit's first bite, acrid in taste and deeply disturbing to him.

He was, however, affected by the hatred coming from his artistry. Like a mother weeps at the bitter words from a child, so he had wept at the pain of it.

The air in Jerusalem was thick with hate. He knew they wanted him dead. They wanted him in hell, the fires forever scorching his claims of divinity. They waited for his arrival at the great feast, setting armored guards at every crossroad. They were salivating at the possibility of an arrest.

Being in Galilee was different. The air was cleaner, and some part of him did not want to leave the salted scents of grassy hills and the sea. But he must leave—it was the path before his feet, and he would not swerve from it. Besides, the hatred of Jerusalem had already reached him there in Galilee. It traveled in his own company, keeping the money purse tucked in his belt.

He'd arrived when the festival was half finished. He would be rushed by no man, no kindred relation. His timing was in complete alignment with the will of his Father. He was unafraid to enter the center of their trap. He knew that his time had not yet come, and he knew that no one could assault him until the moment ripened. When he entered the ancient city, this place of monarchs and priests, he shed tears. Their disappointment in him was like a palpable wall, and he mourned for their blindness and murderous thoughts.

He walked through the outer courtyards of the Temple to the place of teaching, his gait unhindered by whispers and stares. He strode with purpose, determination. He was there to shepherd the lost sheep of Israel. The God-appointed under-shepherds had failed their flock, and now these same under-shepherds were trying to kill their leader.

He sat down on a center platform with his disciples gathered round, a crescent shield in the midst of a mob. His friends were distracted, on high alert for hurled stones and concealed blades meant for the teaching Rabbi.

They were also distracted by their own fate. Would they, too, be arrested? Harmed? Murdered? And for what? Their infant faith flagged on the holy ground.

Jesus knew their minds, and he was not angered. He knew this was hard on them, and he grieved at the suffering to come. From this place of fierce mission and holy sadness, he began to teach the Kingdom. As words poured out from *the* Word, the circle around Jesus swelled. His timbre, echoing on marbled flagstones and colonnades, wove together a colorful tapestry of past, future, and present. The crowd was dumbstruck.

The scholars, too, were amazed. How could One so blaspheming speak with such purity about the Law of God? Their amazement met their hatred, and it bellowed the flame of rage against him. The Pharisees looked around at the rapt faces of the people—*their* people—and their hearts burned hot within them. They could not understand the source of his power, his authority, his deep knowledge. They were the teachers, not he. They were the rabbis, the priests, the interpreters of the Law. And yet he had hypnotized their people and stolen them away.

Jesus sensed their jealousy. He smelled the festering. He felt their hatred—and from that place, he rose up with questions:

"It was Moses, wasn't it, who gave you God's Law? But none of you are living it. So why are you trying to kill me?"

John 7:19

At Jesus's question, the Pharisees sputtered, foaming at the mouth, spittle flying from their lips and landing on graying beards. Jesus couldn't have attracted more attention if he'd set the veil on fire. They denied his accusation before the people while wrath churned furiously from their guts.

Their secret plot was no secret to the people's Rabbi. But

Jesus remained unmoved by their hatred, returning as easily to his teaching as a child to play.

MONEY-BACK GUARANTEE

We want guarantees.

Like the Pharisees, we watch this Jesus, waiting to see what he's all about. We look for the guarantees we need to feel comfortable, but we don't always find them. He provides no pledge that what we want to happen will happen. He is not the cosmic genie, trapped and awaiting release from the world's lamp. We cannot polish him into action or submission. We cannot insert a formulaic prayer or service into the divine vending machine and expect him to eject a particular favor.

He is not the God who will be pushed. He's not the God who receives ultimatums. He can't be bought with severe obedience. He won't be pressured, manipulated, or threatened into giving inappropriate guarantees.

But like the misguided Pharisees, we often forget these things about God. We confuse his openness and affection for us with passivity or weakness. It's from this place that we begin demanding guarantees. It's also from this place that they receive another question from Jesus, one intimately related to the question in John 7.

Mark records that the Pharisees "began to argue with him" (Mark 8:11, ESV). The original Greek of this rather mild terminology is *peirazō* (pā-rä´-zō), which is "to pierce."[10] From the earliest days of Jesus's ministry to the Jewish people, the Pharisees wished him harm. They wanted to nail Jesus to the wall.

Jesus didn't appreciate this, and his strong response is indicative of his displeasure. "Provoked, he said, '*Why does this generation clamor for miraculous guarantees?*'" (v. 12).

The Pharisees were simply expecting God to work the way he had with their ancestors. And why wouldn't they? Signs, wonders, and *"miraculous guarantees"* are how Yahweh demon-strated his constant *chesed* (kheh´·sed), or loyal love.[11]

"What sign do you show us," the Jews asked in John's Gospel, "for doing these things?" (John 2:18, ESV). In their mass exodus from Egypt, it was sign after sign that proved to everyone that their God existed, and that his power could not be trumped. That's why they found no problem with asking Jesus for a sign, a guarantee, *proof* that he was from the same God who gave them manna. "Jews demand signs," writes the Apostle Paul to the Corinthians, "but we preach Christ crucified, a stumbling block to Jews" (1 Corinthians 1:22–23, ESV).

With profound irony, Jesus *did* produce signs. He performed supernatural and divine spectacles that should have converted the most stubborn. But his character and his Cross were the light that blinded them from true seeing. In the end, his charac-ter and his Cross became an obstacle to true obedience.

Jesus is teaching us *why* we, like the Pharisees, are really pressing him. The sign we demand is nothing more than a miraculous guarantee. We require a guarantee that our lives with God will turn out the way we want. When he doesn't give us this guarantee, murderous intent rises within.

GENERATIONS OF DEMANDS

When each of our daughters turned two, we determined it was time to teach them the human behavior of relieving themselves in the toilet. We would be barbarians no longer. Parents under-stand this—two years is long enough to deal with the back end of another person, even a tiny, adorable person who belongs to you and has your nose.

Macy was easy to teach. We sat her on a portable toddler potty in front of her favorite cartoon. We loaded her with juice. Eventually, nature had its way, and the little potty had a sensor that sang when it became wet. That first time of praise and applause, she was happy to comply.

Macy instinctively understood the rationale, the inherent logic behind the potty-training strategy. She digested the cause-and-effect nature: Accident equals wet pants. Wet pants equal an uncomfortable feeling. Transitioning to the toilet didn't seem like such a big deal.

Jo was a completely different story. There was something of an attachment to the way she'd been doing things in her life. Diapers had worked well so far—why change? Why do it the way everyone else did? This kid was born an individual, and she planned to stay that way. We tried the juice, the cartoons, the cute pink potty that sang. Every time Jo needed to relieve herself, she'd stand up, take two steps away from the potty, and squat on the white carpet. This happened over and over, day after day, until we got wise. Wise in potty training means introducing candy.

Candy changed the game entirely. Suddenly, there was a really good reason to try something new. We showed her a bag of exotic treats—the orange marshmallow "circus peanuts." She'd never seen, let alone tasted, them before. We cut the tiniest edge off one peanut and let her eat it. Her eyes went wide.

"If you go in the potty," we told her, "you can have the whole peanut."

She ran to her tiny throne, never taking her eyes off the circus peanut bag, and sat down. Within seconds, we had results, and this kid had her peanut.

Aren't we all like this? We're not willing to trust God's good plan for us until we're guaranteed reward, until we can see it. We all need a sign in the shape of a circus peanut before we're willing to comply. Without that guarantee, we'd rather just stay in the mess of our diaper.

The human need for a miraculous guarantee is exactly what caused our great-grandparents' eviction from paradise. In the Garden, Eve plucked and ate with Adam, their act showing a desperate clamoring for spiritual guarantees of their eternal happiness and well-being. They indulged in that from which they should have abstained. Jesus's question about guarantee is for them.

"*This generation,*" the one Jesus questions in Mark's Gospel, is every generation. Lest we wander off into a discussion about millennials and hipsters, the Greatest Generation and Generation X—we are *all* of "*this generation.*" Jesus looks at those he has made, spanning times and countries and ages, and he identifies us all with this generation of sign-seekers.

What we all really want to know is if our obedience is worth the risk.

Jesus is gracious. He knows we need reassurance. His delight is to bring us the peace that is beyond what the eyes can see. But what Jesus wants us to grasp with his question is that asking for a sign of God *when God is already present* just doesn't sit well with him.

Mark 8 tells us the Pharisees were pushing Jesus for a sign, and Jesus asks them why. What had Jesus just been doing prior to this sign assault?

The context is astounding, laughable even. Just before the Pharisees "started in on him," as Mark records, Jesus had just miraculously provided a Messianic banquet for the famished Jewish people. Jesus hadn't even been able to brush the breadcrumbs from his tunic before the Pharisees gave ultimatums.

The Pharisees were demanding a sign when *the* Sign stood before them, smelling of fish and sun-baked bread, asking questions. They required a miracle when *the* Miracle had just stepped from a boat into their chaotic and God-hungry world. They needed a guarantee that this man was legitimate when the Guarantee of God had just fed his people as Yahweh had in Exodus.

We look so hard for God to come through and show us in plain language that things will turn out okay—all the while we're missing him, alive right here in our space. We are the generation needing guarantees.

Guarantees aren't guaranteed—they never are.

They were looking so hard for a sign that they missed God. They were disrupted by the unpredictability of their own fortunes. Without the money-back guarantee, they moved forward on a path to the back side of the Cross.

DISAPPOINTMENT WITH GOD

We find, to our deep dismay, that far too often the guarantee is just beyond our reach. When we don't get our circus peanut, that Pharisaic place in us is disrupted, and it does not feel good. Our center for personal control becomes dislodged.

This is exactly why Jesus withholds certain guarantees. Being surprised by God creates in us a vulnerability where vulnerability is needed. Our interrupted expectations are his gift. It seems that one of the guarantees he is willing to make us is that he will give us surprises like Christmas presents heaped under the evergreen. He is the God Who Loves to Surprise. I think he enjoys this about himself, but we often don't.

Neither did the Pharisees. They didn't like that the Ancient of Days was born as a peasant in a cave. Lord-Sabaoth works quietly with sawdust and wood for thirty years. His first display of divine power is to turn dirty foot water into discerning, robust wine. He rejects them as the religious establishment and prefers instead the company of sinners. He asks men of wealth to sell all they have. He invites crowds to eat his body and drink his blood.

He tarries when he should hurry.

He's abrupt when he should be polite.

He heals when he should be resting.

He just can't seem to stop.

Unlike Jesus, our reaction to his surprises is far too predictable. We choose to entertain disappointment—dangerous levels of disappointment. Ultimately, this kind of disappointment in God and with God leads to soul-killing fear. We are afraid we won't get what we need and want. This fear gives birth to anger, and anger to boundless hatred, a hatred that ultimately becomes capable of bloodshed.

This is the path of coddled disappointment in God.

Why, he asks, *do you place demands on me?*

He continues: *When those demands aren't met, why do you want me dead?*

His questions burn like wildfire in times of drought. These two questions, brilliantly asked by Jesus to both the Pharisees and to us, work in strategic rhythm. He intends that these questions get to the rigidity of the Pharisee in each human heart.

This whole conversation with Jesus makes me squirm.

The word Jesus used, meaning "to kill," is from the Greek, *apokteinō* (ap-ok-ti´-no). This verb is used nine times in John's Gospel alone, most often describing the lust harbored to murder God's Son. The term can simply mean to end a life, or it can desire something much deeper: "to deprive of spiritual life and procure eternal misery in hell."[12]

What are *we* to do with his question? We all have it in us, this murderous hatred of a God who won't comply with our demands and expectations.

His blood is on every human hand.

CHOOSING TO ENGAGE

Any place in us that is rigid, angry with God, disappointed—this is the Pharisee place, the place that craves the death of God. I am guilty, guilty with Pharisaical guilt, of wanting this unthinkable thing. God gave Moses and all of Israel the command: *"Thou shalt not murder."* As he gave this immortal decree, he instinctively knew that his people would not stop desiring to break it against him.

Anytime I've thought that I'm a better master strategist for my life than Jesus, I have tried to kill him. I've forgotten his brilliance, his ability to provide, his good purpose for me—and I've plotted how to silence him. It's not as obvious as the plotting of the Pharisees.

My strategy of killing Jesus is subtle and quiet.

It's when I silently reach over and take the reins from his hands. It's when I evaluate my circumstances and accuse him of holding out on me. It's when I move forward in decisions, wanting to make things happen in my own intellect or drive. In those moments, I have forgotten who I am dealing with.

I have forgotten too much.

But it doesn't have to end there. When raw disappointment in God presents, we have two options: We can either try to kill him, or we can wrestle with him.

Killing creates distance, but wrestling gets us close enough with God to trade sweat. He hates distance. He wants his arms around us—either an embrace or a full nelson will do.

Wrestling with God is as old as Jacob, who found himself in an all-night headlock with Yahweh. All of Jacob's schemes and deceptions had finally caught up with him, and he was afraid. He knew he deserved what was coming to him in the shape of hair-covered fury. He knew he had sinned not only against his twin, but against the Holy One of Israel. He was disappointed with this turn of events, but this didn't cause him to desire God's demise.

In the midst of terror and utter disappointment, Jacob wanted to know that clinging to Yahweh was enough.

Jacob stayed behind by himself, and a man wrestled with him until daybreak. When the man saw that he couldn't get the best of Jacob as they wrestled, he deliberately threw Jacob's hip out of joint.

The man said, "Let me go; it's daybreak."

Jacob said, "I'm not letting you go 'til you bless me."

The man said, "What's your name?"

He answered, "Jacob."

The man said, "But no longer. Your name is no longer Jacob. From now on it's Israel (God-Wrestler); you've wrestled with God and you've come through." . . . Jacob named the place Peniel (God's Face) because, he said, "I saw God face-to-face and lived to tell the story!"

Genesis 32:24–30, selected verses

Wrestling with God is honored by God (cf. Psalm 46:7ff.). It's looking into God's face and telling him why we're so disappointed and scared. Asking God good questions in the face of disappointment is not a murderous act. God desires to be engaged in holy sparring.

But seeking a way to kill him is utterly unlike wrestling. It is the opposite response. Trying to kill him is the same as trying to silence his voice in our lives. It's cutting him off—his presence, his face, his right to our lives. It's turning our backs to his face, a symbolic gesture that smacks of passive aggression.

Perhaps this seems harsh, a bit melodramatic. However, when we sit with the true nature of rebellion against God, it is shocking. It's a violent, cruel act. I'm not being harsh *enough*.

Trying to kill him is choosing to disengage over engagement.

The scriptures don't sugarcoat what's occurring at the level of the heart. While the Life-Light entered the world to illuminate it, we've joined hands with the dark to extinguish it (John 1:5). This attitude says to the God who created us, "I wish you were dead." God won't give us the guarantees we seek—so we take up our hammers and nail him to the cross to shut him up.

In all these ways, I am guilty of wanting to kill God.

Jesus longs to protect us from ourselves, for he knows we cannot live in this place and be safe. The heart that is full of murder quickly finds itself the victim.

LET GOD BE GOD

In the face of overwhelming disappointment and seemingly terrible surprises, what would it look like for us to put away our weapons and let God be God? What would it look like to let him live?

I'd never been to a street party before Ireland. I'd never seen a whole village get up on a hastily erected stage—in the middle of the town square—and spontaneously perform the perfect choreography involved in Irish set dancing. This is just not the way things work in most American towns.

The evening was cool, as they usually were. The air tasted like brine. It had rained all day, but the rain had turned to a fine mist and a breeze blew in from the sea. As the shadows deepened, the square became filled. People poured from pubs and homes, being pulled by excited children.

By this time, the residents of Caherciveen had accepted our presence with the warmest of welcomes, and they included us as natural, if not exotic, observers of their party. When the musical quartet took the stage, there was standing room only in the square. About six groups of six representing the families of the village crowded onto the lower stage, spanning ages and generations from elderly to adolescent.

When the music started, all feet began a rhythmic stomping that shook the beams and rafters of the set we'd watched being built from planks that day. As if everyone had rehearsed, they whirled and stepped to the beat of the music as one. This went on for an hour or more. When one person would get tired, there would be a fresh pair of legs ready to jump into the dance and take their place. There was laughter. There was singing. There were rosy cheeks and twinkling eyes.

It was all like a scene from a really happy movie, but somehow, it was real.

As much as I wanted to, I didn't dare dance. I couldn't. I didn't know the steps, and as fast as they were going, I would have injured my set partners had I tried. I had an ache, a good ache, that told me something mysterious and beautiful was taking place, and I was on the outside of it.

Our girls, of course, felt the same. They understood that if they hopped on that stage, they'd be crushed, jigged to death by a score of dancers. This did not prevent them, however, from dancing right where we stood.

After the set dancing, all the children were invited to sit on the edge of the stage for the real show. Two young performers of *sean-nós*, a type of Irish dancing that we knew as "River

Dance," climbed the stage. The young man was originally from Caherciveen. The couple had come from Dublin where they danced professionally onstage to honor his home village.

Macy and Jo were in the front, sitting cross-legged next to their friends, the O'Neill boys. The couple's movement began with the first sounds of the instruments. I was watching thunder approach from the sea, coming closer and closer until we could all feel the electric pulse in the hair of our arms and the back of our necks. There were several moments where the male dancer came right up to the upturned noses of the spellbound children and did a leap like a young stag bounding through the forest.

The girls squealed with delight. I had tears dripping into my scarf. The whole moment was shocking, a holy surprise with design.

Jesus wonders why his presence doesn't do the same to us. He wonders why we're so disappointed in him, disappointed to the point of wishing him out of our lives.

Jesus is all the magic and wonder and play of an Irish street party in July. He's the power and thrill of *sean-nós* dancing. He's the passion and rhythm of fiddle and drums. He's invited us to partake in his unpredictability. He's calling us to raise our expectations that have been puny for too long.

In Jesus's words, we are a generation that doesn't know how to live in the Kingdom Among Us. We respond to his invitation, "Thanks, but no thanks." We are ignorant that in him, there is a street party happening right now, and we are missing it. So much joy, so much life, right in front of us.

We just don't know how to take Jesus. We don't know how to honor his aliveness, his humor, his playfulness. He tells us a joke and we don't get it. He invites us to dance and we'd rather sit out. Anyway, we don't know the steps he's dancing, and we're afraid we'll get trampled. We stand in his presence as if we're disappointed or bored, as if our eyes cannot see the dance and our ears are deaf to the music.

In other words, we are disappointed about the wrong things, temporary things.

What if we were to ask Jesus to awaken us to the reality of what he is really like, and then *let him be that Reality?* We can choose to let God be God. Let Jesus be Jesus. Let him be dynamic, colorful, unpredictable. Let him be bold.

Let him be *alive.*

We can dance with him. We're invited to wrestle with him. But we can no longer try to tame him or silence him, and we can no longer wish him gone.

In this way, we will begin to live in the Kingdom Among Us.

Relationships with others are not to be controlled, including our relationship with Jesus. Neither are our own lives. The control we seek, the guarantee we're after, belongs to him alone. The way he molds the surprises of our lives doesn't have to disappoint us—not for long, anyway.

He is not tame. He is not boring. He is not predictable. He is full of vim and vinegar, as my grandfather used to say. His good character and his constant affection are the guarantee he gives.

As the Celtic Christians said, he is the Wild Goose, emphasis on *wild.*

THE PLOT-TWISTING JESUS

In the end, the true Mashiach *was* killed—but it wasn't by the Pharisees. It wasn't by Pilate. It wasn't even by us.

Love slayed the One who would not comply with our shallow expectations.

His love for the Father and his love for us created within him a willingness to lay down his life so we, the assassins armed with nails and hammers, would never taste death ourselves. We would never endure the shame of the Cross.

Nietzsche was half right. Jesus's blood is on us. With profound irony, it is this blood that becomes an eternal guarantee of our righteousness before God.

And still he asks, quietly: *"Why are you trying to kill me?"*

Though I am guilty, I am still beloved. No matter how many times I try to eliminate him from my life so that I can rule, he never leaves. He goes nowhere. He may get quiet, if that's what we want from him, but he never turns his back. Not for a minute. While I'm trying to kill God, he is thoroughly committed to giving me life.

Jesus is kind in his asking. His question is gentle and firm. It works as a red warning light to my soul, a flashing invitation to return to him. He knows our redeemed hearts, that we really don't want him dead. He knows that we struggle to love him more than our own will. He responds to our disappointment in him with gracious questioning. When we've returned to him, he sits us down and welcomes *our* questions.

This is Jesus, our very Inquisitive Christ.

Our wrestling questions are always invited. He's not intimidated by them. He is asking us to put down our weapons of hatred, aimed at his heart, and instead wrestle him for all we're worth.

We will walk away limping and blessed beyond our wildest expectations.

FOR CONTEMPLATION AND DISCUSSION

Lectio Divina Exercise:

Walk into the Temple courts with Jesus. What does it feel like to be so hated? What do you see in the faces of the Pharisees? Relate with them a moment in their disappointment and fear. Feel the shock in what Jesus asks them. *"Why are you trying to kill me?"* How do you respond? What do you do with your desire to kill Jesus? Imagine, instead, leading your disappointment to Jesus. Ask him about it. Wrestle with him in the midst. What does it feel like to be locked in his eternal embrace?

For Reflection:

1. The Pharisees suffered greatly for their obedience to God's Law. How have you suffered by your obedience?
2. Where is the greatest temptation in your life to demand guarantees from God?
3. Where do you see the urge toward *apokteinō*—seeking to kill—in your own heart?
4. How do you view the unpredictability of Jesus? Is it welcomed? Where can you practice letting God be God?
5. What is your answer to Jesus's question: *"Why are you trying to kill me?"*

PART III:

JOINING THE INTIMATE CONVERSATION

CHAPTER SIX

"Still You Do Not Know Me?"

Avoiding Intimacy with Jesus

"I know you well and you are special to me.
I know you by name."

—Yahweh,
Exodus 33:17

The true delight is in the finding out rather than in the knowing.
—Isaac Asimov

Dozens of roses. Study dates without the study. A five-course catered dinner on a downtown rooftop. The day he asked me to marry him, he planned a horse-drawn carriage ride over country lanes. It was all about the advance plan and attention to romantic detail. These principles that produced such elaborate gestures defined our years of dating and engagement.

It was all so magical, so memorable, so *intimate.*

Fast-forward into an avalanche of reality. By our fifth year of marriage, we had two babies—a twenty-month-old attached to the hip, and a newborn strapped to the chest in a modern-day papoose. Our home was bombed with diaper boxes, spit-up towels, and fist-sized teething toys. Sippy cups, baby bottles, and Cheerio dust littered the carpet. I constantly smelled like sour milk, and my best outfit was whatever wrinkled thing wasn't covered in baby vomit. Jimmy had bags under his eyes—not carry-on size, but the kind airports require checking—from staccato sleep. Baby girl commotion and gibberish dominated every conversation and every meal. Their tiny pre-word voices were in our every waking thought.

Jimmy and I were disheveled, exhausted wrecks teetering on the edge of insanity. So many daily necessities were interrupted—including our sleep and hygiene. These girls didn't even let us use the bathroom in peace. The entire world had gone pink and purple.

It was all so terrifying, so strenuous, so . . . *intimate?*

What we're shocked to realize now is that the intimacy between us was greater in the chaos of young parenthood than it ever could have been in the rosy glow of a romantic courtship. How could this be true? One simple reason: You cannot hide *anything* at two a.m. There's a revelation of self that simply happens at that hour.

In the half-lit exposure of too-early morning, we were revealed to each other in a way we never dreamed (or desired). In our intense, pressure-cooked world with two babies, what we'd hidden during our dating years was unlocked and unleashed. I had crazy hair, a crazy body, lots of crazy thoughts—and yet, because he loved me, Jimmy really seemed to enjoy every part of who I was.

This was difficult for me to accept, but I eventually got it. I understood because I felt the same way about him.

I, too, grew more in love with the man I'd married, because I bore witness to some truly heroic acts. I watched him change hundreds of diapers, the contents of which still haunt him. He made me laugh with his horrified faces and gagging sounds. Really, he made me laugh at so many things when all I felt capable of was frustrated tears.

Together, we shared moments of nervous breakdowns as well as hysterical happiness. We brought intimacy to each other in a million ways, from reheating the dregs in the coffee cup to stealing forty-five minutes for a date where we talked about our babies for at least thirty-seven of those minutes.

We were oblivious to this intimacy at the time, but it was there. The intimacy in the reality is what made it all so profound.

It's in these moments, the real-time, real-life moments of deep seeing and even deeper knowing, that intimacy is found—even cultivated. Anyone can present their best on a date. Anyone can display their carefully postured "worst" on social media.

True intimacy is in the enjoyment of transparent presence. It is the vulnerable delight of deep knowing.

But even this kind of relational intimacy with the ones we allow in can disappoint us.

Jimmy and I have now been married for more than fifteen years. We've been friends for more than twenty-five. With years of real-time moments, there's a sense that I get him, completely, and he gets me. He's invited me to know him, and I've done the same. I look at his face and see what he's thinking. I know the backstory to his decisions. He knows why certain things scare me. We love to go on long walks and talk about anything that's on our minds. I know that he will laugh every time I say the phrase "donkey cream." He knows intense boredom makes me obnoxious at Home Depot, so he packs me a snack and sudoku.

We're weird. We know.

But even in the midst of knowing each other, I still look at him and have moments of wondering if I know him at all. At times, I still wonder if he really knows me. Even with the intentional desire to share our lives, we're still prone to completely misunderstand each other's hearts, each other's motives. We second-guess and get each other wrong.

As we change and grow, we can still view each other with the lenses of the past.

We delight in discovering more of the other, but it's still so incomplete, so partial. I am confronted every day that even in the ways I am confident I know him, I still can't limit him to that box in my mind I've labeled "The Way Jimmy Works."

Even in the most intimate of relationships, there is so much we don't know. We can't assume complete knowledge or understanding of any person. No one will fully understand us. We get frustrated when we are misunderstood or just simply missed by those who are supposed to know and love us the most.

Even with the closest of human intimacies, we still find that we're lonely, and that loneliness is unsettling. Along with the loneliness, we find a paradox. We find we're *also* unsettled by the notion of closeness.

We find that we avoid the intimacy we crave.

INTERNET INTIMACY

Try as we might, we cannot deny our need for intimate connection. Unfortunately, we are deeply frightened of that intimacy. It's raw and exposing, and who really wants to be truly naked before another? We're not always safe or invited to do so. When others reject us, we are forced to pursue counterfeit measures, practices that provide false closeness, a forged community to trick our souls.

We've become addicted to this false intimacy, captured by two pervasive examples. First, we are a culture addicted to the rush of exposure to non-intimate sex. According to *The Daily Wire*,

> We dedicated well over four and a half billion hours to watching porn on one porn site in 2016. Just on Porn Hub, humanity spent twice as much time viewing porn in a year as it has spent existing on planet Earth. The site had over 90 billion video views and 44,000 visitors every minute of every day. It all adds up to over 500 thousand years worth of porn consumed in the span of 12 months. Since 2015, human beings have spent one million years watching porn. One million years.[1]

This is our culture's favorite pastime, especially our youth.

Almost 90 percent of college-age males (and close to 30 percent of females) consume pornography either weekly or every day.[2] The Institute for the Study of Labor (as quoted by watchdog website Enough is Enough) found that "those who frequently consume Internet pornography are less likely to marry because they see pornography as a marital sexual gratification substitute."[3]

Porn promises something that marriage could never fully provide.

But we must admit, our cultural problems are not all porn's fault. This drive for intimacy moves beyond sex. Our second cultural addiction is more terrifying than the first, simply because it is clothed in socially acceptable verbiage. We, as a culture, are also addicted to the high we get from "belonging" in false community.

There are 500 million daily active users on Instagram, with 95 million photos being posted per day. This is up 25 million from last year (and just in case you were curious, pizza is the most Instagrammed food).[4] But with all of us taking pictures, posting pictures, viewing pictures, we are more lonely, depressed, and anxious as a people than ever before.

We are still very unseen.

On Facebook, there are more than two billion active users, increasing its database by 500,000 new members every day and six additional profiles every second. According to the *Harvard Business Review*, more than half of registered members from eighteen to twenty-nine years of age check their Facebook page before drinking coffee, brushing their teeth, or using the bathroom after waking.[5] When we must check our notifications before relieving ourselves in the morning, this is the calling card of an addict.

Are we surprised by our fear of real intimate connection with another human being? All we ingest is the junk food of false intimacy and none of its authentic quality produce. We're too sluggish to even try what is good for us. And why wouldn't we be? We can get the sugar rush of inauthentic connection without the work true intimacy requires. We like what these counterfeit intimacies will do for us, and we're simply too full of the fast food to pursue the real meal.

We need intimacy, and we want it to come easily. Many of

us simply don't have the margin in our schedule for more than Internet intimacy. We need to click it, post it, and view it in three seconds or less, because we are too hurried for anything else. Ideally, we'd like to slow down. We'd like margin in our schedule. But where in the world will we find it? What could we possibly get rid of or say no to that might allow us to breathe and pursue intimacy? We wrestle with the expectations placed upon us, and in the end, we determine that everything on our calendars and in our lives is just more important than intimacy.

Because we've inundated ourselves with the false, we no longer know how to engage in the true. But something still rises up in us, something that knows a critical value to life is missing. Thus, we throw ourselves into "trying intimacy," and we quickly fail.

We understand that the soul wants to be known. It's ingrained in our nature. To be known and loved for who we are is among the deepest of human needs. To be unknown feels like death. We must be known, even incompletely, or something in us withers.

We begin to realize that the best human relationship still only provides *partial* intimacy. Our souls need something deeper, Someone deeper. We were created to hold more than we get, but we don't know how to fix it. In sad desperation, we find we no longer remember how to enter into the intimacy that once knit our souls to God's own.

IN THE COOL OF THE EVENING

The conversations always started with the laughter of God.

"Here's a riddle," Jesus began, swallowing his grin like a child. "There's a flower that blooms on every creature's face."

The children walked in silence, repeating the curious statement as they waited.

"I give up," Eve said to her companions.

"Me, too. Tell us," joined Adam.

"A tulip," Jesus said, pausing before laughter exploded from a God-sized belly that shook the canyons and set the cedars shivering. "Get it? *Two*-lip?" he asked, wiping tears from his cheeks. "You should see your faces right now."

The rest groaned, marveling that in all heaven and earth a better joke could not have been created. Adam protested, "But, Jesus, not all creatures have lips. Birds don't."

They all tried to imagine a chicken with lips. It was hard to think of anything else.

"Let there be wit," pronounced the Father.

"Thou shalt not joke-bomb," the Spirit replied.

"Come on. It was funny," Jesus protested.

They all shook their heads, smiling at the weird humor of God. They were happy, being together, walking and talking. The quirky jokes were just part of the deal.

What is difficult to imagine now—enjoying mutual conversation with a visible God—was standard fare. Nothing was lacking in their delight of one another. The Three and the two—a Quinity-in-motion, engrossed in perfect intimacy, created for union. Their silhouette against the setting sun formed one whole, only through swinging arms and moving legs peeked the light.

In the morning of the young world, each was naked, clothed only in the sun's warmth. Each was unveiled to the others, open to knowing and being known. Man and woman, Trinity and humanity—different but unseparated in the Garden's intimacy. The laughter of God created children of mirth and intelligence. The conversations cracked both mysteries and smiles. Dialogue transitioned between matters of flesh to enigmas of spirit with fluid grace. Their talk scraped heaven's jewelry, a wondering in the intricacies of constellations and galaxies. Their conversation dug deep into fresh soils, discussing farming technique and the chemical composition of dirt.

They talked of sex and weather without shame or reaching.

No topic was off limits, not even the tree of which they were not permitted to partake. They talked about this tree, and he gave no chastisement in the conversation. He explained to them its dangers, and they were content in his response.

There was some knowledge not worth knowing.

But in that Garden, their intimacy was already being hunted.

The union was breached with the snake's conversation. He, too, desired intimacy with these wondrous children. He, too, had a joke he wished to tell, a cruel joke where the laughter was mockery, and the tears tasted bitter. Inserting himself between their oneness, he, too, offered a discussion on mysteries. He questioned whether the Trinity was not disclosing full knowledge, crucial knowledge needed to thrive in this new earth. He presented a knowing that was more attractive, more pleasing to them than the intimacy God offered.

With a smile and a wink, he pried open the door to false knowing, a door that humanity could never again shut.

With a bite, the two children swallowed the knowledge of evil. It burned as it descended into the bowels of the soul. The snake, snickering in victory, slithered into the underbrush. He had offered intimacy, but the children now saw him as he was: cold, distant, unapproachable.

His conversations with them would bring nothing but shame.

Though banned from the Garden, though torn from the union they'd once indwelled, the children were still loved by the Triune God. He walked with them, though they could not always see him. He talked with them, though their ears became filled with other, lesser voices. He still offered them the intimacy that had been broken but that would draw them again close to his heart.

He waited with eager patience until the time came to send the Word, the divine Conversation, into their midst. His children treated this Word poorly. They ignored his voice. They rejected his intimacy. They didn't understand his jokes. They nailed him to a Cross to shut him up, for they grew weary with his walking and talking among them.

But this Cross became the reason for the whole world to

laugh, for by it, the Garden gates—long sealed—were flung wide open. Because of the Cross, God would once again commune closely with his children. His Spirit melding in intricate union with their own, they could once again walk and talk together as they had.

They would again know each other as one. It would begin with a question.

INTIMATE QUESTION

In John 14, Jesus returns a frustrated Philip's request with not one but three questions, the first of which cannot be bypassed.

"Have I been with you so long and you still do not know me?"
John 14:9 (ESV)

Philip ate with him. Philip drank with him. They laughed at the same jokes. They talked, for hours, over firelight. Where Jesus laid his head each night, there was Philip. He witnessed the miracles, he heard the stories, he saw the escalating conflict between Jesus and the religious. Philip was his disciple. Philip was his *friend*. And yet, Jesus looks straight into this friend's eyes and asks, "Still, *Philip*? Still *you do not know me*? After all this time? After all these years? Am I still a stranger to you?"

Jesus is asking a man who has walked with him for three years—*closely* walked with him—if he'd even really begun to know him.

Philip had missed what we also miss.

Jesus eagerly offers himself to us, over and over again, but we hesitate to accept his offer. With this question, he asks us if we know him. He invites us to wonder if we really, truly do.

Don't let the wise brag of their wisdom.
Don't let heroes brag of their exploits.
Don't let the rich brag of their riches.

If you brag, brag of this only:
That you understand and know me.

Jeremiah 9:23–24

Without knowing Jesus as he is, we are lost. Our accomplishments, spiritual or otherwise, mean nothing without intimacy, and Jesus is shining a kind light on the lack.

Jesus's question is brimming over with grief. We were made to have complete union with him. *"I am in my Father,"* Jesus tells us, *"and you in me, and I in you"* (John 14:20, ESV). He is describing reality, and we are invited to live as though this reality were *true*. That's our purpose in life. That is the designed end of our every breath and every throb of pulse.

But we neglect our purpose. We choose not to know him. We choose to keep him to the head instead of allowing the knowledge of God access to the heart.

DEFINING OUR TERMS

The verb "to know," found everywhere throughout scripture, is used more than 950 times in the Old Testament alone.[6] There are two primary ways the Greek New Testament discusses this widespread concept of knowing—*oida* and *ginōskō*.

The first, *oida* (oi´-dä), addresses the domain of the intellect.[7] With *oida* knowledge, our mind is replete with data, facts, and rationale. We employ reasoning to attain information.

We play Trivial Pursuit with *oida* knowledge.

We follow navigational directions with *oida* knowledge.

We balance our budget with *oida*.

I studied Biblical languages for my graduate degree. Without *oida*, I would have failed every class. We are called to study the scriptures, to apply our intellect toward the knowledge of God. Theological study and the reading of Biblical literature can be a gift to our souls. We can bring *oida* to church, Bible study—even relationships meant to be intimate. However, when *oida* stands alone, Bible study is just as mundane as assessing our bank accounts.

"He would not permit the demons to speak," Mark records of Jesus, "because they *knew (oida)* him" (Mark 1:34, ESV, emphasis mine). When our knowledge of God stops with *oida*, our knowledge stays with the minions of hell.

The scriptures speak to a different knowledge, one that goes beyond the knowing that *oida* designates. The word is *ginōskō* (ghin-oce´-ko), describing not the mastery of knowledge, but knowledge in process.[8] It could be translated "to *learn* to know."[9] It is a dynamic, active knowing[10] that involves the intellect but also the soul.

This type of knowing describes something deep, something rich, something incredibly intimate between the knower and the object of knowledge.[11] *Ginōskō* contains the engagement of the mind as *oida* does, but it also pursues something hidden. This word denotes a knowledge so deep that it is often an idiomatic term describing sexual intimacy in both the Old and the New Testaments.

You cannot have *ginōskō* knowledge without relationship, and profound relationship at that.

This is vividly illustrated in the Genesis 29 account of Isaac's conniving son, Jacob. True to his name, he becomes embroiled in an unhealthy love triangle that manipulated the master manipulator. In drunken imprudence, he was tricked into consummating a marriage with the older sister of his intended bride. Irate and sheepish as dawn entered their tent, he demanded his rights to the other woman. A second wedding feast was hastily thrown together, and he, too, entered the tent of Rachel and "knew" her. His immediate synopsis, Genesis recounts, was that "he loved Rachel more than Leah" (Genesis 29:30, ESV).

He married both. He knew both sexually. Looking through the eyes of Jacob, his first bride, Leah, was *oida*. Rachel, his second, was *ginōskō*. Both involved knowing, but only one included closeness, enjoyment, and full presence. He literally went to bed with both, but enjoyed true intimacy with only one.

Like Laban's daughters, *oida* and *ginōskō* act as sisters. Members of the same family unit, they invite us to engage at the different levels of who we are.

Ginōskō is intimate knowing, and *ginōskō* is what God both offers and desires. Without *ginōskō*, God becomes math, some technical thing to be mulled and then solved. But God cannot be mastered with the mind. With *ginōskō*, God can be related to, understood, with the whole man.

With *ginōskō*, he can be enjoyed.

In western church culture, we have access to information *en masse*. We live in an *oida* world. We know a great deal. We've attended numerous studies, read copious amounts of books (including this one), but we still miss intimacy with Jesus because we've only engaged *oida*.

Familiarity with God and others is easy. Acquaintanceship requires very little. It's true *knowing* that is the difficult task of relationship. We often see intimacy with God as a luxury item, one that we can afford to pay attention to only when we have a schedule break. Closeness with God, however, is not supplemental.

Intimacy is for more than monks. It is a staple in life with God.

Like soul care, like friendship, like desire—intimacy is vital to the soul. Without it, we live and breathe and relate like a grounded bird, clipped and hindered from becoming anything like our original design.

TRUSTING WHAT WE BELIEVE

The day began with a miraculous healing and ended with the governing authorities plotting murder. He healed the lame man of his lameness, but he chose the Sabbath to do so. This really irritated the Pharisees, because God was not staying within the limits they created for him. In response to their anger, Jesus returns: "*My Father is working straight through, even on the Sabbath. So am I*" (John 5:17). It sounds innocent enough to my ears, but to the Pharisees, this was seething blasphemy.

John writes, "That really set them off. The Jews were now not only out to expose him; they were out to kill him" (John 5:18).

Why?

"Not only was he breaking the Sabbath, but he was calling God his own Father, putting himself on level with God" (John 5:18).

They rend their garments and pluck out their beards at this sacrilege. They sink to their knees and pull down curses from heaven. How dare this bastard child call God his Father?

Jesus does dare, and he spends the next twenty minutes of discourse calling God his Father over and over again, a whopping fifteen times. Jesus knows that this enrages the Pharisees, but clearly he doesn't care. He will not be silenced. He ends his speech to the furious Pharisees with a rebuke and a question:

"But don't think I'm going to accuse you before my Father. Moses, in whom you put so much stock, is your accuser. If you believed, really believed, what Moses said, you would believe Me. He wrote of Me. If you won't take seriously what he wrote, how can I expect you to take seriously what I speak?"

John 5:45–47

Jesus is brilliant in his reply. He allows their *oida* to point the finger. These men prided themselves on being the religious elite. They were the ones others looked to for answers. They knew the Torah backward and forward. They could interpret any passage. They themselves were well versed in Messianic prophecy. And yet, they had their heads buried so deep in doctrine that they missed the Living Word of God among them.

If they had read Moses without tripping over *oida*, they would have seen that he foretold of Jesus in each of the five books he authored. It begins in Genesis 3, where he records that God himself promised to send One who would destroy the enemy for good: *"He will crush your head, and you will strike his heel"* (Genesis 3:15, NIV). In his ministry, Jesus clearly proved that he had authority over Satan and the forces of darkness. With one word from his lips, the demons flop on their backs, exposing their soft, vile underbellies. His command sends evil running for the hills. The Pharisees observed this; it troubled them. What was their response to Jesus being the unequivocal Snake-Crusher?

"Black magic," they said. "Some devil trick he's pulled from his sleeve" (Matthew 12:24).

They completely missed Jesus as the fulfillment of Genesis 3:15.

Moses records the story of Abraham's near-sacrifice of Isaac, and how at the last moment, God provided the ram. He writes of the Passover, and how the blood of a spotless lamb would protect God's chosen people. Moses taught about the manna that fell from the desert sky, miraculously feeding God's people in exodus. It was the Messianic image of the copper serpent that Moses lifted high in the wilderness, saving Israel from the venom of deadly snakes. He gave us the specific dimensions and adornment of the tabernacle. He gave us the law of God. He gave us the symbolic richness of everlasting covenant.

He gave us Jesus.

Jesus is in all of this—every jot and tittle. He is foreshadowed by Moses's writings everywhere. He practically jumps from the page into the beating hearts of our lives.

But only for those who have eyes to see and ears to hear. Only for those with a longing for *ginōskō*.

The Pharisees held Moses up as the one to whom they answered. Jesus saw the irony in this, for he knew that it was he himself Moses looked upon, trembling with worship and awe.

Like the Pharisees, we can believe with mental confidence that the Bible is true. We can read it, study it, memorize it. We can go to Bible studies in cyclical succession. We can have our daily quiet times. We can attend church services and listen to podcasts.

And yet with all that, it is still possible to miss Jesus.

It's possible to believe things *about* God and not really know him at all.

The Pharisees teach us this lesson. Jesus teaches us this lesson, too, with what he asks. Within each one of us lives a Pharisee, garbed in black and frustrated with Jesus.

Jesus desires to confront this in us, to expose the rigidity that leads to vast mistrust. If we don't surrender to the Living Word, allowing him to speak to us and in us and over us, then the written Word will just be lines on a wafer-thin page. The Pharisees could read Moses until their eyes bled. We can, too. But if we're not entering union with God, the scriptures will act as our judge, mirroring how badly we have missed God.

He wants intimacy with us, not religion. He wants our hearts, not only our heads. He wants us to believe him, really believe, when all looks lost and hope is dwindling.

He's asking for our trust, not just our mental assent.

THE DIVINE PRIORITY

To know Jesus, to *really* know him, he is inviting us to experience *ginōskō* intimacy, not simply a relationship born of surface association. *"This is the real and eternal life,"* Jesus explains to his disciples. *"That they* ginōskō *you, the one and only true God, and Jesus Christ, whom you sent"* (John 17:3). What is Jesus saying here? What does it mean to have *"real and eternal life"*?

In clear terms, Jesus is teaching us the content of salvation.

He is saying that the Gospel doesn't just *include* intimacy with God. The Gospel *is* intimacy with the Living, Triune God, and the *ginōskō* Gospel is for all.

Jesus's question shows us that it is vitally important to God that he is known—*deeply* known. We see his ache to be known all around us. The vibrancy of creation cries out for a closer inspection of the Artist. The revelation of himself is both the theme and the purpose of the written Word. From the very beginning, he walked with his image-bearers in the cool of the day, a beautiful portrait of his invitation to be known. "If anyone is to love God," writes Dallas Willard in *The Divine Conspiracy*, "God in his glorious reality must be brought before the mind and kept there."[12]

Knowing God intimately is the reason for our existence. *"When you come looking for Me,"* God tells us, *"you'll find Me. Yes, when you get serious about finding Me and want it more than anything else, I'll make sure you won't be disappointed"* (Jeremiah 29:13, emphasis mine).

He'd rather have intimacy than compliance (Hosea 6:6).

He'd rather have intimacy than facts (1 Corinthians 8:1).

He'd even rather have our intimacy than service (1 Corinthians 13:1–3).

Adam knew Eve and she bore him a child, as did Sarah with Abraham, Rachel with Jacob, and Elizabeth with Zechariah. In wondrous mystery, we are *known by God* in order to bear life: the new life that is birthed by the great intimacy we share.

Intimacy with God invites a decision: full communion or nothing at all. It asks that we stay present with the One we love. Intimacy wants every part, every moment, no withholding.

INTIMACY WITH THE UNKNOWN

Our addictions, as dangerous as they've become, are only the symptoms of why we don't pursue intimacy. The central difficulty, a toxic seed buried deep in Eden's soil, has been suppressed from our awareness.

This central difficulty is found somewhere in the eighteen inches between *oida* and *ginōskō*, the head and the heart: The God we have known is simply not compelling enough for intimacy. He's not even a candidate for worship.

Like our most intimate human relationships, our knowledge is limited and often incorrect. We assume much about God, because of our experiences, because of erroneous teaching, because we've chosen not to seek his true nature.

To know Jesus's true self is completely disruptive, however, and who among us wants to be disrupted? We've chosen to be content with this false image of God because it's convenient.

We've believed the knowledge suggested to us from Eden's rotten fruit. The enemy of our souls also invites us to an intimate knowing of what he offers. He understands that because of our original design, we will all *ginōskō* something, even his lies. Yes, the enemy has plated a god for our consumption that is underwhelming, but he's done something even worse.

He has plated a god that we feel sure will reject us.

If we finally stopped hiding and came into the light of his intimacy, we'd be sick with the fear that he'll refuse to love what he sees. What is now made possible through the Cross is feared by its Christians, simply because we don't know God as he is. In *Hearing God*, Dallas Willard writes,

> Our failure to hear God has its deepest roots in a failure to understand, accept and grow into a conversational relationship with God, the sort of relationship suited to friends who are mature personalities in a shared enterprise, no matter how different they may be in other respects. [13]

Matthew records a conversation between Jesus and his disciples about this false *oida* of God. They'd just taken an awkward boat trip, where the disciples thought Jesus was mad because they'd forgotten to pack sandwiches. The disciples did not understand—not about the bread, not about the Pharisees, and definitely not about what was in the heart of Jesus.

Their *oida* was askew.

Jesus is aware of this, aware that the process of getting him is slow, at best. That's the beauty of *ginōskō* knowing—it invites process, celebrates it even. Jesus is not after mastery, but intimacy. He doesn't give up. He is strategic in pursuing our ability to grasp him more and more, deeper and deeper. *Oida* and *ginōskō* are constantly at play in our lives with God.

When they arrived at their destination, Caesarea Philippi, they beached the boat on a bustling shoreline. Nets, rigging, and sailors dotted the rocks. Women juggling baskets and children weaved among those working. The early morning air smelled of campfires and salt and fresh fish. In the midst of all this, Jesus stood still, watching his people. Each one he saw, he knew by name and story. He knew their innermost thoughts, their core beliefs. That's what makes the question unexpected.

"Who do people say the Son of Man is?" (Matthew 16:13).

He was not after approval. He's not nervously concerned about his status. He asked the question because he wanted his friends to take a moment, a moment in the chaotic middle of stowing a skiff, and think. With his questions, he's inviting us to do the same—to observe his standing in the world around us, in the world that exists *in* us.

"Some think he is John the Baptist," said one.

"Some say Elijah," piped another.

"Some Jeremiah," added a third, "or one of the other prophets" (Matthew 16:14).

His friends told him the truth—some of it. They neglected to mention the bad descriptors—a lunatic, in league with demons, a miracle-man. They delicately shared only what most people would admit of him today: *Jesus, you're respectable but outdated, a distant figure to the real world.*

Our culture sees this image of a stained-glass Jesus and thinks him a good man, but unapproachable, as fragile and powerless as the window in which he is contained. There's an importance in our recognizing that this is how Jesus is viewed. "It is better never to have learned Him at all," George MacDonald said, "than to have learned Him wrong."

We've learned him wrong, and this flawed learning affects *everything.*

Jesus didn't comment on the disciples' responses. He didn't probe further. He waited—quietly, intentionally. He allowed the silence to rest. When he did speak, it was with another question:

"And how about you? Who do you say I am?"

Jesus has to ask, because our false *oida* must be exposed. Without this exposure, there can be nothing real between us. Intimacy can exist only with accurate knowledge. It is something we can receive only as we allow his question to penetrate our souls, uncovering false *oida* within. We can invite him to reveal himself as Moses did on the Exodus 33 mountainside: *Show me your glory.*

As we do this, as we ask for God to teach us the real him, he responds to this prayer with abundance. This is a prayer he delights to answer. He wants to be known, to be shown as he is. But it's a matter of humility on our part. We humble ourselves, listening and watching for the Living God to be revealed. When this happens, and it surely will happen, an amazing thing comes true. We see that Jesus's words to Peter become his words to us:

> *"God bless you, Simon, son of Jonah! You didn't get that answer out of books or from teachers. My Father in heaven, God himself, let you in on this secret of who I really am. And now I'm going to tell you who you are, really are."*
>
> Matthew 16:17

What is more intimate than sharing secrets? Our girls are constantly whispering things to each other, hand covering what passes from one's lips to the other's ear. Revealing secrets, explaining mystery, teaching true nature—this is all vital to *ginōskō* knowing, intimate knowing with God. This is the knowing that existed in Eden's cool evening.

WHERE THE GARDEN MEETS THE DESERT

We are invited to the Garden. We can embrace this intimate knowing offered by God. We can enjoy rich union with the

Maker of our souls. But we cannot keep feeding our addictions to false community and counterfeit intimacy. We must be hungry before we can truly enjoy the feast.

"*Be still,*" the God in the Garden sighs into our chaotic world. "*Be still and know Me*" (Psalm 46:10). Be still and know my love. Be still and know my heart. Be still and know intimate conversation.

Be still and know me in every breath, every second, every circumstance.

The deep, soul-level intimacy and knowing of God requires much. It requires the removal of distractions and vices. It requires consecrated time and space—for the schedule as well as the soul.

It requires a move to the desert.

Most think of the desert as a wasteland, a place of barrenness. But it doesn't have to be. A desert can be many things. It can be found in many places. In Biblical Greek, the word is *eremos* (er´-ay-mos), translated "wilderness or desert."[14] It speaks to a place set apart, wild and uncultivated.

In spiritual terms, the desert is more of a lifestyle than a location, a place of extreme beauty and close intimacy, where the world fades away, and ultimate Reality can be seen and known.

Jesus himself was led into the desert by the Spirit of God. The Three were together in the wilderness, taking nourishment and strength from the unceasing flow of love that passes between them. In solitude and quietness, Jesus made manifest the power of the Living God. It was from this place of power that he was able to renounce the offers of the enemy. For much of his ministry, Jesus sheltered in the wilderness. Mark tells us that Jesus kept to "desolate places" (Mark 1:45). He invited his disciples to join him there often (Mark 6:31; Luke 9:10). "As often as possible," Luke writes in his Gospel, "Jesus withdrew to out-of-the-way places for prayer" (Luke 5:16).

The desert was a welcome friend to Jesus, for it was there he could be alone with his Father. Jesus went in secret to the desert to share in uninterrupted *ginōskō* with the Godhead.

It is to the desert that we, too, must travel if we would share the same.

In one of my favorite books, *A Desert in the Ocean*, author David Adam writes,

> The desert fathers and mothers moved away from wealth and status, away from a church that was becoming popular and growing in power; they moved out of the ocean of hyperactivity and self-justification into the stillness and silence of the desert. They left a people that was seeking to be settled for a life that would be full of adventure.[15]

We all go to the desert in our lives to feel something. We get tired of the status quo that puts us to sleep and pushes our hearts away. Safe and happy is good, but our souls long for more. We desire, on a core level, to go deeper with God, to steal away with him on intimate adventure. We want to be called up into something wild and beautiful and real.

The desert beckons us, as the long, winding road did for Bilbo Baggins or the mystery of the wardrobe for Lucy Pevensie. What would Narnia be without this little girl choosing to press forward into the snowy evergreens toward the lamppost? She could have turned her back and shut the door, but we're thankful she didn't. Without her response, we would not know Aslan.

Jesus's question redirects all reasons for avoiding intimacy with him. *"You have been with me so long,"* he asks, *"and still you do not know me?"*

He wants to know why he stands alone, waiting for our arrival in the desert-garden.

We go to the desert to enter into this Kingdom more fully. We don't have to buy a ticket and board a plane to get there. There is desert in each of us. We can ignore the desert's call to intimate communion with God, but if we do, something hardens over our hearts. We miss the essence of this Gospel of *ginōskō* knowing.

What the world calls barren will yield riches beyond compare.

Just as we cannot ignore the desert and stay as we are, neither can we go to the desert and remain the same. I am changed in the desert. I'm *alive* in the desert. I know that's where I'm most at home.

A PAINFUL DISTANCE

We don't have to wait until we die and stand in the presence of God to be known. God knows us, and he loves what he knows.

> You know me inside and out,
> you know every bone in my body...
> Like an open book, you watched me grow.
>
> Psalm 139:15–16

This kind of knowing heals and restores. This knowing makes the broken whole. As we journey to the desert, we find ourselves knowing and being known along the way.

The existence of the Cross creates the ability to enter this knowing. By his death, Jesus took on God's distance so we could experience God's intimacy. The union they had cherished since before eternity was broken—broken by our sin and his love. The Triune God willingly chose to be torn in two for our oneness with him.

Right now, in this minute, we are offered *ginōskō* knowing. He offers the Gospel of intimate union, the Gospel of an opened heaven and a conversing God. We are invited into the intimate conversations of the Garden in the Desert.

FOR CONTEMPLATION AND DISCUSSION

Lectio Divina Exercise:

Imagine a garden setting, a place where you'd feel most at home with God. Experience the Triune presence with you in this place, quietly entering the scene. How do you feel in this presence? Naked? Loved? Known? Listen as he invites you to go for a walk. How do you respond? If you go with him, what does he say? What do you talk about? Does he tell you a joke? Hear him as he asks you the question: *"Do you want to know me, the real me?"* What is your initial reaction? Listen to your soul as it contemplates the changes it would mean to stay in this place. What do you see in the face of Jesus as he waits on your response?

For Reflection:

1. How have you seen the two different ways of knowing (*oida* and *ginōskō*) at work in your life? In your closest relationships? In your knowledge of yourself? In your life with God?
2. How have you become skilled at avoiding intimacy with God?
3. How does it make you feel that you are fully known, and in that knowing, fully loved by the Triune God?
4. Does it make you uncomfortable to picture God telling a joke to his children? Why or why not?
5. What would it look like for you to live in the desert with God?
6. What is your answer to Jesus's question: *"Still you do not know me?"*

CHAPTER SEVEN

"How Can You Ask— Where Is the Father?"

Introducing the Orphan to Family

Whoever does not have a good father should procure one.
—Friedrich Nietzsche

It's a hard-knock life for us.

—Annie
Lyrics by Martin Charnin

Years ago, I wrote my first essay meant for publication. I was in my mid-twenties, eagerly discovering myself and not enjoying all the discoveries I was making. Though it was about dear old Dad, I entitled the piece "Beyoncé's Trouble." I'll never say why, not for a million dollars or a Pulitzer.

My father's history, and its undeniable influence on my own story, captivated me. Our complex relationship confused me. Therefore, I did what any red-blooded, headstrong writer would do. I wrote my fascination and confusion on the blank canvas of a page. I wanted the world to see in my tangled innards an artistic palette. I wanted blame cast in the right place for why a pea-soup fog now covered a landscape of anger in my soul.

The writing was half decent at best. The content chewed together story and data, and I was having difficulty swallowing the whole mess. The essay portrayed a face of both me and my dad that is better left at the Cross and perhaps a therapist's couch.

The piece began like this:

A grown daughter's emptiness is still her father's possession, an ache that no length of time and no other man can
diminish.

After this, I wrote more. *A lot* more. I pulled weapon words
from my arsenal, defending the position I'd taken regarding the
truth. I told stories, comical stories that invited laughter but had
the acrid aftertaste of pain. The essay continued for eighteen
pages of revelation, weaving a tapestry of narrative anecdote
meant to reveal the good, the bad, but—most importantly—the
true of our father-daughter melodrama. I worked on the piece
for weeks and rejoiced when I finally finished. I sent my creation
proudly into the literary world and held my breath. Months and
a mountain of rejections later, I learned that no editor thought
"Beyoncé's Trouble" was as brilliant as I did. The piece was not
deemed worthy of publication.

For that, I now thank God.

At the time, however, it was devastating. I thought this essay
would be the ascending star of my writing career. After all that
soul-scrubbing work, no one would get to read this modern
classic on paternalistic and filial bonding. I sighed, stacked my
papers, and tried to move on.

But I just couldn't let it go. I wish I had, because this was
when I made a terrible mistake.

In a display of profound immaturity, I sent the essay to my
dad—without preamble, without warning. Imagine opening the
mailbox and finding a hornet's nest that's been poked with
a stick.

I waited, once again, with bated breath. After a few anxious
days, I watched as Dad pulled into my driveway. Even from
behind the windshield, his face stopped my heart. In my youthful
mind, I thought maybe he'd laugh, but he wasn't laughing at this
bizarre glimpse I'd given him into my thought processes. His eyes
were full of something else, something I didn't like to see.

I'll never forget what he said, standing on the steps of my
front porch.

"How could—" he began and had to stop, his face turned into the distance. I feared how he would finish and braced myself for impact. How *could* you? *How dare you? Who do you think you are?* I would have deserved every stone. My truth-telling wasn't all nasty, but neither was it kind. There was an edge to the humor that cut, and my dad was bleeding.

Dad didn't give me the lashing I earned. He asked no questions save one. With a deeper sadness than I'd ever seen in his face, he asked this one question about what I had written.

"How could you have missed my heart so much?"

I felt slapped by the question.

What I had written was the truth—my version of it—and the best I could tell it at the time. As Anne Sexton said, "It doesn't matter who my father was; it matters who I *remember* he was." I felt justified in my flawed remembrances. I had spent more than twenty years observing my dad, a broken human male raising a smaller, broken female. I could sense he had withheld his heart from me in seasons and ways, and it hurt. It needed to hurt. I'd hurt him, too. But in the end, my truth was fallible, informed by partial experience only, and shaped by the self-consumed ways in which I felt he'd missed *my* heart. My memory-vision of Dad was impaired. In my disappointment, I'd become an expert in his failures but had overlooked his kind intentions.

From the vantage point of a grown child (and a parent myself), I can see more clearly the reality.

Dad's love was his best gift to me.

Sure, sometimes the gift was in weird, antisocial wrappings or trussed with all the wrong words. Sometimes the box felt half empty. Any gift given by human hands can only be given incompletely. It can also only be received incompletely. The love he gave, however, was still mine, a gift that living on the fallen planet had obscured. That obscurity led me to miss my dad—not the stories, not the disappointments, but his true heart for myself and my older brother and sister.

My eyewitness testimony, while *mine*, turned out to be

unreliable. Like Adam and Eve and all forebears beyond, I had missed and misunderstood the heart of fatherhood.

THE FIRST FATHER

In the beginning, there was a Father.

This Father existed before time, before particles, before sin's punishing lash. This Father communed with his Son, dwelling with complete understanding. In endless measures, the love between Father and Son was the ancient oxygen of every preconceived notion. Their love lacked nothing. The Father's presence filled the space with robust joy, a joy that begged for others to share. It would not be hoarded in miserly selfishness.

The love of this Father compelled the wondrous deed of creation.

In love, the heavens and earth were spoken into being, forming colossal decanters into which the love of a Father could be poured. Ageless, limitless, fathomless—love flowed from the Father's heart in wild abandon, drenching the newborn cosmos. This Father molded fully formed children of perfect design, children of dust, rib, and breath. With his own hands, he shaped them, giving them a permanent hollow of soul, a place where only the affection of this Father could fill. And fill he did, with excessive supply that gushed from these hollows like a swollen river in early spring. Wearing their Creator's face, these children were the apple of his eye. Both son and daughter never knew a fatherless moment.

It was not to last.

Slithering into the Garden, the Fatherless One whispered doubt into this love-saturated earth, questioning the Progenitor's good heart and intention. Though their Father had never given them a reason to mistrust, the children found him withholding, and they thought it better to live as orphans than remain heirs.

The Garden that was their inheritance, he padlocked with

tears. The never-ending life, gifted to them, was overshadowed by death's yawn. By earth's early morning, all children chose to forsake their Everlasting Father.

All sons and daughters turned their backs to his loving face.

Because of their freedom, this Father would now learn to say goodbye, over and over again, to his children's children. Now this Father would watch in furious longing and unspeakable grief as these orphans would fight for their own survival. Now he would weep as the word "father" would lose its richness and glory, becoming a byword of children maligned.

He watched as Adam raised a son capable of murder. He saw Noah's shame and heard the echo of his curse as Ham reproduced dishonor. He looked on as Abraham, the father of many, sent his unwanted son into the desert to die. A father is meant to protect the purity of his daughters, but he witnessed Lot removing his from safety to be ravaged by perversion. He saw fathers, even good fathers like Jacob and Joseph, create division among their children by foolishness and favoritism. He watched David, Israel's anointed father-king, sow division and reap war among his household of greedy sons.

The patriarchs, charged with bearing an image of the divine Patriarch, miscarried their sacred duty.

This Father knows that outside the Garden, the hollow place will remain, at best, partially filled. The new legacy of fathers is that their children will always misunderstand them. Fathers and children will wrestle with discord, the rancor of mistrust and earning always nipping at their heels like a pair of surly dogs.

He was sad to be called Father, because that name no longer brought good news to his scarred and frightened children.

The first story of the world begins with this Everlasting Father. Every story thereafter is complicated by a fallen father, raising fallen children prone to doubt.

STEREOTYPES

The fathers we are born with, as good as they can be, are not the Good Father. They are not the Everlasting Father—the First, the Best. They cannot love us with perfect love. They will sin against us and hurt us, even when they don't want to, even when they're trying *not* to. They will need to ask for forgiveness again and again. And these are the good ones—the imperfectly good ones that fill the pages of both Old and New Testaments. The ones in my own family tree—Marion and Jack, my grandfathers; my father, Gary; and now Jimmy, my own children's father.

We know, however, that not all fathers are good. Many are more like Walter White than Ward Cleaver. The numbers are so overwhelming we've stopped being shocked. Seventy-one percent of high school dropouts. Eighty-five percent of youth in prison. Ninety percent of runaway teens.[1] According to *Psychology Today*, the common link between them is that none of them had a father in the home.

"I cannot think," said Freud long ago, "of any need in childhood as strong as the need for a father's protection." Lack of fathering protection, however, is precisely what defines childhood for so many. The epidemic of fatherless children is sweeping in tidal waves across American culture. The *Washington Times* reports that fifteen million children have no father in their home. That statistic represents one in three American kids.[2] About six in ten dads report they don't spend adequate time with their kids.[3] The majority of fathers recognize that they are withholding something good, something their children require to be healthy, functional adults: their presence.

No wonder we're cautious about the Everlasting Father. Every child has been taught to mistrust the name. That association of God with Father will always cause a twinge of pain or confusion in whatever spot is tender in our own hearts. This is part of the reason why the world, and even sometimes the church, has rejected its need for Father-God.

We come into God's family through Jesus, but we've been

suspicious about this Deity who wants to father us. In my affection for Jesus, I have felt more comfortable as a redeemed sinner than as a beloved daughter. We cling to Jesus, the saving Son, pushing the Father out of his own home. Jesus saved me; this I've almost always known, but what have we known of the Father? The father-shaped hollow place in each of us questions, "Where *is* he? Where is the Father?" with each new horror story of cruelty and neglect in the home.

We've decided being a son or daughter is no longer necessary when we're already saved by Jesus.

Jesus understands that when he invites us to call God "Our Father," he is taking a really big risk with our souls. That hollow place, however, still screams like a banshee and won't relent. What can we do but march to Jesus with an unspoken ultimatum?

Show us this Father of yours, or we walk.

SHOW-AND-TELL

Jesus's question returns to us in John 14 with a rented room and a strange dinner. Philip has something on his mind. He senses that time is short, and he wants Jesus to cover ground that needs covering before he goes. His request is honest and desperate and filled with an indescribable ache universal to every human soul. He wants what every orphan wants. Philip speaks for me and for you and for the hidden desire of the whole world in his one request of Jesus on this night: "Just show us the Father; then we'll be content" (John 14:8).

Philip's request for Jesus to "show" comes from the Greek verb *deiknumi* (dike-noo´-me), meaning "expose to the eyes."[4] *Deiknumi* indicates a show-and-tell quality of revelation at stake. Philip wants to see with his eyes and finger with his digits the Father in all his goodness and glory. Philip wants every reason he's ever had to doubt that he has a Father—and that Father is *good*—to be shredded right there at the table.

He insists that once Jesus simply complies, he will be content.

This word Philip uses, *arkeó* (ar-keh´-o), describes a state of satisfaction.[5] It's a pushing back from the table with an empty plate and full belly, saying *I've had enough*. Ironically, this word is also the same term used by Paul in 2 Corinthians 12:9 when he records Jesus's words—"*My grace is* arkeó *for you*."

Philip's tired of being hungry. He's tired of being empty. He's tired of being an orphan. He wants to be full.

Naturally, we want what Philip wants. His cry is our cry. From infants to the elderly, we never outgrow this need to be shown a good Father. It's as crucial as drawing breath. Our souls request of Jesus: Just show us the Father. Please. *Then we will be content.*

At least, we *hope* we will be.

We recognize we're unsafe orphans in an unsafe world. There's an ironic sense of safety in knowing this is true, so we cover ourselves with the threadbare blanket of doubt. It's a blanket too thin to warm us, and no matter how we stretch it, it doesn't fully cover. We still lie exposed to the volatile elements of un-belonging.

We require undeniable proof this Father is indeed good—despite all human evidence to the contrary, and then we will finally submit to this Father. We don't know if we can trust him, and we won't come back to the Garden until we do.

Philip's request, rather than delighting Jesus, grieves him. It hurts when our love is misunderstood. Jesus knows this grief. So does his Father.

It's the same grief as this Father in the Garden, looking at children who had completely missed his heart for them because of a few words from a snake.

"*How can you ask—Where is the Father?*" (John 14:9). Jesus looks from face to face around the flickering lamplight, knowing they all feel the same as Philip. We all make this request of Jesus. The problem wasn't with Philip's request, but what his request indicated.

He hadn't been paying attention. The question from Jesus points this out.

Philip saw only with orphan eyes—and like the first kids in the Garden, like "Beyoncé's Trouble," like each one of us, he saw with impaired vision. We can hear this pain in Jesus's question. We can see it in his eyes. We sense we've broken his heart as we've missed him again and again. We view the Father from a position of childishness instead of a child. Jesus continues,

> *"You've been with me all this time...and you still don't understand? TO SEE ME IS TO SEE THE FATHER...Don't you believe that I am in the Father and the Father is in me?"*
>
> John 14:9–10 (emphasis mine)

Jesus didn't play coy with Philip during his incarnation. He made it very clear that the three-year road trip was equal to time spent getting to know their Father. According to *The Evangelical Dictionary of Theology*, over 165 times, Philip hears Jesus call God "Father" throughout the four Gospels.[6]

Philip was there the day Jesus's friends asked him, "Teach us how to pray." Jesus agrees, and begins the lesson with the Father. One scholar writes, "This was not just *a* way Jesus taught his disciples to address God; it was *the* way."[7] Therefore, Jesus, on his last evening with his friends, is grieved to learn that it hadn't yet made a dent.

TO SEE ME IS TO SEE THE FATHER.

OLD MAN RUNNING

His heart was as big as the sea to their west. This was what everyone knew.

He would give the shirt off his back to the cold. He treated a suffering ewe with the same dignity he treated the village priest. He was the paragon of proper stewardship; his life, the model of responsibility. He handled his estate with propriety. He returned impulsivity and anger with wise words. His common sense had earned him respect, and his clever dealings had secured him unrivaled wealth. He was masculine strength with compassion, authority woven with humility.

The old man was a portrait of faultless fatherhood. The whole village agreed. The only ones who didn't seem to understand were the two fools he called sons. How those two could be so different from their father was a village mystery.

The younger boy was handsome and petulant. Since he could toddle, he'd wandered. Even though his father would take the eager young explorer on adventures, tracking wild game and showing his son every secret corner of their expansive property, it was never enough for the boy. He wanted to discover the world without his father. He wanted his own kingdom, where he and he alone could rule. Eventually, the wanderlust caused him to abandon the family estate and name. Most hoped he was gone for good. As charming as he could be at a party, he was a bad egg, and they didn't want him near their daughters.

The firstborn, the elder son, was no one's darling. He lacked all the color and charisma of his brother. He was sturdy, resembling less of his father and more the family mule. He was so sturdy, in fact, he was stuck—stuck so deep in a bog of sanctimonious unoriginality that he'd long since stopped moving. He looked down his long nose at everyone around, even his father. His body lacked the courage to do what his heart desired—to leave the father and renounce his name, chasing after pleasure along with his stupid brother. He had his father's keen sense of responsibility without his father's heart. This made him cold, unyielding. Doing his duty and feigning respect, he held hatred of both father and brother close to his chest with each day that passed.

But oh—how the two were loved by their father! Each of his boys was his favorite. How that could be, no one understood but him.

The father sighed and longed for more—more depth, more intimacy, more companionship with his children. He wished to be seen by his sons as he was, not as they experienced him through the distortion of lack and anger. He wished they would receive the true inheritance that was their birthright: walking with him closely, learning the family trade, wanting for nothing. They seemed only to want his gifts and none of his heart.

It hurt him every day.

Because he loved them, he let them choose. He would never force himself.

He desired heirs, not slaves.

His sons spurned his attention, his affection, his wisdom. They moved around him as if he wasn't there. They didn't seem to see him at all.

He was a father without sons, and it crushed his enormous heart.

He knew it was coming when his boy demanded a share of the estate. The elder son heard his mandate with disgust and waited for his father's appropriate response—to give his brother the back of his hand. To threaten. To tell him to get to work, or better yet, to get out.

His father did none of those things.

What he did do was walk to his desk, open the drawer, and hand his boy the deed to his portion of family property and a heavy leather purse, fat with coin. Before offering these, he looked deeply into his son's eyes. They were lost eyes, full of fear, the eyes of an orphan.

"You are always my son," the old man said. "Always."

The young man jerked the contents out of the father's hands and walked away without a word. Waist belt bulging with premature inheritance, he never looked back.

His older brother watched, raging like a bull provoked. They'd been robbed—the estranged pair left behind. He'd been humiliated for the last time by the boy who was no brother of his. He stood behind his father, fidgeting, clenching and unclenching his hands as the figure walked farther out of stone's throw with their money.

His father stood still.

"Will you do nothing?" the son snarled.

His strange father kept quiet.

"Are you just going to let him do that to you? To *us*?"

Silence.

"Father, what about my rights as firstborn!" He saw his brother now crossing through the gate in the far field. "Don't you care what people will think of you?"

He strode over to the old man, grabbing his shoulder. He would have never dared this before, but justified anger with his father broke restraints that kept his beast muzzled. The elder son was horrified at what he saw: his weak father weeping, tears coursing down his cheeks.

The father should have been ashamed, but he wasn't. He didn't care that with these tears, he forfeited all credibility in his son's disgusted gaze. He wept, and though tears obscured his vision, he could see the distance between himself and both of his boys. The old man lifted his voice, wailing in dirgelike grief. He reached to embrace his son, but the grown orphan recoiled in contempt.

His son took one last look at the tears and walked out his father's door.

The father waited.

Each day, he waited for either one of his lost sons to return to him. Like a woman with child, he quietly watched for signs of their coming. The porch overlooked the western road that swallowed up one son. He knew his boy had forsaken the country of his people, traveling far to create a gap between him and his father.

This same porch also kept vigil over the ewes, tended by his cold and dutiful firstborn. The elder, though under the watchful eyes of his father in the family fields, had created no less distance between them. The old man witnessed his hurried stride, his exasperated air with the frisky young lambs. Even from a distance, his son's face showed disappointment with life. Frustration hardened his frame, outlined by the last fringes of daylight.

But neither son could create enough space where they were unable to sense the presence of their father. It traveled with them as an unwanted companion.

With no guarantees, the father kept watch, attentive with longing, for the return of his sons.

Weeks turned to months, and still he watched. When a debt collector came to claim livestock and land, bearing the boy's signature, the father still watched. When others celebrated feasts and festivals, he watched. When the household took meals and rest, he watched. It seemed to all that he never took his eyes off the western road or western hills.

One day, the village elders arrived to speak to the father about his watching. It was unseemly. The old man was where they'd last seen him—rocking, drinking goat's milk on the portico of his house, watching. The sun was setting pink, a rosy glow reflecting off the wool of his flock.

"This cannot continue," they declared. The old man's gaze didn't leave the road.

"You must forget the boy. Move on." They spat in the dirt, showing the father how distasteful they found the boy's memory in their mouths. "He's dead to you."

The father's eyes didn't waver.

The elders looked at each other and sighed. They turned to leave and saw something in the distance, the same time as the old man. He stood, upending the cups and plates with a clatter, and gasped, "It's him!"

With the village elders watching, mouths agape, he hoisted his robe above his knees and slapped down the stairs, laughing like a child.

"It's *who?*" they asked one another.

No one considered the boy's return a possibility. They stared at the hunched old man running, bony legs pumping like a whipped camel. He cried out, "My boy! My boy!" as he ran. "My boy is home!"

Squinting into the distance, they wondered: How could he even know? The stranger was just a shadowed figure in the dimming light. It could have been anyone.

A good father, however, never forgets his son.

Everyone, including both boys, watched in amazement as their father barreled down the path—through the inner gate, through the outer gate—without stopping. Even when he stumbled, hands outstretched to catch a tangled fall, he simply jumped to his feet and continued dashing down the road with clumsy abandon.

The elders marveled as father met prodigal boy with a clash like heaven. Bags and clothes—even a sandal—flew as the son, standing at least six inches above his father, was picked up in a bear hug and whirled round like a top. They watched when the father, finally releasing his son, removed his robe and swaddled it around the boy's naked shoulders. The old man knelt before him and placed his ring on his son's dirty finger. They watched as he grabbed his arm and ran with him toward the house, shouting scattered instructions to the servants who had gathered inside the portico to view the preposterous scene.

The whole village was invited to the family feast, where a returned son sat sheepishly beside his father at the table's head, still questioning his place.

The whole village watched as the father left the feast and his friends to search for the other son who had left the empty chair by his father's other side.

The whole village heard the son's shouting, his angry accusations through the open doorway. They couldn't fault him. The father's behavior bordered on insanity. It was plainly agreed that both sons and father were out of control.

The villagers shook their heads and clucked their tongues. Neither of his sons deserved the father they had, but then again, the father's actions—his utter obsession with loving these two undeserving sons—was outrageous. His love had made him irresponsible, and the irresponsibility was the shock of the farming community. Where was the wrath? The reckoning? How *could* he embrace his wayward, thankless sons?

"Oh, how the mighty have fallen," they murmured. "Just look at what his love for those boys has done to him."

This reckless forgiveness. This imprudent affection. It was all just too much.

ORPHANS BECOMING HEIRS

These sons had a father who loved them more than life, and they missed him. He was right there loving them, giving them gifts, giving them himself, and they didn't see it. He was right there, calling forth their identity, giving them holy purpose, and they were blind and deaf to him.

Philip had this story in his back pocket for three years. He had intimate, brotherly communion with the Son of God for three years. He was taught heavenly truths by Heaven's Heir himself. He was taken by the hand and brought by Jesus to his Father, again and again.

Philip still missed the Father. So do we.

Within each of us dwells the younger son, the son who mistrusts that life in the Father's house is *arkeó*—enough to satisfy our hunger for more. We also each hold the elder, spending our lives trying to earn what is already ours: the delight of the Father and his abundant inheritance.

Fatherlessness comes with exorbitant cost, consequences both unseen and seen.

Jesus's story meets the universal request, voiced by Philip: "Show us the Father." How we respond to this story, *this* Father, reveals from which child we are living: orphan or heir. In asking his question, Jesus invites us to notice the status of our hollow place, the place reserved for the Father's affection.

We will know its status by the telltale signs of mistrusting and earning. The younger son and the elder. These traits are what define the orphan.

Jesus's question to Philip and to us is clever. Rather than delivering a lecture on the futility of mistrust, he asks a question instead. He poses this inquiry to begin a dialogue with a cautious, hungry orphan.

He longs to teach us a new way. It is the trusting life, and it is good.

Despite this new way, it's still easy to *feel* abandoned here on this fallen planet. With Jesus's question, we are kindly reminded that the feeling, while real, isn't based on reality. We are never abandoned. We have a home better than anything we've experienced here.

Jesus is asking us if we are ready to come back home.

His Father tarries on the porch with anticipation for our coming. He wants us to taste more of our eternal home now than what we are usually willing to receive. When we invite the fathering of God, he enters to fill that empty, angry hollow with more goodness than we ever dreamed possible. As I've re-learned my Father, he has slowly and carefully dismantled the barrier I had erected between us. By choosing trust, I see more clearly the foundation of lies on which mistrust has been built. He wants access to it, this mistrust that strangles our minds and our hearts. He wants to heal us and set us free.

I know that as I go deeper into the Father, the orphan posture will be healed. True peace replaces more and more fatherless bravado. As his child, I can choose to stay with him in his home. As I bring to him my hunger, he takes and nourishes. As I return to him with my dirty rags, he gives me his ring and his robe. I no longer need to carry survival as my burden, for I am safe with him. He's a Good Father, worthy of my trust.

RECEIVING, NOT EARNING

Like the elder son in the story, we all want to earn the gifts we're given.

If we earn love, then we are deserving. No one owns us. We're no one's charity case. If we earn the gift, then no one can take it away from us. That is, not until we stop being worthy.

We've been taught that all gifts come with invisible strings, so accepting gifts is awkward. We are uncomfortable with this arrangement. The more lavish the gift, the harder it is to accept without earning. We want to be in control of our own value and merit. But like the elder son, we forget that worthiness is not something to be earned. Our value isn't based on our accomplishments. We don't get extra points when we do well and points deducted when we make a mess.

As heirs, the Father has called us beloved. We are beloved *because* he loves us. He wants this to be enough. This gift of inherent worthiness, a value that cannot be stolen, is our *arkeó*—holy satisfaction.

> Every desirable and beneficial gift comes out of heaven. The gifts are rivers of light cascading down from the Father of Light. There is nothing deceitful in God, nothing two-faced, nothing fickle. He brought us to life.
>
> James 1:17

His love and his delight are not manipulations from a salesman. The Father wants me, knows me, calls me by a special name. Zephaniah even tells us that this Father sings melodies over us. That's an elusive truth, a difficult reality.

It doesn't make it any less true.

With his question, Jesus invites us to receive our Father's affection. Earning is replaced by the inheritance of the Kingdom. He asks that we bring to him every urge to earn what's already been given so freely.

In a twist of divine conspiracy, this Good Father sent his beloved Son to us—to seek and save all lost orphans. Jesus, the only Son who never missed his Father, never misunderstood him, never orphaned himself, was given up to show every orphan the way home. This perfect Heir received not the Father's love but his wrath, the prodigal's punishment that we alone deserved. God turned his face from this Son so his face could never, ever be removed from us.

The lavish gift of restoration was given at the cost of God's Son.

TO SEE ME

With his question, Jesus reminds all his followers of this vital truth:

To see me is to see the Father.

This is what Jesus said to Philip. This is what he says to us.

That is why he came, to reveal the face of the Father. That's why Philip's question broke his heart. On the night he gave himself over to dark schemes and evil plots, his final conversation with the lads revealed that they still didn't understand. Neither do we.

I have forgotten that all that I love best about Jesus is also true of our Father. The lingering orphan just doesn't want to see. We study and know Jesus to know his Father. We take one with the other.

Jesus took on bone, muscle, and skin to communicate the heart of his Father. Jesus is the Father's show-and-tell made flesh. Every word and act of the Son reveals to us the Father, and that Father is *very* good. Jesus wants us to watch him, and in watching, learn the Father rightly. The Father is just as available to us as the Son. The Father is just as crucial to us as the Son. Jesus's heart grieves when we take him but leave the Father out of pain or guilt or confusion. Talking to this Father, Jesus prays after asking his question:

> *"Father, the world has never known you, but I have known you. These disciples know that you sent me on this mission: I have made your very being known to them—who you are and what you do—And I continue to make it known."*
>
> John 17:25

That is the glory of Jesus, the mission of Jesus—to take us to our Father. That is why he asks the question.

Crowding around him are orphans. On every side he looks into the eyes of the fatherless, the abandoned, the estranged, the homeless. He asks, *"How can you ask—Where is the Father?"*

because he has the profound joy of proclaiming that what we have always craved he has given in full. The fatherless and motherless are parented in him. The empty receive comfort and care in their emptiness. The lonely and alone are brother and sister to God-in-the-Flesh. He opens up his home to us, inviting us to share his name. We have a saved seat at the family table. We are known and cherished in the embrace of Father, Son, and Spirit.

If we are very still and very quiet, we can hear our hollow speak its great need: We're desperate to know this Father.

We need to know the One who loves us perfectly and completely and intimately every single moment. The One who helps us understand who we really are. The One who will teach us everything we need to learn and will never, ever make us fend for ourselves in a love-lost world. The One whose eyes always light up when he sees us, the One who is never ashamed of us or disappointed in us or tells us unkind things about ourselves that aren't true. We need this One, the Father who will never let us down, never walk out of the room, never give up. He is the Everlasting Father, always waiting for us to return home and receive our true inheritance.

"*I'm not abandoned*," Jesus said simply in John 16 before his death. "*The Father is with Me*" (John 16:32). His words indicate shocking trust, *pure* trust, that his Father will show up. Not just any father, but the Father who is always good, always kind, always brimming over with love for us.

It seems too good to be true, that we could be "the focus of his love" (Ephesians 1:4). But it is true, the greatest truth in all the world's lies.

> "*I'm on my way to the Father because the Father is the goal and purpose of my life.*"
>
> John 14:28

That goal and purpose took him to the Cross.

Jesus's obedience as a Son to the Father is his delight. He

longs to welcome all his lost orphans home. As we study Jesus, walk with Jesus, love Jesus, he will teach us how to know our Father. Jesus says, *"The Father wants to give you the very kingdom itself"* (Luke 12:32). We are co-heirs with the Son of God. We are the beloved of the Father, and he wants to give us his Kingdom as our inheritance. We have our Father's affection every day. We can call out to him. It delights him.

The Father's love created us. The Father's love provided atonement for our sins. The Father's love offers us an everlasting inheritance that begins *today*.

The Father's love is the Gospel, the good news of a good Kingdom.

FOR CONTEMPLATION AND DISCUSSION

Lectio Divina Exercise:

Sit with the father on his porch. What does his face look like as he watches the horizon? Relate with him a moment in desire to have intimacy and life with his sons. What does he say to you? What does it feel like to be so unwanted and misunderstood as a father? Listen as he invites you to tell him your own father-story. What has that word meant to you? How has it been lost in your life? How does the father respond to you?

For Reflection:

1. What has "father" represented to you? What is your perspective on its legitimacy and safeness in your life?
2. Where do you see *arkeó*, the feeling of "having enough," in your relationship with the Everlasting Father? What is the status of the father-shaped hollow given to you by him?
3. How does it make you feel that the Father is pouring out his

affection on you—his favorite? Do you see this as true? How do you experience this on a daily basis?

4. In what ways has Jesus, the show-and-tell of the Father, revealed his Father's heart to you?

5. What is your answer to Jesus's question: *"How can you ask— Where is the Father?"*

CHAPTER EIGHT

"Have You Anything Here to Eat?"

Exposing the Belief in an Irrelevant God

"Touch me and see. A ghost does not have flesh and bones."
—Jesus Christ,
Luke 24:39, NIV

*They were in fact ghosts: man-shaped stains on the brightness
of that air.*
*One could attend to them or ignore them at will as you do with
the dirt on a window pane.*

—C. S. Lewis,
The Great Divorce

My daughters don't understand the term "Holy Ghost," and I don't blame them. It's confusing, and more than a little odd. This liturgical name for God comes from Old English vocabulary, translated from the Latin *Spiritus Sanctus*—Holy Ghost. It conjures up a wispy, hovering image, a god that pops from the closet to scare children.

An imaginary friend, on the other hand, is easily understood by children, a favorite companion of childhood. When I was small, my older sister, Alison, and I shared an imaginary friend. Our friend's name was Margaret, and Margaret was introduced to us both by our grandfather, whom we called Pop-pop.

When Pop-pop would come for visits, he'd get out of the driver's seat and open the back-passenger door to let Margaret out of the car, fussing all the way up the front sidewalk. He was reminding her to use her best manners on the playdate with us, his granddaughters. His conversations with Margaret were so real, so convincing. To a five-year-old, it wasn't clear whether Pop-pop had gone crazy or I had. Looking around at everyone's faces, smiling benignly and nodding, it seemed I was the only one with the problem.

One time, I plucked up the courage to ask Pop-pop what Margaret looked like.

"You don't know?" he asked with surprise.

I shook my head no.

"Margaret, come here and stand beside me." I supposed she did as she was asked.

"Just look at her," he said, pointing to his side. "See—she has curly hair and freckles and a little black pair of glasses." Then he whispered behind his hand, "She's a bit short-sighted."

I nodded my head in wonder. Who was I to disagree? I was too embarrassed to admit that I couldn't see her, so I did what any kid would do.

I faked it.

After a while, I pretended that I could also see Margaret. I could hear her. She was my friend, my sidekick, my scapegoat. Suddenly Margaret wanted some Ritz crackers with peanut butter. Margaret was the one who left the sticky mess on the counter that attracted ants. Margaret caught a cold and would be spending the rest of the afternoon in bed, requiring ginger ale and movies.

I wanted to play the game, too.

As adults, we continue to play—only our imaginary friend is God. We look at him like a cosmic Margaret. We see others treating him as though he were real, so we play along, only there's a dark and heavy doubt in our gut. We wonder if it's nothing more than an elaborate game. Is he real? Is he relevant? Does he speak? Does he listen? Is he here beside me?

If God is real—then is he relevant *to me*?

Throughout the scriptures, when God reveals himself, the first thing he must do is comfort his audience. He is holy and awful in the truest sense of the word. To be in his presence is to know a certain degree of discomfort, but I also believe there is another reason his arrival evokes fear.

Like my doubt in Margaret, we don't really expect God to be real.

Our disbelief has more substance than he does, so when he thunders, strides, or treads softly into our lives, we're utterly shocked. We've thought him a ghost for so long his genuine presence alarms. And a ghost God, an imaginary God without substance, has no relevance.

Jesus knows every heart contains at least a fragment of this belief, and he responds as he so often does. He responds by asking us a question.

JESUS EATS

"It is finished." They'd heard him say this with his last exhalation.

They'd watched from a distance as blood and water flowed from his punctured side. They saw his body without breath, without warmth, without color. They saw the light of his eyes snuffed like a spent candle. He was pronounced dead by the local coroner. His body lay swaddled in a cave, the door sealed and watched by sentries. They'd heard some strange rumors, but they dismissed them as conflicting and ridiculous.

Witnessing his cruel death was too great an obstacle to their unripe belief. Yes, it was all very much *finished.* His work. His ministry. The Man himself was finished—and so was their faith. Now hunted men, their lives were over as surely as his. Their courage was finished, too, scattered like his followers, hiding in every nook and cranny of Jerusalem.

They had abandoned their boats, booths, families, and lives for him—and for what? Where would they go now? Jerusalem was too hot, too hostile. They were packing for the trip north, back into the small world of Galilee fisheries where they belonged. Their hearts were stones, heavy and hard in their chests. They gathered their belongings, content to stew in a silence thick as soup.

It was into this silence that he arrived.

Just like that, he walked through the bolted door and back into their wrecked lives. Whatever had been finished, he was just getting started.

They jumped to their feet, screaming and holding their faces like old women.

"*Peace*," Jesus said, a smile splitting his beard.

"They thought they were seeing a ghost," Luke writes with a touch of comedy, "and were scared half to death" (Luke 24:37).

Of course they did. Of course they were. He was dead, and death was usually considered permanent. There's no way this Specter before them could be real.

Aware of his disciples' fears and suspicions, Jesus spoke quietly, as to skittish colts. He offered his hands to them. He lifted his tunic so they could see feet—real, hairy feet, standing on the dusty floor. He was not hovering six inches over the rug.

"*It's really me*," he said. "*Touch me. Look me over.*"

No one moved.

"*A ghost doesn't have muscle and bone like this*" (Luke 24:39). He thumped his chest, and the sound of it was the sound of palm slapping pectoral muscle. None of them dared to come near him. Not one touched him. They were too afraid that their hands would pass through his body like a cloud of smoke.

"*Do you have any food?*" he asked (Luke 24:41).

The absurdity of this question jolted them from their paralysis. One of them cautiously passed Jesus a plate of fish.

They all watched, unblinking, as he squatted on the floor and ate. They never took their eyes from his fingers, going from fish to mouth, pulling apart the white flesh and leaning his head back to drop it into his mouth. It was not until he wiped his messy face with the back of his sleeve and said, "That was good," that they believed.

It's Jesus, after all, and he's no holy ghost.

This is a remarkable scene and a remarkable question from a hungry, post-Resurrection Jesus. Like a boy home from college, Jesus raids the pantry. It's unexpected. It's odd. It's just so *real.* He's supposed to be resting in peace but instead, he pops through walls and requests a meal. I can almost picture him with two fingers, V-shaped for peace, grinning like a kid. *"Have you anything here to eat?"* he asks. No wonder Luke writes, "They still couldn't believe what they were seeing. It was too much; it seemed too good to be true" (Luke 24:41).

By asking this question, Jesus is inviting us to wonder why, at *this* moment, he chooses to help himself to lunch. Like all of his questions, this one is intentional, but it's strange.

It is also exposing.

ONLY THE LIVING

Like my daughters, most of us have a natural dislike of ghosts, even holy ones. We would choose not to fraternize with them. We simply cannot trust anything without substance. We will never give our lives over to anything that doesn't have at least as much presence as our own bodies.

Conversely, there's almost nothing more *human* than eating.

There's an obvious physicality to our digestive process. More than a few organs are involved. All the senses are engaged. However, any child can explain to you the impossibilities of a ghost eating anything. I remember a Mickey Mouse show where animated ghosts ingested food and drink, solids and liquids trickling cartoonlike down skeletal throats into hollow abdomens. The eating was all a farce, because even children understand that a ghost doesn't need nourishing.

Dead people don't eat.

The rules of logic are in play. If it's true that ghosts can't eat, then Jesus must not be one. Only the living consume food. Jesus shows his terrified disciples beyond all doubt that he is a brick wall of real substance.

In this moment, Jesus reminds me of the scene in C. S. Lewis's *The Horse and His Boy* when Shasta speaks with Aslan for the first time:

There suddenly came a deep, rich sigh out of the darkness beside him. That couldn't be imagination! Anyway, he had felt the hot breath of that sigh on his chilly left hand . . .

"I can't see you at all," said Shasta, after staring very hard. Then (for an even more terrible idea had come into his head) he said, almost in a scream, "You're not–not something dead, are you? Oh please—please do go away. What harm have I ever done you? Oh, I am the unluckiest person in the whole world!" Once more he felt the warm breath of the Thing on his hand and face. "There," it said, "that is not the breath of a ghost."[1]

Shasta's obvious disquiet of being accompanied by a ghost reflects the disciples' own discomfort. Aslan must pant his hot breath on the boy's cold hand to get him to a place of belief. Jesus must eat broiled fish to show his disciples he is alive and real.

He must also break into our lives in substantive, unexpected ways to speak his relevance.

God shows himself to be real over and over again. He doesn't want us to pretend he's real, all the while persisting in believing him to be a ghostly figment. He's not Margaret, but we keep behaving as though he is. He's not a hallucination of shattered minds or a psychological by-product of bereft hearts. We've been wrong about him.

He's as real as anything that exists in this world, and we need a God that's real.

EARTH VERSUS HEAVEN

Google screams relevance when God is silent.

We can see and touch the keys of entry into its kingdom of smart devices and instant solutions. We ask questions aloud, guaranteeing our devices speak back to us in response to our every directive. We have no such understanding with God. In the blue light of Google, God's relevance pales, fading once again into the ethereal background of lost spirituality.

It's fascinating what we have Googled—and very telling. I've Googled questions that belong to God.

I remember the day it hit me. It was a particularly hard day of parenting, and I plopped down with my iPhone in a funk to Google, "How do I get my kids to obey from the heart?"

It didn't occur to me to ask God first. It didn't occur to me to ask God at all. No need. I had Google.

The prophet Isaiah describes us when he writes,

Because this is a rebel generation . . .
They tell their spiritual leaders,
"Don't bother us with irrelevancies."
They tell their preachers,
"Don't waste our time on impracticalities.
Tell us what makes us feel better.
Don't bore us with obsolete religion.
That stuff means nothing to us.
Quit hounding us with The Holy of Israel."

Isaiah 30:9–11

We sweat and bleed down here. We need to put food on the table and money in the bank. We need promotions at work to put *more* money in the bank. We need to raise children, watching them stumble and fail and, at times, despise us. We earn income, lose income, spend income, save income. We wrestle with the nagging problems of our interior world or the relationships that aren't working. We do our best to find a little taste of personal happiness in a world that is all too real.

We live in this world, constantly smacked by unkind realities. Our lives, all of humanity, are made up of these realities.

We have a desperate need for a God who matters—and not just matters sometime in the unknown future. We need a God who matters *now*. He needs to make sense to us in the grit and inconvenience of our day-by-day living. We can't stomach the realm of the spirit when our physical, material needs go unaddressed. In the messy minute, we must have a God who is relevant, or we have no god at all. We must have a God of substance—with breath and warmth and life.

John 3 tells the story of a man with needs like our own.

Nicodemus was drawn to Jesus, wanting something from him. He wanted answers. He wanted the Truth. Perhaps he only wanted to be on the right side, in case this Messiah wreaking havoc in Jerusalem was the One. Whatever he was looking for, he wasn't looking for the question he got from Jesus.

> "You're a respected teacher of Israel, and you don't know these basics?"
>
> John 3:10

Giving him no time to answer, Jesus continued:

> "If I have told you earthly things and you do not believe, how can you believe if I tell you heavenly things?"
>
> John 3:12 (ESV)

If Nicodemus could look deeply into the questions Jesus was offering, he might have seen the kindness tarrying just behind the rebuke.

What Jesus asks Nicodemus reveals a toxic poison that is slowly corroding both his heart and ours. His question shows that we can never hear him speak to matters of the soul when we can't accept his relevance to matters of the body. His question exposes the hidden and dangerous belief that what he says, while good, is immaterial for our lives here on earth.

If we go to God at all, many times we go to him as a last resort. We think of him as obsolete, an irrelevancy. When all else fails, we "try" God, perhaps like Nicodemus. In a dark corner of the heart, we still see him as the ethereal Jesus, a ghost without substance for our everyday needs. We think the heavenly things are wonderful, but what we *need* is Someone to tell us how to survive on the fallen planet. I need a God who is not a mirage or a figment of my imagination. I need a Godhead that is present in real time, not a hovering spectacle of no more substance than the morning mist. I must have a Living God or no God at all.

Our souls want a Savior for this earth, not just for heaven. We need a God who walks with the living, not just receives the dead at their time. We need God-with-Us, a God who knows what we go through and can offer practical help. We need a God who gets *life*.

That's a need Google could never meet.

HANDS, FEET, AND BREATH

He shows us his substance with an offer. *"Touch me,"* he invites us, and he means it.

This word in the original Greek, *psélaphaó* (psay-laf-ah´-o), is significant.[2] A compound verb, the term derives from the word *psállō* (psal´-lo), "to strum or play a stringed instrument"[3] and *psēphos* (psay´-fos), "a smooth, worn stone."[4] It's a rock-solid term said by a God with weighted presence, and this God wants to be twanged hard like an acoustic guitar at a country music festival. He wants to vibrate his sonorous, solid presence into every detail of our world.

"Look at my hands," he adds. *"Look at my feet"* (Luke 24:39).

He could have shown his brow pierced by needle-sharp thorns. He could have offered a chest and back cruelly whipped and bloodied by leather cording. He might have shown his purple cheekbone and jaw, bruised from the backhands of mockers. He could have exposed the gaping hole in his side from which the holy blood and water flowed down splintered wood. Instead, he simply holds out his hands and feet. Why?

It's the hands and feet that convey movement and action.

Hands and feet represent real-time relevance. They speak to the intricacies of life. Hands hold and feet travel. Hands touch and feet move us forward. The Jesus who asks us to reach out and take hold of him has holy hands and feet.

It's the hands of Jesus that touched the diseased flesh of the leper. It's the hands of Jesus that wiped tears from the face of his friends at Lazarus's grave. It's the feet of Jesus that walked him into the Samaritan town of Sychar to sit by an all but forsaken well. It's his feet that stood firm in the scorched-earth wilderness when invited by evil to submit.

His hands and feet mattered. They matter still. This scarred, solid God invites us to play the instrument of his ultimate significance, to watch as he works and moves among us.

The first chapter of Colossians reminds us that God is invisible, but in our minds, we forget that invisible does *not* mean imaginary. The presence of God in our lives, in our minuscule moments, has weight. At any given moment, this invisible God lifts the veil, and we behold a most unlooked-for transfiguration. His continuous offer is that we stand on the mountain's peak and experience him as he exists—not a weightless God, but a God of profound stature—larger than the mountain itself. His quiet presence can be known and experienced. This is the end for which he longs—that we see him as he is.

Our souls must see him as the Substantial One.

In that locked room among his hiding friends, Jesus reminds us that he is no ghost. The original word is not Latin, but Greek—*pneuma* (pnyoo´-mah).[5] This term is used New Testament with a range of meanings. It is translated "spirit, ghost, or wind." It can also be translated "breath." This is the same term used in the Greek Old Testament account of Genesis 2, when God *"breathed the breath of life"* into the image-bearer. As humans, we can survive only three minutes without breathing oxygen into our lungs. Three minutes. That's the time it takes to answer emails. There's nothing more relevant, more necessary to life, than breath.

We're startled to learn that in reality, we need Jesus more.

His breath, this *pneuma* we call the Holy Ghost, is more vital than oxygen, more indispensable than breathing. And our need for him is not every three minutes but every breath.

That is intense relevance.

When he asks us what we've got in our fridge, Jesus speaks reassurance to us. We crave what's real, what has quality and substance. Without it, we lose who we are.

THE HUMAN GHOST

We were created in the image of the Substantial One. We bear the *imago Dei* of divine relevance. This is our design. We will always seek what has substance; our very nature presses us toward full relevance. Our old selves, however, are at war with this Kingdom desire for impact. While we all need relevance, we don't always *want* it. We want substance, but we don't want what engaging with substance requires. We want all the impact and none of the responsibility. It's great to have relevance, to be indispensable, but the weight of carrying that relevance on our own is too heavy for our small frames—so we abdicate.

I can shed my God-given substance like ill-fitting snakeskin when it's convenient. When I want independence from God, I must get rid of my Kingdom weight. In so doing, I resign God to nothing more than some imaginary Thing.

We are surprised to find that we can be ghosts, too.

When we disengage with God and others, even our own souls, we pretend that we can float through life as ghosts, concerned only with pleasing ourselves. The great lie of this practice is that our relevance is never neutral. We are constantly impacting the small relational ecosystems that surround us. For people so concerned with reality, we often chuck it faster than our junk mail, hoping we can live without consequences.

When we shirk our impact, we do grave harm to those around us.

We practice this disengagement without being conscious of the damage we are inflicting. In a thousand ways, we say no to God's claim on our substance. In those thousand ways, we become unavailable to staying present and hurt ourselves and those around us.

Children are openly insatiable in their need for substance and presence. As they inherently understand that ghosts cannot eat, neither can they be mothers and fathers. When children sense they are not getting a parent's full weight, they will throw down every single trick they have in their trick bag. Our daughters are this way. If they perceive they are getting anything less from Jimmy and me than full substance, they will protest. Sometimes they protest with words but mostly with behavior, and they will keep protesting until the problem of presence is fixed.

Last week, Jimmy and I engaged in a disagreement about our finances. The conversation had hit the cement slab of temporary irresolution, and we were both so ticked that we couldn't continue. We made the silent agreement to separate from each other *and* vacate ourselves. Jimmy retreated to his workshop, and I to my library to write this chapter.

Life is ironic.

It did not take long for our children to notice that Mom and Dad had become ghosts again.

When the girls figured out that the atmosphere of the house was haunted, their behavioral protests began in earnest. Macy brought an apple into my clean, quiet library, stood next to my desk chair at ear level, and bit into the apple. She stood there chewing and crunching, just watching me type. She bit the apple again, leaning in closer to my face. Apple juice sprayed on my cheek.

I took a huge breath and looked over at her, picturing the steam that must be coiling off the top of my head. She looked right back at me, smiling her knowing smile, and asked, "So, Mom, how's it going?"

She is a smart girl.

Jimmy relayed to me later that Jo had brought Matchbox cars out to his shop, vrooming their tiny wheels over his work surface, his tools, and the walls. The kids couldn't stand even one half hour without the substance of their parents. As children, they point us back to the truth that as adults, neither can we.

MAN-SHAPED STAINS

Relationships require that we be real people, people with weight. It's something that can be sensed with our souls, and no amount of faking it can resolve this lack. Being a person with presence is a choice, something we must keep choosing with each moment.

In C. S. Lewis's brilliant novella *The Great Divorce*, he paints a vivid picture of what it looks like when we reject our substance to live an easier, more self-absorbed life. He writes,

> At first, of course, my attention was caught by my fellow-passengers, I gasped when I saw them. Now that they were in the light, they were transparent—fully transparent when they stood between me and it, smudgy and imperfectly opaque when they stood in the shadow of some tree. They were in fact ghosts...The grass did not bend under their feet: even the dew drops were not disturbed.[6]

Lewis describes people who walk around without any weight. These people carry with them an inability to create positive impact. Not even the grass is crushed by them. We dwell as these "man-shaped stains" because we simply do not want to carry the weight and depth we were designed to carry.

This was never the way it was supposed to be. In the beginning, God molded Adam from the things of substance—wet earth and God's kiss. We became a living soul wrapped in body. We were never meant to be anything less than creatures with weight and bearing. "His very breath and blood flow through us," writes Paul, "nourishing us so that we will grow up healthy in God, robust in love" (Ephesians 4:16).

With God, we are robust. Substantive. We are relevant.

Without him, we are hardly human in nature. When we neglect our lives with God, we live as vacuous souls, great empty spaces that cannot receive or give love, life, beauty, or strength. We can't pretend to be real, and we can't fake presence. We need the Substantial One to seal the rift from which our substance leaks. The image-bearers of God must practice putting off the ghost. We can intentionally choose to live from our true substance. When we exercise our relevance, we are choosing to allow God to fill the abyss of nothingness we've invited into ourselves. Jesus wants us to be real in a world becoming emptier of life each day.

We do this by taking seriously his invitation to grab hold of his substance. We must have the courage to touch the Living God.

EXERCISING SUBSTANCE

Paul writes,

> You don't need a telescope, a microscope, or a horoscope to realize the fullness of Christ, and the emptiness of the universe without him. When you come to him, that fullness comes together for you, too...Entering into this fullness is not something you figure out or achieve...you're already *in*.
>
> Colossians 2:9–11

We are invited to live in all the fullness of Christ. "You're already in," Paul tells us. We don't have to figure it out. We get to just *live* it. We were made to live it. Again, from *The Great Divorce*, C. S. Lewis describes the ground-trembling weight of those in union with God:

Because they were bright I saw them while they were still very distant, and at first I did not know that they were

people at all. Mile after mile they drew nearer. The earth
shook under their tread as their strong feet sank into the
wet turf. A tiny haze and a sweet smell went up where they
had crushed the grass and scattered the dew.[7]

It is these bright ones who represent our true substance, or
divine relevance. They shake the earth. They leave imprints in
the turf. They have impact beyond reckoning.

We are the shining ones. Taking hold of his substance, we
leave our glorious mark wherever we move. That is exactly how
he made us to be.

We must return again and again to Jesus's offer: "*Touch
me.*" That compound verb contained the word for a smooth,
worn stone (*psēphos*), last used in Revelation 2. Speaking to our
eternal identity, Jesus says this:

> "*I'll give a clear, smooth stone inscribed with your new name,
> your secret new name.*"

Revelation 2:17

As Jesus invites us to reach out and feel his stone quality, his
solid nature, so he has given us the same. Our substance is as
solid as a rock, and it is set in permanence in his Kingdom. By
grabbing hold of his substance, our own substance is invited to
return. We begin to know who we truly are in the weight of his
constant relevance.

I AM SUBSTANTIAL

In Genesis, we read the narrative of a dusty, tent-dwelling
pilgrim named Abraham. This narrative describes with sardonic
humor the mingling of a theophany and the eating of lunch.
Old Abraham is just sitting, swatting flies and sweating. The
last thing he expects is company. Who could move in this heat?
Who would *want* to?

The text begins, "GOD appeared to Abraham at the Oaks of Mamre while he was sitting at the entrance of his tent. It was the hottest part of the day" (Genesis 18:1).

Remembering his manners, Abraham says to God, "Master, if it please you, stop for a while with your servant. I'll get some water so you can wash your feet" (Genesis 18:3).

Once again, we see a God wearing feet, feet that move him toward us every moment. Abraham continues, "Rest under this tree. I'll get some food to refresh you on your way, since your travels have brought you across my path" (Genesis 18:4).

God answers, *Why not?* Like Father, like Son. This God enjoys a good meal.

Abraham runs into the tent and awakens a dozing, ancient Sarah. He runs into the cattle pen to rustle a calf. He runs to the goats for milk and the larder for curds. With flour up to Sarah's elbows, they hastily prepare lunch for their Guest. With great ceremony, Abraham bows and sets God's plate in God's lap, and yells, "*Bon appétit*" with a flourish.

He then squats under a tree to watch what God will do next. What *does* God do next?

This God with a belly and feet eats. He tucks into the meal with gusto. Between mouthfuls, he happens to mention, *By the way, Abraham, I'll be back again this time next year. By then, Sarah will have a baby boy.*

And somewhere from behind the flap of the curtain tent, an old lady howls with laughter.

This is when the Substantial One loves to show up for us, right in the middle of the hottest part of the day. He comes because he wants to talk. He does the same for us all the time, only we don't always invite him to sit and eat.

"*Behold, I stand at the door and knock,*" he's saying to us. "*If anyone hears my voice and opens the door, I will come in to him and eat with him, and he with me*" (Revelation 3:20, ESV).

The God of substance is at the door, waiting to be asked in for a meal.

KINGDOM RELEVANCE

Our God gets human reality.

Jesus is privy to what we need, and he offers us exactly that. Jesus, in his kindness, does not neglect the physical in order to push the spiritual. He does what no one else can do for us: He integrates the physical and the spiritual together as one. He makes us fully human, able not only to survive here but to *thrive*. He does this so that we can sweat and live and bleed and make money here on earth out of a secure sense of God's wholeness.

That is relevant beyond fathoming. He is relevant beyond fathoming.

> He had to enter into every detail of human life. Then, when he came before God...he would have already experienced it all himself—all the pain, all the testing—and would be able to help where help was needed.
>
> Hebrews 2:18

God invites the belief that what he has to teach us is for right here, right now.

The lessons are for today. They are for this morning and for the workday and for bedtime. There is no problem we face, no question we ask about our lives here on earth that Jesus doesn't answer in the Sermon on the Mount alone.

Test it and see. And then remember that there's *more*.

> We don't have a priest who is out of touch with our reality.
>
> Hebrews 4:15

He is the God of right now. He is the God who took on our skin covering and became human. He's not "out of touch with our reality." He can give us all we need for both earth and heaven, for both present and future.

He wants to give to us our substance as a gift. Receive the

earthly things from him. Receive the heavenly things from him, too. He waits to be invited for lunch.

FOR CONTEMPLATION AND DISCUSSION

Lectio Divina Exercise:

Sit with the disciples in their locked upper room. What do you see as you look around? What is the mood of Jesus's friends? Watch as Jesus walks through the locked door. Feel the weight of his presence. How does he look as he greets you? His companions are frightened, so Jesus asks for something to eat. What does his face look like as he asks, *"Got anything to eat?"* How do you respond to this request? What are you thinking as you watch Jesus eat his meal?

For Reflection:

1. Consider a fast from technology. For a set time, abstain from all screens and devices. When you feel tempted to check your phone or social media, be intentional instead by conversing with God about your needs. How difficult is this for you? What do you discover as these mediums are unavailable to you? Journal your experiences of this fast.

2. Where is God asking you to *psélaphaó*—"touch" him? In what circumstances is he asking you to experience his substance?

3. What are your thoughts about the post-Resurrection Jesus you encounter in the disciples' locked room? What is the personality conveyed in this moment?

4. How do you view your own substance? In what ways do you vacate your substance to avoid consequences and demands?

5. What is your answer to Jesus's question: *"Have you anything here to eat?"*

PART IV:

ENTERING A DEEPER COMMITMENT

CHAPTER NINE

"Do You Want to Be Well?"

Considering the Offer of Healing

The hands of a king are the hands of a healer.

—J. R. R. Tolkien,
The Return of the King

"You revive my drooping head."

—King David, to his Shepherd,
Psalm 23:5

Two men in coveralls begin at dawn, herding the rams—horns first—into the sheep pen near the house. The sound of Charlie the sheep dog's commands and the mournful wails of plump livestock rend the west Irish morning in two. The whole flock is so thick with wool they can barely walk on their broomstick legs, legs that look like they'll snap right in half. They bounce off each other's bloated bodies, tripping up the hill with loud complaints. It's amazing how much the sheep sound like frightened humanity. By their tortured bleats, it's clear they're expecting imminent doom. Survival instincts are on full alert, nerves prompting them toward escape at all cost.

Sheep-shearing day at Sean O'Neill's farm is a day like no other: difficult for the shepherd, terrifying for the sheep.

If it were up to them, they'd never submit to shearing. They'd keep growing fatter and fatter with fluff until they couldn't move, couldn't stand, couldn't even eat. I had been watching them for days in the fields—they strained simply to bend their necks for a blade of grass. They've been plodding along in denial, when in reality, they're bound and oppressed by something so obvious.

Imprisoned with abundance. Disabled by warmth. Sick with wool.

What they don't realize is that if they're not sheared, they'll never get to experience freedom of movement, the brisk, salty breeze running along their curved backs. Still, they'd rather stay trapped in the straitjacket to which they've grown accustomed. Why? Because the idea of submitting to shearing terrifies them. It might hurt a little. It might hurt a lot. They simply prefer their woolly prison to experiencing the terror of the electric razor and giant, shiny shears.

That's why sheep need a shepherd.

Sean, the farm owner, loves his sheep. He knows what's best for them, and what's best for them is to be sheared. He knows the scary instruments alarm them, but he has a velvet-glove approach as he speaks to them and handles their frightened hides. He is calm. He knows they don't want it, that they'd run as far from him as possible, but his genuine affection for his flock makes him utterly committed to their well-being.

For the Yanks from the suburbs, it's an amazing process to witness. The rams, stocky and indignant, are taken first, one by one. Sean explains to us with a wink and a whisper that the ewes and lambs are watching. They're listening to the messages being communicated in sheep dialect by the rams. He's hopeful that once it's their turn, all the ewes and their sucklings will acquiesce with a modicum of compliance.

Ideally a three-man job, the shepherd and his mate wrestle the first ram to the ground. Grunting and sweating and Gaelic swearing are essential. Once the sheep is prostrate, they flip him on his back. Sean kneels on the ram's bull-like chest, pressing his full weight down, roping the hooves. As the shepherd, he wants this sheep to see his eyes and hear his voice. They know him—know his hands, his cadence, his face. The shepherd's mate makes quick work with razor and shears, concentrating like a painter breathing art on a canvas that can kick your teeth out.

If the ram could talk, he would probably confirm that shearing does indeed hurt—but only a little. It's a good pain, the kind that holds the hand of birth and growth and healing.

In less than three minutes, the ram is bald as a baby, shaking with rage and looking, well, *sheepish*. Undignified doesn't begin to cover it. It's incredible to behold the difference in size and shape.

Like an assembly line, the second ram is ushered in, then the third, and the same process is reenacted *ad nauseam* until the entire flock look like pigs instead of sheep. Once complete, we survey the sheep put to pasture. They are foraging in groups of two or three, contentedly chewing. They look a bit silly, but their relief is palpable. It's noticeable that they're no longer panting as they were under the weight of wool. They can breathe again. They can graze again.

Their shepherd had scared them as he does each summer, but they were back in the forgetful posture of trust. He really did know what was best.

We all, like sheep, are sick with wool. We're simply drowning in what ails us.

Sometimes we're able to deny it, filling our lives with devices and vices that dull the pain and distract us from our problem. We don't always see that we're sick. Eventually, however, the hurt we carry won't be quieted, and we discover it's worse than we realized.

We are a culture of sick sheep. Some of us carry it on the outside, fighting ailments that range from annoyance to debilitation. There is no denying that the western world is sick. In the United States, for instance, the National Health Council reports that more than 130 million adults and children are plagued with incurable, chronic conditions, including mental illness. This number reflects more than 40 percent of the inhabitants of America.[1]

Not all of us, however, carry our sickness in a physical way. Some of us are simply soul-sick. We carry our ailments on the inside, our interiors unhealthy with the nature we weren't meant to bear.

We all, like sheep, are scared of shearing. We don't want what restores. We don't want to be healed. It might hurt. Instead, we spend money we don't have on temporary and ineffective treatments. Researchers predict that by the year 2023, this country will spend $4.2 trillion in treatment costs and "lost economic output."[2]

After we are depleted of time, energy, money, and strength, we find ourselves still stuck with the weight of our wool, and we're suffocating.

WAITING IN VAIN

Sheep cannot shear themselves. We cannot heal ourselves. We need Someone else to step in and take the role of Shepherd-Healer. When Jesus introduces his question in John 5, we hesitate before answering. We hesitate because we're surprised to find that we don't really know the answer.

"Do you want to be well?"

Sean O'Neill's flock didn't have a choice. The shepherd didn't ask them if they wanted a good shearing. He didn't ask their permission to make them well from what weighed them down. They were forced into their healing.

Jesus doesn't do this.

Yes, we all, like sheep, need healing, but the difference is that our Shepherd will never force health. He honors our dignity, our God-given ability to choose entry into the process of restoration of body, mind, and soul.

John invites his readers to observe this as Jesus entered a first-century refugee camp. The sick were fleeing from themselves, and the Sheep Gate in Jerusalem was where their flight had led. Hundreds of Jews—oozing, festering, disease-ridden, draped across tiles, leaning against columns. The maimed and crippled were not permitted to enter the Temple, a Temple that allowed entry to dying sheep but not sick Jews. They were kept outside, where the livestock tramped in but never came out. There were hundreds at the pool, holding their breath, looking for the moment a celestial being *might* descend and fan the sacred waters with angel's wings. At least, this was the legend. It was a fool's hope, but that was all they had left. In *The Gospel According to John*, D. A. Carson writes that historians have found that the water of this natural fountain was fed by "underground, intermittent springs, which caused the water to turn red at times and [it was] thought to be medicinal (chalybeate)."[3]

The sick were spending their dwindling energy camped around a therapeutic hot tub, one that made them no guarantees. They'd been duped, taken for a ride by their own awkward attempt at self-healing. "A large number of the sick," writes John, "blind, lame, and paralyzed," lay whittling away their hours, waiting for a miracle (John 5:2).

They would wait in vain. They were wasting their lives beside this dank pool at the Sheep Gate, in the outer wall of Jerusalem at Bethesda, from the Hebrew *"bet esda"*—translated from the verb "to pour out."[4]

Unfortunately for this man, nothing was pouring out at the moment. Not even a trickle.

Our man would wait as long as his life lasted to roll into those stirred waters, only to find that they could not heal what ailed him.

None of John's four previous determiners applies to this man. In the original language, the other terms, *"sick, blind, lame, withered,"* are not used to describe him. John labels him with an interesting Greek term, *asthéneia* (as-then´-i-ah),[5] a compound adjective—*a*, the negative prefix signifier (meaning "not"), and *sthenoo* (sthen-AH-o), a verb denoting both physical vitality and strength of soul.[6] This man had neither.

In other words, this man wasn't just sick. He was *unwell*.

Due to language and context clues, many scholars agree that this man was unwell as a result of poor lifestyle choices. He was sick because he'd made himself sick. He'd been living crippled in his sin-sick body for thirty-eight years, which happens to be the same number of years that God's people spent wandering around the wilderness of Sinai.[7]

John's intended connection is not a difficult leap.

The scriptures are filled with the paradigm of cause-and-effect relationship between sin and physical health, from Job's friends to Jesus's disciples when they asked about a man born blind: "Rabbi, who sinned, this man or his parents?" (John 9:2, ESV). Through his prophet Moses, God himself warned his people about the congruence between disobedience and *asthéneia*:

> *"If you will diligently listen to the voice of the LORD your God, and do that which is right in his eyes, and give ear to his commandments and keep all his statutes, I will put none of the diseases on you that I put on the Egyptians, for I am the LORD, your healer."*
>
> Exodus 15:26 (ESV)

In the case of Job, the blind man of John 9, and many, many others, sickness is not a result of personal unholiness. The same is true for the hundreds at the Sheep Gate in John 5. This courtyard was bursting with those who suffered in innocence, those who did not bring upon themselves the sickness that kept them there. There were many there who were ill simply because they lived in a world made sick by the fall.

But the man of John 5 was living with the consequences of his own decisions. He was sick with them—and yet, *this* is the man Jesus chose to engage. His sin did not prevent Jesus's coming. This man didn't approach Jesus. He was one of the few who were healed by Jesus's initiation recorded in the Gospel accounts. He didn't beg Jesus for a miracle like so many others. He couldn't.

His *asthéneia* prevented him from doing anything to secure his own healing.

Whether by cruel hands or our own hands, the wellness of Garden days has been snatched and replaced with *asthéneia*.

In the end, the result is the same: All we know is something in us isn't right, and we're not sure we want to do anything about it.

HEALING EXCHANGES

Like the man at the pool, we lie in our mess, waiting for something to happen. We settle for temporary relief, a self-sufficient fix in our addictions and idols. Meanwhile, we grow accustomed to living with chronic *asthéneia*. The part of us that chose this unwellness with our parents' first bite of diseased fruit fools us into thinking we'll be okay, so long as we limp along on our own terms. Jesus knows this is how we think, deep in our dark places. He knows this is what the man at Bethesda was thinking, too.

Jesus doesn't simply heal the man. With the steady hand and precision of a surgeon, Jesus knows how to separate falsity from true condition. He does so with this man, using a question as his scalpel.

"Do you want to be well?"

The answer seems obvious. The question seems superfluous. This man has been ill and homeless for thirty-eight years. Of *course* he wants to be well. But this question is not a stupid question. Jesus has something more than a cure on his mind.

Jesus doesn't assume that the man is ready.

He's been ill for decades, and his entire identity is wrapped up in his illness. For Jesus to heal him, he will have to give something up that he may not be willing to abandon yet. Jesus knows this, so he asks the man if he's ready.

"Sir," the man says, "when the water is stirred, I don't have anybody to put me in the pool. By the time I get there, somebody else is already in" (John 5:7, ESV).

In other words, Jesus—*don't interfere.*

We remembered in the previous chapter that Jesus has hands and feet, active appendages meant for our good. This man has the

Son of God before him, his hands stretched out to restore him to a full life, but the man's not really sure if he wants a new life.

Neither are we.

Jesus's question today reminds us that we're sheep, and we are not necessarily ready for the shearing we desperately need.

Do you want to be well? The answer changes for me depending on the moment.

When Jo was six, she broke her arm in a freak accident. We had just moved to Florida's northeast coastline only three weeks prior. She snapped both bones located above her wrist, and she was set in a cast to her shoulder for ten weeks.

Sand, saltwater, and subtropic humidity do not mix well with a first-grader in a cast.

She couldn't go outside without profuse sweating. She couldn't go to the beach or jump the waves because she wasn't supposed to get wet or sandy. She couldn't play with her arm stuck out in front of her like a lopsided Frankenstein. She was distressed and cranky.

Needless to say, Josephine required quite a bit of pampering.

We scratched every itch. We gave her sponge and sink baths. We let her watch inordinate amounts of television. We overlooked a lot of bad attitudes. Our other daughter, Macy, would often lament, "I wish I had a broken arm."

Yes, I thought. *Me too.*

As a family, we did our best and counted down the days with a homemade paper chain until Jo's cast could be removed, and she would be free. The day finally arrived. Jo's mangled arm was restored. The smelly cast was sawed.

Unfortunately, her attitude smelled worse than her cast.

Our sweet-hearted little daughter had grown accustomed to a certain level of treatment in her infirmity. In ten short weeks, an identity was formed, and she was reluctant to say goodbye to it and return to life in the land of the fully functional. A six-year-old is capable of feeding herself, bathing herself, dressing herself—but this girl didn't want to do any of it. In an odd moment, she claimed she could no longer walk and would need to be carried. I reminded her, in a strained tone, that she had broken her arm, not her legs.

No matter. The invalid-queen required carrying.

"To be sick," wrote English author Charles Lamb, "is to enjoy monarchical prerogatives." We resist the healing our souls crave because it requires a change of identity, a relinquishing of an ironic superiority. Our pride must be put to shame.

In true healing, we no longer get to be self-consumed. Like Macy and me, there's desire to become broken, to grow even sicker than we presently are, because then we're not expected to behave as well people. This justifies our sin tendencies, our reverse pride, our coping mechanisms.

This is why Jesus asks: *Do you want to be well?* This tiny word, "well," is packed with powerful meaning. In Greek, it comes from the adjective *hugiēs* (hyoo-GEE-ace), meaning "whole."[8] It is an important Biblical term, used four times in John 5 alone. It conveys a sense of completion, a life with no lack.

To receive healing from Jesus is to choose an exchange. We exchange our *asthéneia* for his *hugiēs*. We exchange our sickness for his wellness. We choose to be made whole and holy. Like sheep, we know that once he touches that place that needs grace, we will never be the same. There's no going back. We can't live life the same way with the same paradigms.

Healing, by nature, necessitates change. It brings transformation. We can medicate our souls' illness without ever receiving healing. If one can be healed without being changed, then what happened wasn't healing at all—just a temporary fix.

The Healer's love isn't satisfied with a *little* of our hearts, or only a portion of our lives. He loves us with jealous, ardent love that desires the whole. It's the kind of love that heals with a single touch of his hand, glimpse of his face, breath from his mouth. It's the kind of love that transforms an entire life. Once healed, that life now lives with a different purpose.

We may not be ready to do this. Jesus knows this. He asks us to speak honestly with ourselves. Honesty is a good place for healing to begin.

HEALING HURTS

Like O'Neill's sheep, we instinctively know that the healing offered to us will also hurt. We're more frightened by the deeper pain that we don't know than by the chronic pain that we do. We read stories like *The Voyage of the Dawn Treader*, and we understand something undeniable about the nature of true healing—to cure what ails, some digging is required. Eustace shares the process of being "de-dragoned" by Aslan. The lion requires the naughty Eustace to "undress" himself. In other words, Aslan wants the dragon-boy to try to heal himself of his plight. Eustace begins peeling away his suit of scales like sunburned skin, and he finds the job quite easy. The only problem is that each time he sheds one layer, another layer is found underneath. After three or four sheds, Eustace is in despair, realizing that he cannot rid himself of the dragon.

> "Then the lion said—but I don't know if it spoke—'You will have to let me undress you.' I was afraid of his claws, I can tell you, but I was pretty nearly desperate now. So I just lay flat down on my back to let him do it. The very first tear he made was so deep that I thought it had gone right into my heart. And when he began pulling the skin off, it hurt worse than anything I've ever felt."[9]

Jesus desires to bring healing to every part that's sick—body, mind, and soul. He is after our wholeness. In order to be well, truly well, Eustace needed Aslan to do the painful work of healing. The man by the pool needed to allow Jesus to heal more than his body, and he wasn't prepared for the pain.

"He heals the heartbroken and bandages their wounds," the psalmist says of God (Psalm 147:3, NLT). But the nature of sickness is that it is tender. It is sore. It throbs when it's touched and screams when it's prodded. To receive healing from Jesus takes courage, because there is an ironic element of pain in healing. Just like the sheep, just like Eustace, we find that to be made well is also an invitation to undergo painful work.

Our bodies and souls are fiercely intertwined, and for the outside to be well, the inside must undergo treatment. *"First clean the inside of the cup and the plate,"* Jesus advises us, *"that the outside also may be clean"* (Matthew 23:26, ESV).

We must see ourselves as we truly are—lame, broken, bleeding.

We must acknowledge all the ways that have brought us to this point of need—sin, wounding, the enemy.

None of these things are pleasant. It's scary to behold our true, chronic condition in the light. It feels like death. We were never meant to do this on our own, but we hate to do it in the omniscient presence, with the One who misses nothing.

It's overwhelming to look upon our sickness of soul, to carry our heavy baggage to Jesus and let him open up the cases we've been carrying for so long. Jesus knows we're afraid to do this, and he has compassion. He asks us to go with him into this place anyway. He already sees what's inside us, and his love doesn't waver at the sight. Like the man at the pool, our sin infection never prevents Jesus's coming.

He promises to be with us each step in the painful work of healing.

We may not be ready for this. If not, Jesus is patient. He will never give up and will never leave. But again, he asks the question because he seeks the honest answer.

HEALING REQUIRES

When Jesus approached the invalid of John 5, he was offering more than a cure. He was extending an invitation into friendship with him. He was inviting this man, abandoned and alone, into his companionship. He was inviting relationship.

Jesus did heal the man of his physical wound, but he didn't force himself on the wound of the soul. Later in John's narrative, we find out that the man who could now run, leap, skip, and high-step used these new legs to run to the religious authorities, for some reason eager to tattle that Jesus had healed him on the Sabbath. He went out of his way to do it. Why? Perhaps he didn't want to live his life with a different purpose. He wanted healing without discipleship, without submission.

He wanted healing without relationship.

That is, however, what true healing offers, and that is what true healing requires: deep, intimate, personal relationship with the Healer.

That level of intimacy is overwhelming. It's terrifying. Instead of welcoming the gaze of Jesus, the friendship of Jesus, the affection of Jesus, we avert our eyes and stare at a pool that will do nothing for us. The pool doesn't require anything from us but time.

But Jesus asks for it all. This is what he wants, though he very rarely gets it. *"They screw their eyes shut so they won't have to look,"* Jesus said in Matthew, *"so they won't have to deal with me face-to-face and let me heal them"* (Matthew 13:15).

To be healed, we must come face-to-face with God himself. This takes great courage, courage we may not yet possess. We discover that we are not yet ready to be made well.

In order to put our healing in his hands, we have to know his goodness. Sometimes, he seems so untrustworthy, cruel even. The shearing can be so frightening, the metal clippers and the terrible buzzing of the electric razor can make us gasp in terror. We think we'll never survive the good intentions of our Shepherd. The sheep dog that chases us and snaps at our heels and herds us back to the fold when we try to stray—we find this treatment unfair, an infringement on our livestock rights. We're also aware of the rod and the staff. This looks like a crooked instrument of torture. Mostly, we just think we'd be better off if the Good Shepherd would allow us to care for ourselves, to do our best for ourselves.

But this is not so. In *A Shepherd Looks at Psalm 23*, Phillip Keller writes,

The day I bought [my sheep] I realized that this was but the first stage in a long, lasting endeavor in which from then on, I would, as their owner, have to continually lay down my life for them, if they were to flourish and prosper. Sheep do not "just take care of themselves" as some might suppose. They require, more than any other class of livestock, endless attention and meticulous care.[10]

We are not the kind of creatures who can simply muddle through life on our own and be okay. We were designed for the Shepherd's healing hands. When we stray from him and rebel, we find ourselves in all kinds of dangerous situations, far worse than shearing. It is in the affectionate gaze of Jesus that we are safe.

We must never forget that the Good Shepherd became the sacrificial Lamb of God. He, too, was led through dark, deep places. He, too, was to be sheared, the weight of our sin upon him like a waterlogged wool pelt. "Like a sheep being sheared, he took it all in silence" (Isaiah 53:7). Jesus willingly took upon himself the sickness of filthy wool, the terror of the shears, so that we could be reunited with him forever. The Son of God has become the sick, desperate, miserable poor of this world so we can be well.

Because of this Lamb, no sickness will ever be able to snatch us from his flock.

He asks us if we're ready, and we screw our eyes shut. We close our eyes to his healing so we won't have to see what's in his face—Love, fierce and holy Love. The kind of love that scares us with its intensity and requirement for every part of who we are, for he has given every part of himself to secure our healing.

Many of the places we may be led into will appear to us as dark, deep, dangerous and somewhat disagreeable. But it simply must be remembered that He is there with us in it. He is very much at work in the situation. It is His energy, effort and strength expended on my behalf that even in this deep, dark place is bound to produce a benefit for me...It is He who makes sense and purpose and meaning come out of situations which otherwise would be just a mockery to me.[11]

His healing may feel like cruelty, but it is not. It simply cannot be. It is impossible for him to be cruel. He is always kind, always loving, and he knows what we need—even if it seems the opposite of what we would want. It is not in his nature and character to treat us with anything but loving care. "But the fact is, it was *our* pains he carried—*our* disfigurements, all the things wrong with *us*. We thought he brought it on himself...He took the punishment, and that made us whole. Through his bruises we get *healed*" (Isaiah 53:4–5, emphasis mine).

We can trust his intentions for our wellness. If we don't know this to the very core of our beings, then we will continue to deny the healing our souls require.

We can answer yes to Jesus's question because he knows what sickness feels like. We can answer yes to Jesus's question because he is trustworthy.

ORIGINAL DESIGN

God kissed his Garden children and blessed them. With flowers in her hair and dirt on his hands, the two were his dream made flesh. He looked at them intently, and what he saw was good.

No, not just good. What he saw was *outstanding*.

Each limb was supple and strong. Each finger and toe well formed to grasp fruit and tread the spongy earth. Oh—and their faces. What upturned noses! What deep wells in their shining eyes! Their bodies radiated health. The man's was like a solid oak—stretching and strong, housing a power that would make the ground tremble with joy as it was worked by his hands. The woman—how lovely she was. As graceful as a hind, the fierce beauty of a lioness, her frame was his soft glory. He delighted in them as a mother adores the infant at her breast.

But he could see more than what was framed on the outside. Like a clockmaker looks at a watch, seeing cogs and wheels, he could see the ticking of their perfect systems. As he gazed upon them in love, he saw robust, beating hearts that pumped platelets to the outer frontiers of their forms. He saw lungs that filled with the breath he breathed out for them. He saw the special system he'd given them toward fruitful multiplication pulsing with potential and passion. He saw lobes and cortices, encased in the helmets he'd made with his own hands, sending messages of a good reality to every moving part. Muscle and tendon, arteries and organs, all working in orchestral harmony—a full-bodied symphony of vigorous health.

He also saw even deeper, to the space between bone and marrow, flesh and spirit. He saw their inner well-being, two souls at complete rest. There were no shadows touching minds or darkening hearts. The congruence of their bodies and spirits reflected each other like a still lake on a warm summer evening. What was true on the level of soul exuded throughout the physical form. He saw each part in deference to the whole and rejoiced that his children were unfragmented creatures. His design was flawless, his living art unspoiled. They were like him—whole and holy.

He wished it could have remained.

The Sick One, watching for his moment, coughed toxic words into the air around the Garden children. The stench of lies clouded their faces, and they inhaled. The fruit they ate was poison, wreaking wild havoc on body, mind, and soul. Their perfect health evaporated with the morning mist. Now when God looked inside them, the potential for life was braided together with the potential for dysfunction and disease.

Hearts would palpitate.

Tumors would invade.

Minds would become dark places, centers for sickened thoughts.

The body and spirit would fight a constant war with each other.

The Sick One looked in his direction, laughing with ugly mirth. Now they would be *his* children, the progeny of he who is unwell.

But in God's great heart, the seed of hope was buried in the rich soil of his love. Before the beginning of time, he'd already made a plan for the rescue of body and soul. When the time was ripe, he would wrap their frail flesh around his uncontainable glory. He, the Healer, would walk among them, breathing in their polluted air, touching their contaminated bodies. He would give them a foretaste of what was waiting for them in the endless ream of eternity.

He, the Well One, would invite their sicknesses to plague his health. He would bear syndromes on his shoulders, and in so doing, he would destroy its death grip on his children forever. The back of the Sick One was broken. It is broken still, and his certain end is simply a matter of time.

IN THE PARTIAL

Because she is a teacher, my mother's all-time favorite movie is *The Miracle Worker*, the story of Anne Sullivan's healing work with Helen Keller. When Anne began her work with Helen, she did not see the angry, feral, hopeless child that others saw and had dismissed. Anne saw a little girl, living beside the dank pool of her own incommunicable world. She saw a soul that needed to be introduced to light, color, words. She saw a child in need of healing.

An ardent teacher, Anne never gave up on Helen, even when Helen gave up on herself. Because of Anne Sullivan, Helen Keller found the words that had been trapped in her muted mouth. Anne Sullivan gave her a voice.

By patient love and deep relationship, Anne Sullivan healed Helen's soul—but the healing was only in part. After her time with Anne, Helen was still blind. She was still deaf. Anne could not undo these things. Helen still lived with the physical disabilities that made her different from the other children.

Helen Keller's healing was partial.

Helen was made for a world without sickness and decay. Helen was made to run without stumbling and hear the sound of a nickering horse. Helen was made for the Garden. So was the man of John 5.

So are we. We are made for "that Day":

> "The sun of righteousness will dawn on those who honor my name, healing radiating from its wings. You will be bursting with energy, like colts frisky and frolicking...on that Day." God-of-the-Angel-Armies says so.
>
> Malachi 4:2–3

Unlike the mythical creature at the Bethesda pool, the wings of the Healer are operational. They are real. We need to remember that the hands of Heaven's King are the hands of a healer. Even when we turn him down and reject his offer of healing, he is not swayed. He doesn't relent. He stays. He will wait as long as it takes. He returns us to his question often, not being rebuffed at our unreadiness to be healed.

However, even as we say yes to Jesus's healing, we choose to live with a hard truth, the Helen Keller truth: There will always be more to heal this side of God's Kingdom. *Hugiēs* will remain partial until God no longer tarries.

On this side of Jesus's Kingdom, we can and will taste healing. We can be well. But all hurt is not fully healed until we are returned to the glory of the Garden, walking with him face-to-face, living out our healing in every part. Until that time, the wholeness is, paradoxically, partial. The wellness, too. And the healing. Living with the partial, we still suffer from *asthéneia*.

But we do not suffer alone. He suffers with us as he waits. He holds the partial in his hands, binding us up with him until fulfillment belongs to his people.

BACK TO PROSPERING

There are still echoes of the Garden in our souls. We instinctively know that our bodies, hearts, and minds were not made for *asthéneia*. He created Adam and Eve with complete *hugiēs* in which to live and love and work. He proclaimed their utter goodness. "*Prosper!*" he said (Genesis 1:28). Prospering is a condition of those who are well, inside and out.

With his question, Jesus takes us back before the Sick One introduced us to the diseased fruit. With his question, Jesus is asking us if we're ready to return to life in the Garden. To our "very good"-ness. To prospering.

To well-being.

In the Garden-restored, the fruit will not be rotten, and it will carry no diseases to poison body or soul. The very leaves we find there will be agents of wholeness.

> The leaves of the tree [of life] were for the healing of the nations. No longer will there be anything accursed, but the throne of God and of the Lamb will be in it.
>
> Revelation 22:2–3 (ESV)

In the coming Kingdom, at the fullness of time, we will no longer suffer from *asthéneia*. We will be *hugiēs*—whole. Fully. Forever. "*Behold,*" says God to his people living in the partial. "*I will bring to [them] health and healing, and I will heal them and reveal to them abundance of prosperity*" (Jeremiah 33:6, ESV). His children are invited to return to the Garden, where no enemy assault, no disease, will ever infect our souls again. Because of this rescue, true healing can never be snatched away.

Any sickness we experience now is just the lingering effects of an already-toppled regime. It has no real hold on us any longer.

Any healing we experience now is a foretaste of the fullness of what is yet to come. We submit to the partial while we wait with longing for the whole.

Jesus is asking the question, and the question is for us. He wonders if his sheep are yet ready to be sheared. He asks if the sick are ready for healing.

He wonders if we have the courage to be well.

FOR CONTEMPLATION AND DISCUSSION

Lectio Divina Exercise:

Sit with the man by the pool. How do the two of you feel as you compete for a miracle cure? Relate with him a moment: How has it been for you to be sick for so long? Watch as Jesus approaches you. Hear him as he asks you the question: *"Do you want to be well?"* What is your initial reaction? Listen to your soul as it contemplates the changes it would mean to be healed. What do you see in the face of Jesus as he awaits your response?

For Reflection:

1. What has *asthéneia* represented to you? What is your perspective on its effects in your life—physical, mental, spiritual?
2. Where do you see the fear of shearing in your relationship with Jesus? What is it about healing that scares you the most?
3. How does it make you feel that you were created *hugiēs*—whole and holy? Do you see this as true? How do you experience this on a daily basis?
4. In what ways have you made sickness a part of your identity?
5. What is your answer to Jesus's question: *"Do you want to be well?"*

CHAPTER TEN

"How Many Loaves Do You Have?"

Investing in Kingdom Life

"Give, and it will be given to you.
Good measure, pressed down, shaken together, running over, will
be put into your lap."

—Jesus Christ,
Luke 6:38, ESV

No one has ever become poor by giving.

—Anne Frank,
Anne Frank: The Diary of a Young Girl

Our most patriotic Fourth of July was celebrated deep in the heart of Irish sheep country.

In the seaside village of Caherciveen, we found a community much warmer than its weather. They treated us as long-lost Yankee relatives come home for a holiday. By the time July 4 drew near, we decided to throw a small party for our new friends—but not just *any* party. We wanted to invite the Irish to a traditional American Independence Day—with *all* the trimmings. If any other nation knows how to celebrate freedom from tyranny, it is most certainly the Irish.

The morning of the Fourth, we awoke to rain. Wet weather never seemed to keep the Irish indoors, so we didn't allow it to dampen our spirits, either. We grabbed the grocery list, our well-used wet gear, and headed into the village to shop.

What we discovered was that Americans *not* in America are limited in patriotic shopping venues. In western Ireland, there are no Walmarts, and we loved that lack. This left our small market in Caherciveen as the only option for fifty kilometers. We divided the list between us, wished each other luck, and commenced the hunt.

I began with hot dogs. I asked one teenage boy stocking shelves, "Excuse me. Could you point me in the direction of hot dogs?"

Between my accent and the unfamiliar request, he stared at me like I was speaking Swahili. "Hot what?" he asked with a thick Gaelic brogue.

"Hot *DOGS*," I repeated—louder, hoping this might serve to clarify. His face told me it didn't. I then attempted the unpleasant task of describing a hot dog to someone who's never had one. By the end, even *I* didn't want to eat one.

After asking two other employees and then wandering the aisles, I finally found them. These "hot dogs" came four to a pack, were labeled in Gaelic, and apparently filled with unicorn meat because they were as expensive as caviar. These were the Irish cousins of hot dogs, and apart from the wet, cylindrical shape, the familial tie ended there.

Jimmy was in charge of getting sparklers and fireworks. Apparently, when he asked about them, he received the same look I did when asking for hot dogs. They don't exist in Caherciveen. He walked the streets of the village, quickly discovering that there was no chance of sparklers, fireworks, or any other incendiary device beyond lighter fluid. Out of desperation he bought some emergency candles to light.

Finally, we put our daughters on the hunt for the colors of Old Glory. There were no pennants, flags, streamers, or balloons of red, white, or blue. I blame the lingering, bitter taste of imperialistic oppression. There were plenty, however, of emerald-green novelty items. We got what we could and headed for home.

None of us said what we were all thinking: This Fourth of July was going to be bogus. I'd had to sell a kidney to afford hot dogs.

On a whim, we made one final stop at our friend Helen's bakery. We'd tasted her crown-shaped queen cakes before, and we were desperate to believe in their magical abilities to cover over the wrongs of this party.

As we removed our supplies from the car, Jimmy's cloying optimism collided with my depressive funk. We readied the cottage with dirty looks and cranky children. I asked myself a hundred times why in the world we had invited people over. I was unpacking groceries when Jimmy, dripping wet, came into the kitchen from the courtyard.

"We have a small setback," he said.

I braced myself, holding a hot dog in each hand.

"The grill won't light."

I looked out the window. Fire would be a miracle in this rain.

"No problem," said I, ripping hot dogs from plastic sleeves with hostility.

In conclusion, we microwaved ten packs of Irish hot dogs. They were neon pink when I pulled them out, slapping them on a serving plate. I looked around at green balloons and pouring rain, sighing as I blotted the sweaty hot dogs with a tea towel.

Like most things in life, this was not going to be what I wanted it to be.

Regardless of our food issues, the emergency candles, and our green balloons, it was a great party. Our friends arrived, and our friends had fun. Jimmy and I kissed and made up, and we were even able to enjoy the night without embarrassment. There was music, storytelling, and an odd sense that we were with family. Many had never consumed a hot dog before and were kind enough to say they were "brilliant." This weird Fourth of July ended with the singing of "The Star-Spangled Banner" and queen cakes.

I wanted to cancel the whole party, but I thank God I didn't. Our ironic, Irish-American Fourth of July turned out to be a treasured memory.

We didn't have much to offer our friends, but we gave

what we could. We invited them into our celebration, into our different customs, and they received what we offered with joy. As I had hoped, Helen's magic covered our lack, and friendship was the dish *du jour*.

Our simple availability was more than enough to make everyone forget the hot dogs and foiled plans. It was the giving, the open-handed offering that made everyone return home full.

DEFINING OUR LOAVES

They were in the middle of nowhere. No villages. No markets. Nothing.

Jesus had once again invited them into the desert, and others had snaked behind like a midsummer's creek, pulsing with babies and laughter and suffering. These were the poorest of the poor. These were the desperate and homeless and unemployed. These were the sick and demon-plagued and filthy. These were the ones who didn't have two mites to put together, let alone two meals.

His disciples were frustrated. They wanted peace and quiet, but Jesus just kept healing, blessing, and teaching. The rock cliffs towered over their heads, echoing his holy and wholly mystifying words.

His disciples cleared their collective throats. They pointed to the position of the sun. They patted their rumbling stomachs, but day turned to night turned to day. Three whole days had passed, and like Jonah, they were all getting a little bit cranky. Jesus turned to his friends and said,

"I hurt for these people. For three days now they've been with me, and now they have nothing to eat. I can't send them away without a meal—they'd probably collapse on the road."

Matthew 15:32

The disciples couldn't believe their ears. They couldn't believe his presumption, his audacity. With building impatience, they asked him to explain his thinking.

"But where in this deserted place are you going to dig up enough food for a meal?"

In other words, *we have no hot dogs.* Jesus answers their question with his own.

"How many loaves do you have?"

In the original Greek text, Jesus asks about the disciples' *artos* (ar´-tos)—their bread.[1] The presence and symbolism of bread is of great importance in both Old and New Testaments. In Biblical culture, meat was the luxury of the wealthy. According to *The Evangelical Dictionary of Theology*, bread was the staple of the poor, and thus, it was indispensable nourishment for the vast majority.[2] Acquiring and possessing enough loaves was the necessary pursuit of the populace. The assembly gathered before Jesus and his friends were no strangers to hunger.

The Biblical text tells us that the crowds of men, women, and children of Matthew 14 and 15, numbering in the tens of thousands, had no bread. They had no loaves of their own. What little they'd had, they'd consumed long ago. But their hunger went deeper than bread, so they stayed at the feet of Jesus.

To have daily bread at one's disposal was to flourish, and these were not a flourishing people.

This word for loaves, *artos*, cleverly derives from the verbal root *airō* (ah´-ee-ro), meaning "to raise up."[3] Unless otherwise intended, the ingredients required to make loaves of bread must go through a rising process to be useful for consumption. The bread-making process takes time. It takes a rising agent, such as yeast. It takes muscle for rolling, kneading, and pounding dough until pliable. Making bread is a process of availability, of intentionality toward sustaining oneself.

Loaves are a product of this intentional pursuit of nourishment.

When Jesus asks us to number our loaves, he is asking us to evaluate our availability and intentionality toward his Kingdom work. As with *airō*, he's inquiring if our greatest gifts and assets are prepared to rise to meet him where he is working.

Our loaves are our time. Our loaves are our stamina and energy. Loaves are what we think about, what we dream about, the goals we pursue. Our loaves are the balance of our savings accounts as well as the way we spend our weekday evenings. Our loaves are our giftings, our talents, the possessions that make up who we see ourselves becoming. Our loaves are the things that we treasure, the things that fill our visions and souls.

The loaves we possess are the matters we pursue for our own nourishment.

Jesus is asking us what we have in our personal bags of glory. He's asking if we might be willing to give to him our own necessary pursuit of loaf acquisition.

Don't shuffle along, eyes to the ground, absorbed with the things right in front of you. Look up, and be alert to what is going on around Christ—that's where the action is.

Colossians 3:2

He wonders what we're prepared to offer in co-participation with his Kingdom. He is asking if we're ready to look up with open hands.

He wants to know if he's welcome to decide what's best for our loaves.

FORGETFULNESS

The disciples' question in Matthew 15 seems legitimate. "But where in this deserted place," they asked, scratching their heads, looking around, "are *you* going to dig up enough food for a meal?" (Matthew 15:33). In other words, this is your problem, Jesus, not ours.

They are in an uncultivated area with no place to acquire the supplies they need. They are strangers to this mass of humanity swarming around their Teacher, and Jesus seems to have placed impossible expectations on them to produce a feast from famine.

We, the readers, can empathize with the situation. They're fresh out of hot dogs, and they don't see it as their responsibility to get more. We know what it feels like to be put in an impossible situation, a situation where we can't possibly perform but we're expected to do just that. Therefore, we agree that the disciples' question to God's Son is bold but valid.

But we'd be wrong. We'd be forty-six verses wrong.

Forty-six verses earlier, located near the end of Matthew 14, Jesus did produce a feast from famine. Just forty-six verses ago, Jesus had just provided a lavish, Messianic banquet for upward of 20,000 men, women, and children. He had just satisfied bellies that had rarely experienced fullness. He also suspended the scientific realities that hold the world in orbit and traveled across the Sea of Galilee on foot. His signs point to a generous and powerful God, a God that is Immanuel—*with us*. He has assured the people that alignment with him would mean unceasing provision and continual abundance. He could and would slake the ever-increasing hunger and thirst of our souls.

Historical time lines put these two miraculous feedings in A.D. 30—the feeding of 5,000 (Matthew 14) in midwinter, and the feeding of 4,000 (Matthew 15) in early spring.[4] These forty-six verses in between represent a matter of months, if not weeks. Forty-six verses' worth of time.

But to the disciples, it's like it never happened. In *this* wilderness, they seem to suffer from an outlandish loss of short-term memory. "Where in this deserted place," they challenge, "are you going to dig up enough food for a meal?" (Matthew 15:33). They had already forgotten what Jesus could do with a few loaves of bread.

In between the time of winter's frost to spring's buttercups, these disciples forgot the unforgettable revelation of God. They were suffering from spiritual memory loss, a degenerative disease that befuddles, bewilders, and creates inexplicable bouts of forgetfulness.

I am frustrated for Jesus in this moment. How does he deal with such preposterous lack of remembering? We wonder why he hasn't fired them and gotten newer, better disciples long ago. But he doesn't do this. Nobody gets fired. Nobody even gets berated.

They simply get a bellyful of question, a question meant to be received with a determined humor and a humorous determination on the part of our Lord.

I'm betting this question sparks a memory in their minds. Mark records the presence of this question in his account of the first feeding, right before Jesus used a boy's meager supplies to serve a banquet: *"How many loaves do you have?"*

But the story doesn't stop here. In Matthew's next chapter—after *two* miraculous feedings—the disciples are in a boat, *still* struggling to remember what Jesus can and will do with their loaves.

And they began discussing it among themselves, saying, "We brought no bread." But Jesus, aware of this, said, "O *you of little faith, why are you discussing among yourselves the fact that you have no bread? Do you not yet perceive? Do you not remember the five loaves for the five thousand, and how many baskets you gathered? Or the seven loaves for the four thousand, and how many baskets you gathered? How is it that you fail to understand that I did not speak about bread?"*

Matthew 16:7–11 (ESV)

Jesus is patient with our forgetfulness, showing humorous grace instead of hostility. He doesn't walk away in a huff. He doesn't lash out in frustration. His eye doesn't even twitch.

He simply asks questions.

Because of their spiritual memory loss, the confused and forgetful disciples of Matthew 15 were unable to offer Jesus the few loaves they possessed. They were afraid to give.

They were hindered by their perception of false poverty.

Because of our own memory loss, we hoard our precious loaves, unwilling to enter his Kingdom work with open hands.

EVALUATING OUR LOAVES

He doesn't ask, "Will you give me your loaves?" He asks, "*How many?*" This is strategic on his part. It's a question of careful sifting and calculation.

It says much about God that he asks us to weigh the value of our loaves before offering them to him. He does this because he understands that we are *already* in a constant state of evaluating what we have to offer. We look within, we look around, we measure and appraise. Estimating by a constantly fickle standard, our loaf worth is determined by the quality and abundance of others' loaves.

Western culture, and especially the western church, is plagued with LCD—Loaf Comparison Disease. This disease has reached pandemic levels as we compare our spiritual giftings, callings, and ministries to those around us. I am embarrassed to admit how difficult it is for me to celebrate the success of another. Instead of blessing the loaves of others, I find myself pulled to diminish their accomplishments or denigrate my own in the light of other loaves' goodness.

Psychology Today names this pull to compare "social comparison theory," which states that "individuals determine their own social and personal worth based on how they stack up against others they perceive as somehow faring better or worse."[5]

It is the nature of fallen humanity to compare who we are to others. We size one another up, using our own finely crafted standard of measurement. We evaluate ourselves against others in every possible way.

Career success. Financial status. Physical attractiveness. Reputation.

Gifting. Spouse. Friends. Education. Behavior of children.

Ministry and service. Spiritual maturity. Doctrinal knowledge.

This research also discusses that those who enter into this vicious comparison trap "often experience feelings of deep dissatisfaction, guilt, remorse, and engage in destructive behaviors."[6] We know these destructive behaviors. Lying. Posturing.

Exaggerating. Overspending. Highlighting the faults of others. Self-promotion. The list of these behaviors would equal miles of bread loaves laid end to end.

Our flesh needs to feel on top. We can always find someone to compare ourselves to who makes us look better in our internal mirror. When we accidentally make a comparison that leaves us feeling worse, it burns. And then we must seek another false comparison to bring us back on top again. It's an ugly cycle, and Jesus invites us to stop.

Jesus does not support our flesh comparisons. He will not indulge them. It's more false than comparing apples to oranges; it's attempting to compare apples to screwdrivers or puppies. It doesn't make sense to try.

Our God-stories are written by the same Hand but with different settings and plots and character developments. He does not pass out generic lives. With deft insight and unceasing affection, he eagerly writes each individual story, and he offers it to each one as a rare gift.

Our comparisons are not only incorrect, they are a complete exercise in futility. Our lives are not the same. Our *loaves* are not the same. They cannot be measured against one another.

Paul agrees. Noticing this tendency to compare our value to others in the church, he writes, "When they measure themselves by one another and compare themselves with one another, they are without understanding" (2 Corinthians 10:12, ESV).

It's foolish and irrational thinking.

The New Testament shows us that we share these behaviors with the disciples. In Mark 9, there were hissed whispers behind the back of the Teacher. The handpicked friends of Jesus tried to hide from him that they were fighting. In the wake of the record of their embarrassing public failure to provide relief for a troubled boy, they could go nowhere else with their faulty loaves than to comparison. They simply *had* to get back on top at the expense of the others. They didn't want Jesus to know that.

Meanwhile, Jesus just kept walking, listening to the heated

undertones behind him, talking to his Father about these men who would carry the Gospel to his people.

When they got to the house where they were staying, they all settled down for a meal, trying to forget a horrible day. Jesus broke the bread and the awkward silence with a question, swallowing his grin as he tore the loaf in two.

"*What were you arguing about along the way?*" he asked, casually dipping his loaf in olive oil as he unwrapped another Gospel question.

Mark's account is true comedy. He writes with understated irony, "The silence was deafening." We, as the reader, can almost hear the crickets chirping in the background. "They had been arguing with one another over *who among them was the greatest*" (Mark 9:34, emphasis mine).

He asks them and he asks us this question to give us yet another opportunity to come to him with our need to have our loaves on top. If the lads had done this in the first place, then perhaps it wouldn't have led to an argument over whose throne would be a few inches higher on the heavenly platform. But they didn't bring their broken loaves to Jesus, just as we choose to keep ours to ourselves—and it led to more brokenness.

As I struggle to evaluate my personal loaf situation, the continual presence of the double-headed snake, shame and pride, whispers nonsense in my brain, seeking to aid in the private evaluation of what I have to give. I argue within myself of whose loaves are the greatest.

I have shame that my loaves are so paltry; I have pride that they are mine, and mine alone. Depending on the day, the hour, and the company, my evaluation changes like Irish weather. I compare myself to others whose loaves look a bit thin, and pride swells in my chest. But as the wind shifts, so does my evaluation once again. Shame descends the moment I'm confronted with loaves that I observe are better, more hearty. I take stock of my supply, and I see that I am lacking what is needed.

The flesh is rife with Loaf Comparison Disease. We must be on our guard.

When we find our loaves lacking, we must go directly to Jesus. There is nowhere else that is safe. He'll take us in that state. He'll love us in that state. He will provide an accurate evaluation.

This question of counting our loaves is only appropriate for Jesus to ask.

We are constantly invited by the world, the flesh, and the enemy to give our loaves in an unhealthy manner. There's so much pressure, even from the church, for us to say yes and spend ourselves in places and ways Jesus does not intend for us. This question is an intimate conversation between Jesus and his friends. This is a question for which deep relationship is a prerequisite. We are not designed to spend ourselves for every social justice cause or volunteer for every need in an organized church program.

We need to ask Jesus where he's deploying our loaves.

Jesus is our Guide, and he is our Questioner. He is the only one with the authority to help us measure and weigh our loaves, and then invite us to give them away.

He understands that without his exposing question, my loaves grow rotten with mold. These stale loaves are nourishing food for no one—not others, not even for myself. Before inviting us to share our loaves, Jesus first offers to help us see our loaves correctly. He wants us to decipher them with his math.

He wants us to see our loaves with his eyes, to risk his evaluation of what we possess.

RISKING OUR LOAVES

As Jesus asks this question of me, I look around and see the famished eyes of those who want my bread, the bread I've worked hard to acquire. I look into my bag and see the loaves within. I see the face of Jesus—undemanding and yet expectant. To reach into my bag and hand my loaves over to Jesus is an enormous risk. What if by doing so, I forfeit my own ability to survive? What if I don't have anything to eat when I'm hungry?

What if I starve because of this foolishness?

Much of the time, I find myself deciding to give some loaves to God—but not all. It's common sense to share a little *and* keep a few tucked away for a rainy day. What if I give all my loaves to God, and then he doesn't come through? I'm left holding an empty bag, hungry and disillusioned.

I'm afraid that I'll have nothing if I give him my loaves. So were the disciples.

> He charged them to take nothing for their journey except a staff—no bread, no bag, no money in their belts.
>
> Mark 6:8 (ESV)

Who is this God who expects us to go on journeys to unfamiliar places without a suitcase or snacks? Who is this God who invites us to give him every loaf we have down to the last crumb? A very real part of us is terrified that once we turn over our loaves to him, this presumptuous God will take our offering and leave us with nothing.

We read the Genesis 4 account of Cain's spurned grains, and this fear is confirmed. In what seems like a case of divine loaf comparison, we find the synopsis of God's findings rather cold: "The LORD had regard for Abel and his offering, but for Cain and his offering he had no regard" (Genesis 4:4–5, ESV).

What we don't understand is that the downfall of Cain was *not* in what was given. It was in the withholding. He offered God the lesser fruits of a begrudging heart. He was willing to part with what he considered second best. Cain discovered, with building rage, what we also discover with the partial giving of our loaves—half-hearted gestures are not befitting of Kingdom sons and daughters.

WITHHOLDING OUR LOAVES

God gives us the choice to hoard our supply. He knows we can choose to work by the sweat of our brow, grinding day in and day out in this world that has not yet bowed its knee. We can ask him to keep his hands off our stuff.

He honors that choice. But as a good Father, he also has no regard for it.

We saw this when our kids were very small. I recall one instance when our seven-year-old, Macy, and her six-year-old sister, Jo, grappled with this choice. We were taking a 500-mile road trip to Florida, and for this trip, we had purchased two ginger ales for the girls. This was their first time having a carbonated beverage, and they were more excited about the cans of soda than they were about the beach. When the time came, Jo asked for help opening her ginger ale, but Macy wanted the independence of "doing it myself."

We should have known better.

The tab was popped just as we hit a divot in the highway at seventy-five miles per hour. A violence of spray spewed forth, causing Macy to startle and drop the rest of the soda. In one-tenth of a mile, the soda was opened and the contents had vanished into pleather crevices. We had one sticky, wailing daughter in the backseat.

In general, our parenting style does not demand that we immediately replace the spilled soda. In this case, however, our hearts were very tender toward our daughter's brokenhearted response. This was to be a rite of passage for her, and she was denied this rite by a pothole and tiny fingers. Therefore, I turned to my other daughter and asked the fateful question: "Josephine, would you please kindly share your drink with your sister?"

In other words, how many loaves do you have?

What Jo didn't realize was that our plan was to stop at the very next gas station to replenish the special drinks and bless our children. Generosity begets generosity, and the blessing of others is often a precursor to being blessed oneself. We wanted to use this as a teachable moment, to show her how the Good King works in his Kingdom of Goodness.

But Jo had a choice, and she was struggling to make the right one.

My second-born looked at me, a hardening coming over her eyes and into her hands. I literally saw her fingers grasp her can tighter, creating tiny indentations. She looked over at her sister—taking in her tears, her sadness, her stickiness. She looked down at her can of sweet, bubbling liquid, weighing the contents of it in her grip. She said nothing as a war was being waged in her little soul.

In that moment, our sweet daughter with the birthright of sin nature said, "I don't want to."

Of course she didn't. We understood that. But the question wasn't if she *wanted* to share. It was if she was willing.

In the end, she shared, but she was not happy about it.

When we share in this manner, we are sharing from the perilous place of Ananias and Sapphira. We are sharing from a kinship with Cain.

We don't want to give our loaves to God. We want to hoard them for ourselves, because we don't understand the Kingdom principle: Generosity begets multiplied generosity. I am not advocating a prosperity gospel. There's no toll-free number listed here for personal donations.

What I am recognizing, however, is the observable way God's Kingdom works.

Proverbs states,

One gives freely, yet grows all the richer;
another withholds what he should give, and only suffers
    want.
Whoever brings blessing will be enriched,
and one who waters will himself be watered.

                                        Proverbs 11:24 (ESV)

Jesus echoes,

"*Give, and it will be given to you. Good measure, pressed down, shaken together, running over, will be put into your lap. For with the measure you use it will be measured back to you.*"

Luke 6:38 (ESV)

Good measure.
Pressed down.
Shaken together.
Running over.
Our cups overfloweth.

In Kingdom economics, there is a mysterious and holy correlation between our generosity and God's. What we give, God will meet with abundance. This is so much bigger than money and possessions. This is where our capacity itself is enlarged by God's wealth.

God knows our fears, and he invites us to number them among the loaves, too.

Like Jo, like the disciples of Jesus, we have the choice put before us to share our loaves. Jesus is after that place in us that *will* share, but the sharing mirrors nothing of his Kingdom heart. It is a begrudging, stingy sharing, and for this sharing, the Kingdom has no regard.

When the feeling of lack is acute, and we're sure we have nothing to offer those who are hungry around us, *that's* when Jesus asks this question. He asks with a playful grin, to help us see where our trust is hidden, and he asks at the most inconvenient times.

He asks when our sister spills her soda, when our friends disappoint us, when our local church lets us down. He asks when we see the suffering and pain and undying thirst of those in our lives who desperately need more of God.

How can anyone have the power, the *freedom*, to live with such lavish, joyful surrendering of their loaves? Is this even possible?

We all carry Cain in us, and because of this, we no longer know how to share our best with God.

We need to be taught how.

SHARING OUR LOAVES

Children were scampering, playing hide-and-seek among the rocks. A fussy baby was being soothed by his mother. Families were milling together, always keeping one eye on Jesus. Matthew records thousands had gathered, drawn like a magnet to the Carpenter who fixed both furniture and bodies. They were lost sheep, seeking a shepherd. They were the homeless, the restless, the hungry looking for a meal.

Jesus's friends had little more than pocket lint to offer the languishing crowd that filled the hillsides, a pulsing carpet of grass. The depth of need around them was overwhelming. They knew—on a gut level—their inadequacy to feed, to nourish, to love. They had no memory of all that God could do with just a few loaves. Their bags were light, and their hearts were closed.

In reality, none of this mattered. They were in the presence of an unseen feast, a meal behind the veil. They had in their hands the Bread for which all souls hunger, and Jesus was about to show them this once again.

The disciples, wanting a little rest, a little food for themselves, were thrilled when Jesus called them in from the hills. They had been wanting to suggest to Jesus that the crowd be sent on its way.

"Rabbi," Philip began, "don't you think it's time for the people to go home?"

"Yes," said Peter. "They've got to be hungry by now."

"I know I am," chimed Andrew, well known for his vigorous appetite.

They all nodded their heads in agreement, watching the face of their Teacher. They did not like his response.

"*I hurt for these people,*" Jesus said, staring out over the crowd.

"For three days now they've been with me, and now they have nothing to eat."

He paused. No one volunteered anything to say. His words were met with expressions as friendly as the stones at their feet.

"I can't send them away without a meal—they'd probably collapse on the road."

Matthew 15:32

With that, he raised his eyebrows and waited, clearly expecting a reply.

A million thoughts rushed into their minds, but they clamped them behind mouths shut tight. It would not do to yell at Jesus. They all looked to Philip, who seemed to be comfortable asking questions of Jesus when no one else dared.

"But, Jesus," he sputtered, checked exasperation outlining his tone and face, "—where in the world? We are in the middle of nowhere," he said, gesturing wildly around him at the rocks and hills. The word "god-forsaken" was on his lips, and he swallowed hard. "How could you get enough to feed all these people?"

Jesus knew that it occurred to no one that this was even a possibility. Nevertheless, he seemed to be enjoying this conversation, for he smiled, volleying the question right back to his friends.

"How many loaves do you guys have?"

They groaned inwardly, sighed outwardly, and went to get their bags while Jesus watched, enjoying a joke they didn't get.

From the satchels of twelve men, seven loaves were made available to Jesus. And true to their trade, a few salted tilapia were produced as well. They gave these to Jesus with a shrug. Their loaves barely filled his hands. He looked at their weary, dirty, frustrated faces, and it was more than just the crowd that owned his compassion.

"Sit down," he invited them. "Please—all of you sit down." He waved over the crowd. To his disciples, he said, "You boys rest. I've got the meal."

Like an unhurried chef, he set out his ingredients, surveying them on a smooth, flat stone the size of a kitchen table. He laid his hands on baked rock, enjoying the lingering warmth under his palms. His gaze held the loaves and fish he'd been given.

"Yes," he said to himself. "*This will do well.*"

Raising his chin, he exposed to the men his sunburned neck as he looked into a coral evening sky. He said nothing for a time—just stood looking up, focusing on something Unseen. He smiled into the firmament, the creases around his eyes becoming deep desert gullies.

"*Thank you,*" he said into the air, thick with Kingdom. "*These loaves are good, and I bless the Giver.*"

The disciples, the crowds, were quiet as the grave. All cocked their ears to the sky, hoping to hear the heavens reply. No sound came but the warbles of kingfishers, trolling the coast for their dinners. Jesus turned his gaze to where they were sitting, the twelve men he loved. He looked deep into each face. His expression held a lifetime of words.

"*Thank* you," he said to them. "*These loaves, your loaves, are good. I bless the givers.*"

Something in each of them caught in their throats. They forgot their frustration.

What happened next came with the quietness of the setting sun. There was no thunder clap. No crashing tidal wave. No rush of a mighty wind. No lion's roar from heaven. Every gaze was glued to the brown hands of Jesus and the food on the rock.

His movements were simple. His face wore a huge smile. Jesus picked up one loaf and called Philip and Andrew to the table. Before their eyes, he broke the loaf into quarters and gave them each two shares. Ignoring their incredulous stares, he instructed them to do the same.

"*Break the loaves and pass them around,*" was all he said. He invited no arguments. This he did with each pair of twelve.

There was a space between the reality of lack and the reality of abundance. This space made his disciples squirm. Their stomachs grumbled, knowing they would get nothing to eat. As they broke, they expected natural law to rule the moment. The loaf portions would get smaller with each tear.

This did not happen.

Each piece, as it was broken by their hands, became larger. With wild eyes, they handled the bread, sniffed it, wanting to find the seam that surely contained some magic trick they couldn't see. Like children unwrapping gifts, they tore the loaves apart with abandon. Hunks of bread were falling on the grass around them. The faster they broke, the faster they distributed. The more they distributed, the more they had in their hands to give.

Murmurs in the crowd turned to shouts.

"Look—the bread!" was the music bouncing off the canyons.

Children smiled as they greedily ate what their bellies desired. Laughter, that day, was passed along with fish and bread, and loudest of all was the laughter of Jesus.

LIFE MULTIPLIED

God created the world *ex nihilo*, out of nothing. He didn't need a starter kit. He spoke all of creation into existence with the Living Word (Psalm 33:9). He brings forth life where nothing is living. He creates in a void, in a vacuum. He doesn't need bread to produce food to feed many. He made manna fall from the sky every day, with no assistance from the Israelites whatsoever.

He doesn't need a base substance from which to work. He doesn't need particles or molecules, bread or fish, to make something new.

But still, with profound mystery, the Kingdom holds its breath as it waits on the loaves in our pocket.

The Apostle Paul encourages,

Be energetic in your life of salvation, reverent and sensitive before God. That energy is God's energy, an energy deep within you, God himself willing and working at what will give him the most pleasure.

Philippians 2:13

The Greek word for "energy" is the verb *energeō* (en-erg-eh´-o)—from *en*, a complex preposition implying connection, and *ergō*, the verb "to work."[7] This Biblical idea of God's energy is vastly beyond what our energy can produce. It is an unseen energy that expands as it meets an offered gift. It takes the gift, the offering, the planted seed, and creates from it a harvest that surprises its recipients and the principles of economics. It is the hidden energy at work as late winter blooms to life. It is the creative energy of the fertile womb.

The life-giving energy of God is his unlimited presence, his unlimited resources, *at work* on our behalf. In him, we have life, and life multiplied beyond the restrictions of mathematical theory.

It's an extravagance many of us have not yet tasted.

Oh, the utter extravagance of his work in us who trust him—endless energy, boundless strength! All this energy issues from Christ: God raised him from death and set him on a throne in deep heaven in charge of running the universe, everything from galaxies to governments, no name and no power exempt from his rule. And not just for the time being, but forever. He is in charge of it all, has the final word on everything.

Ephesians 1:17–21

This is our Co-worker, our divine Colleague. Into forever, he offers us this Resurrection energy, an energy that elevates all those who risk entering into intimate participation with God. Our loaves, the ones that were fit only for the grave, by his *energeō* are made good for heaven.

He takes delight in us and the Abel gift of ourselves. As we give him our bread, his "endless energy" creates a feast. As we give him our gifting, we see what was profane become exceptional and holy. We see how his unforced rhythms produce thirty-, sixty-, one hundred-fold more than what we put in. As we give him our lives, he returns them back to us with utter extravagance, lives of which we could imagine only in our dreams of the Garden.

> *"When you're joined with me and I with you, the relation intimate and organic, the harvest is sure to be abundant."*
>
> John 15:5

He invites us to behold the divine multiplication of energies when we invest in his Kingdom heart. Like the widow of Jarephath in 1 Kings or Elisha's companion in 2 Kings, he shows us the manner in which a good Father meets the giving of sons and daughters. He shows us with a haul of fish that breaks the boat, coming from a once-empty net. He shows us with barrels of elegant wine instead of disappointed guests. He shows us with a picnic in the hills that came from the pockets of a few men.

From the beginning, he's been teaching us how to return to the Garden, where all good things are offered and multiplied.

THE BROKEN LOAVES OF GOD

The incarnation gave us everything we need to surrender our loaves back to God.

Taking on our flesh, God's Son taught us how intimacy with his Father was *his* bread. Full communion with God was the life-sustaining loaves in the midst of satanic temptation, in the loneliness of ministry, in the rejection of his people. Because Jesus feasted on the goodness of his Father at all times, we are now invited to the Kingdom table. This table is laden with the fruits of opportunity to enter more fully into an intimacy that is available only to an heir—co-participation.

The beautiful paradox of the Gospel is that God, the One who owns the divine rights to every loaf we possess, rained down endless manna from the Cross. Withholding nothing, not even the divine *Artos*, he gave us a feast that would satisfy us forever. This he did in utter freedom and great joy. Jesus took his body, his loaves, and after blessing them, he tore them in two. These loaves he offers to all who have none of their own.

Take, he invites us. *Eat.*

These loaves are my body, broken for you.

Jesus is the Bread of Life, the hearty *Artos* that was both broken and distributed for us (John 6:35). He displays for us all the unfathomable, stunning generosity of his Father. When we consume the *Artos*, this Jesus in whom all true loaves dwell, something happens in our souls. Something in us, long mal-nourished, becomes satisfied. That deep, dark place in us where we identify with Cain is transformed into an Abel heart. We "taste and see that the LORD is good" (Psalm 34:8, ESV), and because of this, we can offer our loaves as Abel offered his sacrifice: from a heart that is whole and holy.

As the Bread of Life, Jesus, too, emanates this divine raising agent, a holy *airō*—a God-ability to elevate all that he receives into his scarred hands. He delights in rising to meet our in-tentionality, our availability with his Resurrection power. We become connected to God in deep intimacy when we join him where he's about Kingdom work.

As a father invites his child into a project meant to cultivate connection between the two, God desires the intimacy that comes from laboring closely. He wants side-by-side cooperation, the comfort that comes from parallel work.

This offer to work shoulder-to-shoulder in intimate *energeō* with God is the offer of the Gospel.

He proclaims this truth over us:

"I'm no longer calling you servants because servants don't understand what their master is thinking and planning. No, I've named you friends because I've let you in on everything I've heard from the Father."

John 15:15

He wants us to not only understand his work, but to participate with him in it. We are no longer simply the hired help. In Christ, we are co-strategists with the God of heaven.

In the mysterious economy of God, our loaves matter. Our loaves are intricately involved in his eternal plan, in his predetermined work. It is because of this that we *get* to give our loaves with freedom and joy. It is only from knowing this God that we can. It is only by knowing and living in his great, generous heart that we can give from a place of freedom and joy. It is from this place that we can surprise ourselves by responding: "Have what's mine and bless it. I am counting on your goodness."

From this posture, we become eyewitnesses to the exponential math that will wash over the world. Loaves compared, loaves spent only on ourselves, are wasted. They feed no one. But as heirs who trust in the heart of the Father, we get to waste every loaf for the love of God. He receives what we give, and then he applies Kingdom economics. With our small supply and his endless wealth, he multiplies a feast where all souls, including our own, may be fed and satisfied.

Before the loaves have even left our hands, he's already raising up abundance.

FOR CONTEMPLATION AND DISCUSSION

Lectio Divina Exercise:

Imagine the hill country surrounding the Sea of Galilee. Look around and see the thousands who wait for a meal. Notice your own body: Are you hungry? How many loaves do you have in your bag? Listen as Jesus invites you to give him whatever you find there. How do you respond? If you give them, is it from a place of trust and freedom? Watch him as he takes your loaves and multiplies them. What is your initial reaction? Listen to the shouts of the crowd around you as they are fed with your loaves. What do you see in the face of Jesus as he watches you disperse his multiplied supply?

For Reflection:

1. What are the *artos*, loaves, that you possess?
2. In what ways have you experienced Loaf Comparison Disease (LCD)?
3. How are you suffering from spiritual memory loss in your life with God?
4. How does it make you feel that *energeō*, the life-giving energy of God, has already met and multiplied your giving?
5. What would it look like for you to give your loaves to God with freedom and joy?
6. What is your answer to Jesus's question: *"How many loaves do you have?"*

CHAPTER ELEVEN

"Do You See These Great Buildings?"

Choosing Against Self-Promotion

*"For which of you, desiring to build a tower, does not first sit down
and count the cost, whether he has enough to complete it?"*
—Jesus Christ,
Luke 14:28, ESV

There's so much space here
With all my walls down.
There's so much space here
With all my walls crumbling down.

—Melissa Helser,
"Redemption Rain"

In the Valley of Shinar, the ground was tough, dry, and cracked as the working hands of its people. Though fed by twin mothers, Tigris and Euphrates, the valley sprouted more dust than crops. Lean livestock groaned over flood-flattened plains. Surrounded by competing clans, the people fought to possess before being possessed. Mothers raised fierce sons and work-hardened daughters. Men gathered in dens, defiant and posturing. They all, as one, desired to make their names great among the land.

No one talked of the Great Flood. Generations came and generations went, and no one even remembered.

"Let us make a stronghold in our own image," they said to one another, unaware that Heaven was listening. "Let us make bricks. Let us make paste."

With exceptional skill and elaborate communication, they spent their days making and laying bricks.

Such common purpose and single-minded focus.

Their concentration invited pleasure within the Creator. Their determination, though now used for this godless purpose, was a gift he'd given them from the start. They would need this determination to work the land and grow life. But they'd forsaken the holy mandate, exchanging cultivation for construction.

God witnessed stone laid upon sunbaked stone, held together with the slime of their mortar. He watched as his people grunted and sweated toward their own gain. Soon, very soon, their abilities had built them a wall, tall as the soaring cedar. From this altitude, they could see the full breadth of their valley, even the glint of water that flowed through far tributaries in distant borders. Giddy with triumph, intoxicated with success, they wondered aloud if they could build higher.

They cried as one. "Let us make a tower that climbs to the threshold of the gods."

They desired sight—to see with the oracle of height what the future would bring to them. They needed also to be seen. God and man alike would see and know the weight of their strength, their invulnerability. Never again would they wonder if they were enough.

For scores of years—grandfathers teaching fathers teaching sons—the sweat and blood of men mingled with brick, trickling between stones in the winepress of toil. Their tower, ziggurat-shaped and immovable, was meant to eclipse the sun in both elevation and glory.

The Creator saw each day, each brick.

He wept rain upon their precious mortar and bare heads. Forgetting their Creator, they offered sacrifices to the gods that would return the heat of the sun to bake their stacked clay.

The Flood-God watched from a distance closer than they could imagine. For more than one hundred years, he watched. He watched until he would watch no more.

They didn't know it yet, but their fortress—the prize of their eyes and the fruit of their hands—would be ruined. Not by armies. Not by weapons. It would be torn down by the violence of confusion.

HEROD THE GREAT

Towers and temples alike are touched by ruination.

In 586 B.C., Solomon's Temple was torn down by Nebuchadnezzar and his unstoppable Babylonian army. It wasn't until 19 B.C. that a full-scale, funded project to restore the Temple to its former glory was initiated, and it was under the unlikeliest of kings: Herod I.

More than ten thousand skilled laborers were employed for the task, and incalculable resources gathered. "Herod wanted to convert Judaea into the greatest kingdom in the east," describes *National Geographic*. "A key part of his plan was the transformation of Jerusalem, whose walls he extended, and whose public areas he filled with monumental buildings."[1] Josephus, noted Jewish historian, described the Temple's unparalleled grandeur in his writings:

> It was a structure more noteworthy than any under the sun. The height of the portico was so great that if anyone looked down from its rooftop he would become dizzy and his vision would be unable to reach the end of so measureless a depth.[2]

According to historical record, it was not only the marble, gold, and stature, but also the stonework that created a sense of awe. The highly skilled stonemasons were so precise with these massive stones that nothing, not even a sliver of parchment, could be passed between them.[3] The *Jewish Virtual Library* states, "Such fine maneuvering of the stones is incomprehensible given that even today's modern machinery cannot move such heavy stones."[4] The average stone size used in the wall weighed ten tons.[5] To put this in perspective, Google tells us that the average African elephant represents only seven tons of weight. These mammoth-sized stones were moved by brute force and sheer genius.

The Temple was a marvel unmatched, a spectacle to the first-century world. It certainly was to Jesus's disciples.

But what Jesus saw was very different.

Erected by a man who referred to himself as "the Great," the Temple was planned by Herod with power-lust in his heart. The hands responsible for the design and extravagance of God's dwelling were also the hands that massacred the innocents in Bethlehem. Israel's king aborted the lives of hundreds of Jewish babies to uncover God-Made-Flesh and murder him.

When Jesus looked at the Temple, he wept. What Jesus saw when he entered Jerusalem was another Valley of Shinar. Jesus witnessed glory corrupted, and it provoked another profound question from God's Son.

In Mark 13, awash in the light of the Temple, Jesus asks us to consider with him the forgotten stories hidden underneath the rubble heaps.

THE GLORY OF THE SUN

The elders said it was folly to look upon the Temple at midday. Greater than the sun, it blazed in glory heat, warming the great locus of God's eternal city. With flawless, creamy marble and golden spires to prevent barn swallows' repose, this center of the Jewish universe gleamed with uneclipsed majesty.

Many men wept at the hallowed sight. Peter, a country fisherman from Galilee, was one among them.

The friends of Jesus sat outside the Temple gates, waiting for the Temple to return their Messiah. He had entered in the morning, and by lunch, he had still not appeared. The disciples were left outside, gawking as the sun rose upon the building at their backs. They could feel the heat radiating from smooth walls. Their hearts were captured by the shining beauty, ablaze like a beacon upon Jewish hills.

"Look, Rabbi!" Peter shouted when he saw Jesus, yelling and pointing like an impolite child to the expanse of marble and bronze. "Just look! Isn't it wonderful? The gates, the stones, the buildings! See how they steal the sun's fame?"

He paused long enough to see Jesus's face. He expected to see the same openmouthed wonder and fascination that had taken hold of him and his companions, but Peter was disappointed. What was written on the face of Jesus was an expression of granite determination, jolting him more than the Temple's splendor.

He beheld the set jaw of an angry God.

"Do you see these great buildings?" Jesus questioned his friend in Mark 13.

Peter nodded, looking from the gate, to the stones, to the spires, then back to Jesus. "Of course. Yes, I see them," he said, waiting for Jesus to reveal a great secret of architecture or symbolism.

"They will all be thrown down."

NATURAL INSTINCT

The first Temple's architect, King Solomon, was a man intimately acquainted with ruination, penning the proverb: "Pride goes before destruction" (Proverbs 16:8, ESV).

He understood the principle that favor from God can turn the abundantly blessed into the arrogant godless. This can happen more quickly than we anticipate. In chapter 10, Jesus's question invited us to experience co-participation with God. He encouraged us to offer our loaves and then watch as the unending supply of God meets this offering.

This is a beautiful Kingdom principle, but it is also a dangerous one.

As we survey our multiplied bread and contented crowds, it

is easy to forget where the feast originated. We eat our fill, and from that fullness can come a dangerous sense of satisfaction. We can easily begin to feel the stealth movements of pride, those voices that whisper that the feast was created by our own supply and ingenuity. Within a moment of swallowing the God-given meal, we forget God and begin erecting great buildings that will help us climb higher than we ever dared.

We find quickly that a little self-promotion is all that is required.

One of the greatest joys I have in life is that my daughters are best friends. They've shared a room since Jo, our youngest, was born. Just a toddler in a youth bed, our firstborn, Macy, slept perpendicular to her new sister's bassinet, singing child-crafted lullabies to Jo at bedtime. When Jo was old enough to scale the bars of her crib, we'd find the two lying side-by-side like a litter of puppies, contentedly snoring under one blanket. Even though we've now offered them rooms of their own, Jo still begs Macy to sleep with her every night.

Now closing in on adolescence, Macy and Jo understand each other in a special way, interacting more like twins than siblings. They protect each other's secrets. They make the other laugh. They seem to have a system, and it's a system that works well. We are ecstatic (and more than a little surprised) as parents by this closeness. But that's not to say the girls never argue. Their fighting can get high-pitched, scratching, tear-clumps-of-hair-out ugly. The arguments are almost always started around the perception of unfair treatment.

Someone's getting shortchanged, and that is a fight worth picking.

The shortchanging happened in our home this year when both girls wanted to audition for their school's Christmas play. This was their first audition, and they were apprehensive. They ran lines together and practiced their roles. We overheard them saying supportive statements like, "You're going to be great," or "If only one of us gets a part, I hope it's you."

Jimmy and I watched all of this with a mounting level of

concern. We know how the real world works. When auditions were over, only one of our daughters received a callback. It was fascinating how quickly support evaporated into self-promotion.

Instantly, the one who did not receive the callback diminished the accomplishment of her sister. What once was the epic role of the century now suddenly became "dumb." This play had lost all quality and flavor, and she didn't really want to be a part of such a mediocre cast.

On the other hand, the daughter who received the callback walked a little taller, became an expert on all matters drama-related, and felt freedom to direct her sister. She sensed an innate superiority and wanted everyone to know it. She got a taste of being promoted, and she wanted more. In subtle ways and means, she invited her sister to understand that she was better, more talented, *worthy*.

All of this self-promotion exposed by a two-line role in an elementary school Christmas play.

This behavior warranted conversation, some parental shepherding—but we were not alarmed. Promoting ourselves, at the expense of our siblings or friends, is quite natural as children. It happens as soon as we have the smallest taste of self-awareness. We want to be treated fairly. Really, what we want is to be treated *better* than those around us. We are born demanding the biggest slice of the pie and the better role in the play. Observe any child for more than an hour, and this becomes obvious.

Self-promotion is as natural and unconscious as breathing, and it doesn't stop when children grow up.

As adults, we simply become more polite, disguising our need to self-promote with family, career, even ministry. We need to know we *at least* measure up to others. We are driven to act on our own behalf, making enough of a name for ourselves in the circles that matter most.

TOWERS AND TEMPLES

This practice of self-promotion is ancient, going back to Genesis 11 and beyond.

In the Greek Old Testament, the word used for "tower" is *purgos* (poor´-gos), denoting a structure specifically "built to repel hostile attack." This tower in the Valley of Shinar would allow its dwellers "to see in every direction."[6] We all want protection. None of us can live exposed to the whims and strategies of our enemies. It is our instinct to build for ourselves a stronghold, a structure designed to keep us safe and give us an edge over those who come against us.

Unfortunately, even those around us we love and trust can become our enemies if they thwart our need to promote ourselves.

Likewise, deep within there is every soul's ache to get close to God, close enough to see whether he's angry or whether he is pleased. Toward that effort, we build temples, sacred structures that seek to elevate us. We imagine our beautiful, elaborate temples prove us worthy of God's blessing.

It's all quite natural. Because something comes naturally, however, does not make it required. Nor does being natural inherently make an urge good.

We find that the natural is often most susceptible to corruption.

We self-promote because our flesh compels us to do so. In boasting of our own value, we follow in the nature and footsteps of the enemy. He boasted that his beauty and glory were equal to God's, deserving of better position. He launched a full-scale attack to erect his own monument, with heaven's floor as his foundation. The desire for personal glory prompted a catastrophic rebellion of one-third of the spiritual realm.

This one moment of self-promotion led to the fall of all humankind.

The nature of post-Eden humanity is that we all covet

structures, built to serve our undeniable need. The God-given desire for significance rears its ugly head, screaming that we must secure for ourselves an ironclad legacy.

When all is still and quiet, I hear the rumbling deep down for towers, castles, and temples—the "great buildings" erected for personal honor, protection, provision. Each structure offers us something different, and we go about gathering materials to build what the moment requires. These structures we build serve as more than protection. They are also designed to draw the eye to our own glory. These structures speak to the watching world that my life is impenetrable, a success, *worthy*. I want a self-tribute I can touch and see, something that cannot be easily toppled.

I need something that shows that I am someone who cannot be overlooked.

I want a kingdom of my own. We all do. What we want is something that reaches all the way to heaven and beyond. We want to build something that scrapes the rim of the sky. All throughout history, fallen humans have followed in the footsteps of Shinar inhabitants, seeking to build *purgos* and temples of our own.

Unfortunately, these structures are not as stable as we had hoped.

ANCIENT RUINS

Ruin. Both a verb and a noun, this small, four-letter word holds so much disappointment. Yet throughout history, we as a people have been drawn to ancient ruin sites with a strange attraction we simply cannot shake.

I had limited experience with ancient ruins before our sabbatical in Ireland. At our cottage, we were situated less than a mile from three ruin sites, dating from 600 B.C. to A.D. 1400.[7] I, too, became fascinated by both their palpable regret as well as their pervasive presence around us. We spent part of every day at one of these three sites. They were the ancient playground of our daughters. There was no tourist office, no ticket-taking, no price gouging. It was as if they were completely forgotten by the world bustling at their crumbled feet.

Cahergall and Leacanabuaile Forts, two ringed strongholds, varied in height and diameter. While still relatively intact, these forts were forlorn, deserted, and fraught with lonely danger. A fall from the top ledge of Leacanabuaile could kill a man. Cahergall, her smaller cousin, was pocked with dark tunnels under its base. We talked of the days when flags and banners would have flown from the ramparts, when bows and arrows were sent spiraling through the mist to stall enemy assault. We imagined what stolen booty was hidden away underneath the crushing weight of stacked rock. Despite our daughters' pleading, we did not explore the melancholy passages. With centuries of secrets buried within, I was afraid of discovering something we didn't want to know.

The third ancient site, Ballycarbery Castle, was the most "ruined" of the three. Built with interlocking stones, it boasted of using the blood of bullocks to seal the rockwork from wind penetration.[8] At the time of the castle's full glory, it must have been absolutely intimidating, jutting out from the coastline like a stone-wrapped fist.

The broken castle told of fairy-tale magic, of lords and ladies and great heroic quests. It was at Ballycarbery that we climbed the staircase with great gaps in both stairs and wall, ascending with caution into the cylindrical tower. With wildflowers growing between the castle cracks, we imagined we were Rapunzel or Quasimodo, imprisoned by evil enchantments. The dark, cold stones cast a spell over its remains.

We could see all three ruins from the kitchen windows of our cottage. Sipping Barry's tea, we watched each evening as the descending sun cast eerie shadows behind them. The movement of the river and the sea peeking through their stony crags made them like living, glinting graveyards. All three of these structures were designed with strength enough to survive the elements:

merciless coastal gales, lashing rain, the relentless weathering of time. They were built hearty, like all things Irish.

They were meant to safeguard, a beacon to warn of enemy onslaught. They were meant to shelter—goods, livestock, families. They were meant to be symbols of wealth and power, erected manifestations of personal value and worth. They were, like Babel, meant to make a name for their bearers.

They were, all of them, abandoned and ruined.

TOWER-TOPPLING GOD

Our towers, castles, monuments, and temples will never deliver what our souls crave. They are painfully temporal, fated to fall. We spend so much of our time, our energy, our gifting in self-promotional building projects. For a while, they may cause others, even ourselves, to gasp in wonder and jealousy.

For a very little while.

Like Herod's Temple, what we and others see may glitter in the sunlight. Like Ballycarbery Castle and Leacanabuaile Fort, we may seem impermeable to suffering and loss. Like the Tower of Babel, we may be elevated above the known world in extravagant beauty and power.

Jesus sees the reality behind the extravagance.

He looks at these structures and sees them for exactly what they are. Our pride-structures are nothing more than an ugly, razor-edged wall, a barrier between us and him. Our buildings of pride, while lovely to our vision, are an eyesore to heaven. We think they'll take us closer to God, but in the end, they always become competing towers to his glory—and he will not allow them to stand.

His question reminds us of this reality.

"Do you see these great buildings?" he asks. *"They will all be thrown down."*

That look of fierce determination is on his face, and he will not have anything erected between us and his heart.

*"And I will break down the wall that you have smeared
with whitewash, and bring it down to the ground, so that its
foundation will be laid bare."*

Ezekiel 13:14 (ESV)

History teaches us this again and again.

No one calls the *purgos* of Genesis 11 "the Tower of Shinar."
No, this debacle was named by the nature of its defeat. By *sugcheō* (soong-kheh´-o), a Greek term described as "to confound
or disturb,"[9] Yahweh cleverly introduced linguistic confusion to
halt construction. God took one look at his wayward children's
plan and stirred up divine mess. He created babble where strategy governed. He injected chaos into a well-ordered plan.

Less than forty years after his death, Jesus's prediction regarding the Temple was fulfilled. Only seven years after the Temple's
completion, Romans burned their way through Jerusalem to its
religious and cultural epicenter, tearing down the Temple, stone
by stone, until almost nothing was left.

He makes it perfectly clear. All walls will come down, one
way or another.

We were meant to have whole, integrated lives that could not
be fragmented into competing affections. *"You can't worship two
gods at once,"* Jesus taught. *"Loving one god, you'll end up hating
the other"* (Matthew 6:24). We cannot build our monuments of
glory *and* be his disciples. The two are mutually exclusive. Our
structures are in competition with our intimacy with God, and
he knows they're not getting us any closer to his heart.

"TO LOOSE-DOWN"

With his question, Jesus is giving us a glimpse toward the future
of all our walls: The "great buildings" around us will all be
"torn down"—*kataluō* (kat-al-oo´-o) in the original language.[10]
The root verb, *luō*, means "to loose."[11] It is paired with a
preposition, *kata*, that provides the direction of the loosing. The

buildings will be loosed, and they will be loosed in a manner ruled by the laws of gravity.

Gravity dictates that the stones will not be scattered or crushed. They will fall to the ground around us as rubble.

This is what Jesus does to our *"great buildings."* He *looses* us from the heavy weight they place on our shoulders, and he does so in such a way that not one stone is lost. He liberates us from their vise-grip on our souls. He frees us from their power and influence over our lives. In his kind determination, Jesus assumes the role of skillful demolitionist. He lovingly shatters our pride monuments.

He makes it his business to topple our towers and take down our walls, but he does so with respect, even humble joy. He wants to be invited to this holy deconstruction.

The prophet Isaiah predicts of the Messiah:

[He] will rebuild the old ruins,
raise a new city out of wreckage. They'll start over on the
    ruined cities,
take the rubble left behind and make it new.

Isaiah 61:5

In his kindness, Jesus removes our walls, and then he re-builds something grand with the fallen rubble. No other god is like this.

He alone can see what the cleared space will make room for—something eternal, full of true glory. In dismantling the in-tentions of the Shinar people, God employed a "confounding." But in the original language, this term serves as a clever double entendre.

Sugcheō also means "to pour together," which is precisely what God does.

As he dismantles our great buildings, he is "loosing" the rubble for a different purpose: a pouring together of his life with ours. God is always desirous, always ready to mix his material with our own to create something truly grand and beautiful.

Rather than causing confusion or chaos, God's confounding invites union.

It is a holy pouring together of the Creator and creature, introducing something much greater than our "great buildings." In the absence of the tower that ironically blocks our view, we find we can now see clearly without it. With this divine loosing, Jesus is inviting only one kind of promotion in this world: to promote him. We look to him and see his beauty, his glory, his holiness. Then we look *with his eyes* and see that he has freely given to us from his storehouse of gifts:

He has made us beautiful.

He has designed us for glory.

He has clothed us with holiness.

Self-promotion, tower building, monument erection—they're all quite natural. What God designs for us is *super*natural, those postures of the Kingdom that require height, but not derived from our own towers.

The antidote to self-promotion is the emulation of God's Son. He has already shown us how with a towel and a basin.

> [Jesus] got up from the supper table, set aside his robe, and put on an apron.
>
> John 13:4

A SUBVERSIVE ECONOMY

Literature keeps a secret about who is truly "great." It's the simple country hobbit who saves Middle Earth. The beautiful girl covered in ash becomes the heiress to a kingdom. These great stories echo the Biblical narrative, showing us that it's not the power-hungry, the rich, the monument builders who are royalty in God's Kingdom. It's the shepherd boy who becomes the king, the teenage girl who carries Heaven in her womb. It's the foot-washing God who inherits the Kingdom.

It is those who choose a different way than self-promotion.

We've discovered along the way that the economy of God is disruptive. He takes our loaves and multiplies them, making much of the little offered. So, too, God takes what looks great to our human eyes—our towers, castles, and temples—and dismantles them, exposing a crumbling and ill-laid foundation. In an epic reversal, it is those who choose to pour themselves out at the feet of Christ, rejecting their natural instinct toward self-promotion, who are exalted in God's comic economy.

"For who is greater," Jesus asks, "the one seated at the table or the one who serves?"

The answer to Jesus's rhetoric is so obvious it's laughable. Any survey would show that the better seat is the seat of honor, the seat being served.

The better seat is the one offering power and authority.

The better seat is the chair where cravings and whims are plated and brought before the exalted.

But is it the greater seat?

Jesus answers for us: "You'd rather be served, right? But I've taken my place among you as the one who serves" (Luke 22:28).

The better seat is not the way of the subversive economy of the Kingdom.

> "You've observed how godless rulers throw their weight around," he said, "and when people get a little power how quickly it goes to their heads. It's not going to be that way with you. Whoever wants to be first among you must be your slave. That is what the Son of Man has done: He came to serve, not to be served—and then to give away his life."
>
> Mark 10:42–45

God, the only One with supreme right to be served, in a shocking display of humility wrapped himself in flesh and a towel. Not demanding service, he chose to serve instead.

THE WET HANDS OF JESUS

The sun lowered behind Bethany's hills. The last hint of day clung to treetops, glinting gold off the distant Temple. The preparations had been meticulous. Dishes steamed on the low table—charoset apples, rosemary and bitter herbs, roasted lamb. The aromas filled the small chamber with anticipation. These country lads had come clean, careful to scrub away the dirt from the creases of their hands and under their fingernails.

The young men felt heavy, emotion caught in their throats by the candlelight and aching symbolism of the night. Gut and heart churned in equal intensity, desiring to feast on Passover spread, but ever more so on the glory of the new Kingdom come. They gathered round the table, leaving the place of honor for Jesus. They watched and waited for him to initiate the ceremony as had ten thousand patriarchs before him.

Without blessing the food or the company, Jesus stood, leaving the table with a lopsided smile and no words. He went over to the corner table and unfastened his belt and robe. Taking the folded linen lying next to the basin, he wrapped it towel-like around his waist.

They watched in silence as he carried the supplies of a slave to their table. Bringing the basin and pitcher of water to Philip's place, he slowly poured water into the bowl. They assumed that Jesus needed his feet refreshed and cleaned before the meal could begin. Peter signaled to the house servant, who quickly sprang into action.

Jesus looked at the boy and shook his head.

"Thank you," he said, *"but I can manage."*

They all gasped as they watched him get to his knees beside Philip. He looked up into his friend's confused face. *"Philip,"* he asked, *"may I have your feet?"*

"But, Lord!" Philip protested with a jerk. Several of the disciples jumped to their feet in outrage. "You *can't!*"

"But I must." Jesus showed his teeth as he smiled at Philip. *"Will you let me?"*

Philip hesitated before nodding and offering his hairy legs and feet into the wet, waiting hands of Jesus. With strength and vigorous splashing, Jesus wiped away the dirt, cleansing and refreshing the traveler's tired feet. They watched intently Jesus's every movement—his hands, the top of his head, the water sloshing over the sides of the basin.

This awkward display, the sight of a kneeling Messiah, made them cringe in their seats.

This Jesus did for each of his friends, wrestling at Peter's place with both feet and ego. It took a long time, the food long cooled on the table. After every man, he emptied the basin of dirty water and filled it with fresh. He took his time, intentionally cleansing the grit and animal filth from the feet of fishermen and friends. As he washed, he whistled an old melody of Jewish mothers. The earlier tension that had filled the room floated through the open window into velvet night.

They couldn't believe it, but Jesus seemed *happy*.

Much later, the lads remembered how Jesus had also washed the feet of Judas with the same attention he had for them all.

After he'd finished, he untied the towel and hung it to dry. Cinching his robe again and wiping his hands, he returned to the table. He sat down with a question, keen as a curious child.

"Do you understand what I was doing for you?"

The boys looked from one face to another. It was clear that understanding was lacking.

"You call me 'Rabbi,' and that is good, because that's who I am— your Teacher."

"Yes, Jesus," they murmured, nodding their heads in agreement. They waited for the punchline, as his face seemed to indicate a joke was being told.

"Since I, your Rabbi, was eager to get on my knees to clean your feet, I want the same eagerness in you. This way of relating is my gift to you."

THE EMPTYING GOD

The chronology of his last meal with them is profound. First foot-washing, then feasting.

As they ate the bread and drank the ceremonial cup, Jesus told them how his body would be broken, and his blood poured like wine.

This was his last night with these men. He was preparing his body, mind, and soul for immense suffering and pain. He had poured his love and words and work into this rough band of twelve. He had called them friends. He had washed between their toes.

But they still didn't get it. Neither do I.

As much as I'd like to deny, I am the disciple who bickers and argues and fights for my own rights. I am the disciple who forgets my cleansed feet and fiercely intends to build my "great buildings."

The Son of God had gotten down on his knees before the dirty, silly, clueless poor of this world. Jesus—Almighty God, Maker of Heaven and Earth, God-of-the-Angel-Armies, the King of all kings—gets down on his knees before us.

Self-promotion isn't even a category for Jesus.

> Think of yourselves the way Christ Jesus thought of himself. He had equal status with God but didn't think so much of himself that he had to cling to the advantages of that status no matter what. Not at all. When the time came, he set aside the privileges of deity and took on the status of a slave.
>
> Philippians 2:5–6

The term used for "*set aside*" is the state of *kenosis*, an emptying. He emptied himself of the need for titles, status, and power in order to take on flesh-and-bone. As in Genesis 11, he poured *sugcheō* out, but the *sugcheō* was himself.

It is in this disruptive pouring that we are filled.

In a profound reversal of fates, it was the Son of God, Heaven's Prince, who gave up his better seat at the table's head. God, the One for whom all true monuments, and castles, and temples could and should be built, tore down his Temple to destroy the barriers we erected between us. Jesus, the One who treasured closeness with his Father at all times, allowed the wrecking ball of wrath to demolish him. He was, indeed, lifted up above all else—not by a tower but by a Cross.

Jesus was talking about *"tearing down"* his own body, but many couldn't see it. Jesus had challenged the Jewish leaders to tear down their own temple and see what he could do with it. And that was what it was—*their* temple. It no longer belonged to God, and he wouldn't allow it to become a permanent obstacle between his people and his heart.

It's hard for us to see it, too. We deserve to be torn down for our pride, for our rebellion. Jesus didn't, but he submitted to this tearing in our place. His body, his unbroken intimacy with the Father, was toppled to break down the barrier between us forever.

He would like us to understand something important: All personal building projects lead to loss.

In the Kingdom of God, however, it is precisely *with* this flesh-emptying that we gain the world. Once emptied of the need to self-promote, we find God. We find life. We find ourselves. With his question, he is challenging the way we seek entry into his Kingdom. We don't have to build towers and temples to get access to Jesus.

He is already here, right at our feet.

Jesus has shown us the way. He has not required something from us he was unwilling to do himself. Like Jesus, we *get* to receive the call to foot-washing, wall-toppling, and taking the "greater" seat.

A SEAT AMONG THE RUBBLE

To rise above the striving, wanting vision and glory, is not a godless desire.

We don't want to be bogged down in the mud of this earth. Jesus understands our undeniably deep need to be lifted up above our circumstances, our weaknesses, our thoughts. We crave a lifting from these things, but Jesus makes it clear with his question: Striving and self-promotion is not the way to get it. God is the only One who can lift us above what holds us down. No tower, no striving, will ever fulfill that deep soul need.

How is it even possible to lay aside self-promotion as we grapple with the desperate drive in each of us to be on top? There is only one way this can be done.

We choose trust.

We choose to trust that God is good. We choose to trust the story and significance we have in him. We choose to trust that God wants to give us a kingdom within his own, a place where we have become the person we need to be in order to handle a seat of honor.

He offers us the lifting we need, issuing a continuous invitation to come up the mountain where he provides a clear view and fresh air.

> And he went up on the mountain and called to him those whom he desired, and they came to him.
>
> Mark 3:13 (ESV)

We are invited to practice the discipline of taking the lower seat, to bridle this urge of self-promotion in ourselves. We get to learn oneness and union with God in the small things, like serving someone else dinner while we wait patiently for our own. It is in this that we, like the Temple of old, will truly reflect the glory of God's light.

In holy irony, Jesus was willing to be ruined by God's wrath, stone by stone, so we never experience personal destruction.

It is not our souls that are destroyed—just our walls.

We get his kindness, his lifting, his divine *kataluō* that is pain-ful only for the moment. We begin to discover that he takes the rubble and exchanges it for something far greater. We also discover that we have no need for great buildings. God *himself* is the building for which our souls long.

God is our Stronghold, our Tower. Only he can set us up above our enemies and give us a clear view. "The name of the LORD is a strong tower; the righteous man runs into it and is safe" (Proverbs 18:10, ESV).

God is our Castle, giving us shelter and warmth. He is our Monument, the tower that cries glory and honor and praise into the watching cosmos.

God is...the castle in which I live,
my rescuing knight.
My God—the high crag
where I run for dear life,
hiding behind the boulders,
safe in the granite hideout.

Psalm 18:1–2

He is our Temple, the place in which we dwell in close-ness with the Divine. In beautiful paradox, he invites us to be *his* Temple, the space in which he comes to dwell and bless humanity. "You are God's Temple, and...God's Spirit dwells in you" (1 Corinthians 13:6, ESV).

It is only in choosing the lower seat that we give God permission to topple our great buildings. In God's surprising, unlimited, subversive economy, in this choosing we will be lifted to the only place that is safe—his heart.

Jesus's question is an invitation that invites a specific response: *Tear down my monuments. Break down my walls. You have my permission. I want nothing between us.*

He honors that response, and we will get the height that we need.

We know that the towers, castles, and temples erected every moment around us are temporary. We also know that as Kingdom heirs, we need not fear denying our impulse to self-promote. Our high places are eternally secure.

Until that day, we have the great mountain-heart of God.

He will lift me high upon a rock.

Psalm 27:5 (ESV)

FOR CONTEMPLATION AND DISCUSSION

Lectio Divina Exercise:

Picture yourself in a wide, stretching valley. Before you, a large building project is underway. From what you can see, it looks like the project is going well. You see a set of blueprints laid out on a nearby table, and you note that before completion, the building must go much higher. You notice in one hand, you hold a bristled brush. In the other, you hold a bucket of mortar. There are bricks at your feet. You realize that you are the builder, and the project is yours. How do you feel about your project? What are you hoping it will provide? In the distance, you see Someone walking toward your building. It is Jesus. What is the look on his face as he surveys your building and the materials in your hand? He asks and gestures to your project: *"Do you see this great building?"* As you turn your attention to the foreground, it dawns on you that this is not a building at all, just a wall. Jesus has stopped on the other side, and you can no longer see him. What is it that he speaks to you next? What is it that you want him to do?

For Reflection:

1. What is the *purgos*, "tower," that you are currently building?
2. What great buildings of others have caught your eye?

3. How does it make you feel that *kataluō*, the "loosing-down" of rubble, is what Jesus has in mind for your walls?

4. What would it look like for you to kneel before others, taking the lower seat?

5. Have you ever experienced the freedom of choosing not to self-promote? Have you ever experienced the joy of finding God's *sugcheō*, the "pouring together" of his life with yours to elevate?

6. What is your answer to Jesus's question and statement: *"Do you see these great buildings? They will all be torn down."*

CHAPTER TWELVE

"What If Salt Loses Its Saltiness?"

Tasting the Everlasting Covenant

"Can that which is tasteless be eaten without salt?
My appetite refuses to touch them; they are as food that is
loathsome to me."

—Job 6:7, ESV

The salt moans, mountain
of buried light,
translucent cathedral,
crystal of the sea, oblivion
of the waves.
And then on every table
in the world.

—Pablo Neruda,
Ode to Salt

By the sixth day, the earth was teeming with salted life. The oceans swam in it. The fresh water tasted its presence without offense. The soil was sown with dynamic levels of salt—more for the date palm and barley, the asparagus and spinach. Less salt, much less, for the branches that would yield thirst-quenching juices of apple, plum, and peach.[1] The Salt-Giver sprinkled salinity into the cosmos, seasoning water and sky, terra firma and rock. Even the roaming livestock of land and the monsters of sea were salt-bearers, both needing salt and giving it back into the embrace of surrounding elements.

Salt, like crystalline oxygen, was the air breathed. It was the holy element of preservation, of consecration, in every moment, every dewdrop, every stone, every pore.

As all creation watched, the Salt-Giver stooped to cup freshly salted dirt. With the precision of pedological science and the creativity of Renaissance art, the Godhead measured steaming soil and sculpted. The sculpture awoke to God's warm whisper, *"You are the salt of the earth,"* breathed into upturned face. With the bone and marrow of this man, another figure was formed, one whose salt would sustain her uniquely through the process of receiving seed and bringing forth life.

"This is salt of my salt," said the man, and he spoke well, for God had whispered over her this blessing, too.

Creation rejoiced, for *here* were creatures, salted like themselves, and yet bearing the image of the Salt-Giver. Creation looked to the pair—and animal instinct told them their delicate balances would remain sacrosanct under the children's care.

Into this brackish paradise slithered a creature who cared nothing for salt save its bitter properties. This serpent sowed brimstone and destruction into the soil of mind and heart, killing the wellspring of balanced life that was implanted by the Creator. He showed them the forbidden fruit, and in it, they saw a better salt than they had tasted. Beads of sweat broke upon their humbled brows with the first bite. The body, once contented, would now crave all lost salt.

The sweat of their toil would drench the sown crops. Their tears, too, would water the earth at their humbled feet. They would taste the acrimony of extremes—chasing enough of the salt that framed them, then choking on its bitter overabundance. Always an imperiled balance, saline inequity threatened like a bursting nimbus over their bent heads.

Salt was in both the meat and vegetable that the first brothers laid before the Creator. Salt was in the flood's havoc and the rainbow's refracted light. Salt was in the parting of heavy seas and drawn by Egyptian whips, cruelly lashing the backs of the slave. Salt was in the fodder of sheep and the rancorous, undrinkable water of the desert. Salt—intended as a blessing, now marred by wrath. The boon of creation bore and bears still the mark of the curse, the breaking of Eden's salt-covenant.

Salt is in every birth, in every death, in every human moment in between.

PRIMAL POTENCY

I have personally tasted the primal potency of salt, introduced to my senses in Ireland.

Living my life landlocked, I never knew salt had such a distinctive smell, such a unique feel. I had traveled to various coastlines before—Florida, Maine, the Caribbean, even the Mediterranean coast in southern France—but nothing prepared me for its exposure while living in County Kerry. Salt flourished, an abundant crop like sheep and heather. The windows of our cottage collected a daily crusting of sea salt. When we opened the kitchen door to the courtyard, the constant blowing of a salty breeze nipped our lips and eyes. Lacking a clothes dryer, we hung all our wash on the line placed at the eastern side of the cottage. When we removed the clothing pins, our wash retained their suspended shape, stiffened by salt's presence in the air.

Salt was an unyielding white cloak, seasoning our hair, our boots, everything under heaven's gaze. Its unseen presence held hidden power, biting and cleansing, refreshing and coaxing alike.

We are creatures of salt, living constantly at its mercy. As humans, approximately 0.4 percent of our total body weight is made of salt combinations. This may not seem like much, but it is a percentage similar to the salt concentration of seawater.[2] We live with a salted blade to our necks, a dance of salinity that requires just the right amount of balance. With the fluctuation of salt loss by constant sweating, our bodies become vigilant guards in maintaining that balance.

We will never stop needing salt. The body's instinct to acquire this compound is potent, "a deep-seated biological drive as fundamental and almost as powerful as those of thirst, sex, and maternal behavior."[3] In one experiment done with sheep, normal salt supplements were withheld from the livestock. After several days, it became clear that the sheep were aware of their salt lack. In order to rectify their body balance, these creatures drank just enough seawater to counteract the body's lack of salt. Once the balance was achieved, the animals would stop consuming the saltwater.[4]

Without the medicine of salt, we die.

It just so happens, however, that our medicine doesn't taste unpleasant at all. We want more than we should, and too much salt can prove dangerous to the body's health. "In modern industrial society," states an article in the *New York Times*, "salt has become cheap and plentiful. And the ancient instincts that made it seem so desirable now prompt humans to take much more than they need."[5]

The instinct, once a life-sustaining drive, now incites us to excessive consumption. "Over time, this can stiffen blood vessels," caution scientists at Harvard Medical School, "leading to high blood pressure, heart attack, or stroke. It can also lead to heart failure."[6]

Salt has a profound impact on the beating human heart. Too little salt, and we die quickly. Too much, and death stalks us slowly. The right balance of salt is a matter of life and death.

THE COVENANT OF SALT

The story of humanity is our attempt to maintain this balance through religion.

Since the beginning of civilization, people have looked to both heaven and earth for the salt needed to thrive. In the Far East, worshippers prostrated before Shiotsuchinooji, the Japanese god of salt, while thousands of miles and oceans away, Aztecs sacrificed to a different salt deity, Huixtocihuatl. To the ancient Babylonians, salt was the captive of the goddess

Tiamat. In Greece, her name was Salacia. In Rome, Amphitrite. These gods required exacting homage from their people before allowing precious salt to sieve between their stingy fingers to earth below.

To these early people, salt was more than a table condiment—it was the lifeblood of culture.

In hot, arid climates, salt took the place of refrigeration, expended to preserve meats and fish that would have spoiled long before they were consumed. It was also seen as a healing agent, an antiseptic to cleanse wounds as well as prevent infection.[7] Salt had incredible value, traded as currency in various cultures.[8] Humanity has always been willing to pay for salt's value. Our word "salary" derives from Latin *salarius*, "salt."[9]

Salt preserved more than food, sustaining health and relationship, a crystallized symbol of "hospitality, friendship, durability, fidelity."[10] Even today, salt retains this meaning. In modern Arabic, the words for "salt" and "treaty" are the same.[11] One Biblical scholar writes,

> "To eat bread and salt together" is, in the East, an expression for a league of mutual amity. When the Arabs made a covenant together, they put salt on the blade of a sword, from whence every one puts a little into his mouth. This constitutes them blood relations, and they remain faithful to each other even when in danger of life.[12]

Salt was an essential part of all Jewish rituals in both Old and New Testaments, a sensual symbol of both life and blessing (Ezekiel 16:4).[13]

This started with the first breath of new life.

On their emergence from the womb, Jewish newborns were rubbed all over with salt, acting as a protectant from both bacteria and evil spirits.[14] Salt was a key ingredient in Passover rites, as well as all sacrifices made to Yahweh. The Israelites were commanded to "present all...offerings with salt" (Leviticus 2:13). "As the neglect of sacrifices was a breach of covenant on their part, so also was the neglect of salt *in* their sacrifices."[15]

The taste of salt was a permanent fixture on Jewish lips and hands.

God placed salt at the highest place of honor, initiating a new covenant, the Covenant of Salt, with his people (2 Chronicles 13:5). This sacred covenant, used for "particularly holy and inviolable obligations,"[16] was known to "denote an indissoluble alliance, an everlasting covenant."[17]

The Covenant of Salt was special, known by the people as "eternal and unchangeable before God" (Numbers 18:19). As salt was to be a permanent presence on the Hebrew table, so Yahweh wanted to express his continuous table fellowship with his chosen people.[18] In other words, he wanted to eat with them, drink with them, be with them in daily life until the end of all things.

In the life of Jesus, we see that he still does.

BREAKING SALT-COVENANT

With the sun shining on their backs, they sat on the grassy hillside, a tight ring of fellowship. Though they were surrounded by strangers, these were his friends. These were the ones he ate with, drank with, laughed with. These were the ones with whom he would leave his words, his questions, his very Spirit.

Over the ledge to their right, they could see the sparkling waters of a quiet sea. They could smell the salt in the air that teased their faces and beards. Jesus took a deep breath and sighed out, relishing the freshness of the seaside. He looked at his friends and said to them quietly, intimately—"You *are the halas*," he said. "*The 'salt' of this earth, of these people.*"

His friends, too, filled their lungs with the salty breeze. It awakened them, like plunging into the waters of the sea itself. It made them feel new, fresh, like boys again.

"*Let me tell you why you are here,*" Jesus continued, forbidding any dismissal of his words. He wanted his companions to understand. He didn't want there to be any confusion. This profound metaphor, packed with a God-punch of flavor and meaning, was being illustrated before their very senses. *"You're here to be salt-seasoning that brings out the God-flavors of this earth"* (Matthew 5:13).

They were, in this moment, tasting communion with the God of Salt, and this tasting would make salt of the fishermen and friends. This holy moment, the leaning in close to converse, the trust and intimacy between them, this was the salt their souls required. This was the place from which the whole world could be seasoned.

Like his first disciples, we, too, are the *"salt of the earth."* We are partakers of Salt-Covenant with the God who made us, participants in the exchange of intimacy and oneness.

Our lives with God are meant to compel curiosity about the goodness of both King and Kingdom. The way we talk *with* God and *about* God *"brings out the God-flavors"* inherent in all the daily moments. Jesus is saying that as we live and walk and work in this world, we are coaxing out the already-existing presence of God. The way we live is intended to season and preserve those around us for the Love that pursues every soul.

We are invited by God to make life with him taste good.

We were made to do this for one another, preaching the gospel of salt with every breath we expel, every bead of sweat, every tear the world wrenches from our hearts.

Something, however, has damaged our salt. Instead of *"bringing out the God-flavors,"* we find our lives dull, our faith uncompelling. We reject the intimacy, the closeness so freely offered to us. We find that we break the covenant that defines us, and in the breaking, our flavor is lost.

"Any one of you who does not renounce all that he has cannot be my disciple. Salt is good, but if salt has lost its taste, how shall its saltiness be restored? It is of no use either for the soil or

for the manure pile. It is thrown away. He who has ears to hear, let him hear."

Luke 13:33–34 (ESV)

If the standard, as Jesus stated, is the renunciation of absolute control over our lives, then we are in grave danger of becoming unsalted. We have lost our saltiness, again and again, by getting up from the feast with God and walking away to find our own flavor.

When I am not prepared to lay my life on the table before God, I break Salt-Covenant. In the hands of covenant breakers, even a gift becomes a scourge. Instead of a Garden, we enter a barren wasteland, a salt flat of the soul from which we cannot flee (cf. Deuteronomy 29:23). We are all the tasteless prodigal who runs from our own salt nature like it is a plague, not a present.

We forget our promises, our trust.

We forget God's promises, his trust.

As much as I desire to be good salt, I know I cannot stay good. I can't stay fresh. I can't keep myself from sinking into dullness by neglecting intimacy. Day after day, moment after moment, we could weep at how easily our salt becomes inedible.

We will never keep perfect covenant, not this side of his Kingdom. We fear the judgment we deserve. We hear it as he asks, *"What if salt loses its saltiness?"* Jesus questions our salt's longevity because he knows what we also know: We cannot uphold our end of Salt-Covenant.

We find, after receiving twelve of his questions, we still have no answers for Jesus that will satisfy our own guilt.

This needs to be acknowledged, spoken aloud.

Without salt, doctrine and liturgy lose their meaning and substance. Without salt, we introduce to a salt-deficient world the wrong Jesus. We look at our lives in the spotlight of all Jesus's questions and taste a grievous truth:

We are covenant breakers, and we cannot restore our saltiness with ritual or religion, no matter how hard we try.

THE SALT GOSPEL

The salt gods held the throat of the world in their stiffened grip. The people looked to the skies, the waters, the earth, praying deliverance from a tyranny of dark lack: lack of protection, lack of justice, lack of balance. Though their bellies were greedy, the gods' stony faces—meant to shield and provide—were silent, and the offerings left for the flies to feast.

Into this atmosphere the Godhead peered, their eternal plan savory, ripe. The Spirit, with eyes alight, scattered Salt into a submitted vessel. In holy mystery and uncontainable joy, the Son entered earth's woe and a woman's womb. Unlike the ancient gods, he, the one true God of Salt, chose to become salt like humankind, as one of them.

On his advent into Bethlehem's night, he submitted his tiny body to be rubbed down with its grit. Shivering in the cold sweat of a naked, limestone cave, he cried the salty tears of a newborn in the swell of his mother's arms. He drank the milk of her breast, tasting with human tongue the salt of its nourishment. He would submit, again and again, to the humble circumstances of his people. He would eat what they ate. He would bleed sodium-red and sweat the elemental compound sodium chloride.

As the Salt of the earth, he would touch his faded people with flavor and color. He would heal their imbalance. He, the God who breathed oxygen and emitted carbon dioxide, never broke the Salt-Covenant. Instead, he would invite them to new covenant, a new nature that would once again resemble the Giver of Salt.

But before this could be fulfilled, this Salt would have to be trampled. He would have to take on the identity of salt—unfit, worthy of the dung pile, the trash heap. He would be hated, despised, mocked by his own unsalted people, the very people he had come to restore. As the ultimate sacrifice of Salt, he would decide to drink the cup offered him.

This cup was not filled with the wine of gladness. No, the cup given to Jesus was one of destruction, the cup of wrath. This was the cup of broken covenant, filled with the tears of a grieved God. This cup also held the bitter salt of a groaning earth and a groaning people, those who had long since lost their ability to taste God-flavor.

In one great climactic moment, the choice stood before the Son: to take and drink from the brackish cup, signaling and sealing the mingling of his holy blood with the Father's will. It was the brine of both wrath and love, mixed together in sacred potency, the swilling draught that only the Son of God could take to his holy lips and drain to the dregs.

In his question of the cup, there was agony. There was grief. There was a recognition of the hell to come, but there was no hesitation. For Jesus to break covenant with his Father, as the perfect Son and the perfect Salt, never even crossed his mind. He would accept the everlasting covenant with his Father's will, for it was not in him to deny his Father or his children.

In the garden's flickering light, he made his decision. *"Do you think for a minute,"* he asked his friends and us, *"I'm not going to drink this cup the Father gave Me?"* (John 18:11).

Jesus's choice to drink this cup would answer the terror of the world:

Will the Godhead ever divorce?

Will Jesus, as the Salt of heaven, ever lose his saltiness, forsaking his Father's will?

Will we be cursed forever, bearing this sin nature that has muted our flavor?

The entrance of the first question, hissed from serpentine lips, had answered these questions for millennia, twisting the hearts of all who had long mistrusted the love of God.

As Jesus allowed himself to be manacled and taken from the garden, he answered each question with a NO that trembled the world and tore the veil. With sweat, blood, and tears on his face—each containing the compound of created order—this Son took the offered cup from the Father's hand.

He drank of it to the last drop. The salt that heals flowed from the splintered wood of the Cross.

For all eternity, Jesus knew the mind of the Father. There was never a need to question. Jesus spoke what he heard the Father speak, and he did what he saw the Father do. The beauty of the rescue was mingled with the mystery of this moment, the world's horror becoming unutterable reality.

On this dark day, the Son no longer had access to his Father.

He could no longer see his Father's eyes. He could not hear his Father's voice. The sin of the world, borne on the incarnate God's shoulders, stood as a barrier erected between them. He *must* ask his Father a question, the only question he uttered from the height of the Cross: "*My God, my God, why have you forsaken me?*" (Matthew 27:46, ESV).

It's impossible to fathom the dread of this moment for both Son and Father.

Jesus cried out this question "with a loud voice," wrenched from the bowels of his soul. Psalm 22, a Messianic psalm, gave voice to the sufferings of Jesus, the unseen reality of broken relationship with the Divine. He took up the Messianic mantle, with all the pain, and wrapped it about himself like a cloak to keep warm.

> Why are you so far from saving me, from the words of my groaning?
> O my God, I cry by day, but you do not answer.
>
> Psalm 22:1–2 (ESV)

We are rescued at a terrible cost.

What would be unbearable to us, Jesus bore. What would be hell for us, Jesus endured. The perfect intimacy was broken so we could be made whole. The continuous flow of relationship was stanched so we could be brought home.

In Gospel irony, that cup given to him by his Father initiated a different Salt-Covenant, a heavenly treaty that could never be undone. Out of the ashes of a sin-severed relationship, a covenant between the Godhead was voiced again, a binding oath to remain forever in their oneness, in their deep and unshakable union. It is this very oneness of the Godhead that holds the world together. It is from this oneness that we are held together.

Instinctively, our souls know this.

"For even if the mountains walk away
and the hills fall to pieces,
My love won't walk away from you,
my covenant commitment of peace won't fall apart."
The God who has compassion on you says so.

Isaiah 54:10

Mirroring birth, his body was again rubbed with salt, but this was the embalming of the dead. The blood of his suffering was wiped clean from his frame by soaked rags. His body would once again be placed in an unkind cave, cut from the limestone hillside of Judea.

This trampled Salt would do what no other salt could do. Once deemed unfit, he would pour flavor back into himself in Resurrection power, a holy *artuō* (ar-too´-o), "seasoning."[19] This *artuō* would make vibrant what was once flat. It would make whole what was broken. It would redeem the entire salt-deprived world by its seasoning.

Because of this Salt, we never need face becoming salt-unfit. He's taken the wrath, the dung pile, so we could be sown in places of goodness.

Jesus has restored our saltiness. He rescues us with a satchel full of questions.

He puts himself beside this saltless place in us, the part that huddles in the silted earth, waiting for the recompense of affronting a Holy God.

He kneels down and asks us to accept his saltiness on our behalf.

His Gospel restores our salinity. By his incarnation, all of creation and its creatures will be restored in final triumph to its original design.

The Salt-Covenant is everlasting, and in Jesus, it can never be broken—not by us, and not by him. "If we are faithless, he remains faithful—for he cannot deny himself" (2 Timothy 2:13, ESV).

Within the fine print of this covenant, we are promised a daily renewal of our salt natures.

> The steadfast love of the LORD never ceases;
> his mercies never come to an end;
> they are new every morning;
> great is your faithfulness.
>
> Lamentations 3:22–23 (ESV)

SALTED, PURE, AND HOLY

As newborn babies, we return to the covenant helpless, in need of nourishment. He doesn't hurl accusations. Instead, he scrubs us down like infants in his goodness, reminding us that we are okay in the longing for balance, in the waiting. We are still *good* in the process, still good in the partial.

We are still good in the questions of Jesus. This is exactly what his questions remind us. We don't have to fear losing our place in his Kingdom. He will always flow his fresh seasoning into our lives, reviving us to once again bring out the God-flavors of this earth.

> *"Take for yourself spices,"* the LORD spoke to Moses. *"With it you shall make an incense, a perfume, the work of a perfumer, salted, pure, and holy."*
>
> Exodus 30:34–35 (NASB)

This is the holy work of covenant. He takes our lack and mixes it with the saline of Calvary, creating a perfume that can flavor the whole earth, a dynamic fragrance, *"pure and holy."* If he's invited, he stays with us and takes the punishment, offering us fresh seasoning—again and again, seventy times seven into infinite forgiveness and endless love.

Because of this, we *get* to relinquish full access to our lives. We can, in loving trust, invite him to scatter us as he pleases into the soil of this world. This holy, salt-giving God is like no other. He has decided to bear responsibility for both sides of the covenant. He will keep both his promise and ours.

At the tidal wave of his Kingdom, the salt of broken covenant will no longer sting our eyes. On that day, the Salt-Giver "will wipe away every tear" (Revelation 21:4, ESV). All the salt we have lost, all the grief we have shared, will be restored to us one hundred-fold. We will leave the partial behind for full union with him.

Until that day, Paul writes in Colossians 4:6, "Let your speech be seasoned with salt" (ESV), exhorting the Salt of the earth to sprinkle questions into our relationships and conversations in a salt-deprived world. We can embrace our image-bearing identity as his fellow questioners. In this role, we mirror him, becoming inquisitive to our own souls and the souls of others.

THE FLAVOR OF QUESTIONS

There is a truth about the nature of God, perhaps, we did not know, a truth as old as earth.

The Son of God is a curious God, and he has been asking us questions—really good ones—all along the way.

Like the disciples on Emmaus Road, we have Jesus with us on our disappointing journey of life, asking us questions, wanting to be with us where we are. Like those disciples, we don't recognize that it's him.

We have viewed his questions with suspicion, feeling that a lack of answers is what affects our salt balance most acutely. We seek *answers*, answers that would draw us back into covenant.

Without answers, we wrestle with our unworthiness, our incompetence, our lack. We think God must wrestle with this lack in us, too.

This is not the way of the Kingdom. Jesus teaches us that questions are not to be feared but welcomed.

His questions show us, time and again, that life with God is not about answers—it is about intimacy. With this and all his questions, he welcomes us back to Salt-Covenant, to the promises made in Eden.

He is both question and answer. With his questions, he invites us to this holy process, this invitation to let *him* be our answer—forever and amen.

Questions show that he is, at the core of his deep, wide heart, fiercely relational. His constant questions are divine proof of his desire for oneness. He did not sculpt us from salt-mud and then walk away to be God. He craves dialogue. He initiates conversation.

He knows us.

He loves us.

He wants more with us.

"Let me tell you why you are here," he says. You are here for *this* conversational intimacy with me. You're here for *this* sense of identifying with me, at home in my Kingdom. This process of becoming again true sons and daughters. *This* returning to the salt balance you were designed to have.

Questions invite covenant faithfulness. Questions draw us back into close relationship and the right balance of salinity. Questions are not to be rushed, for it is in the irony of questions that our lives are freshly salted.

It is these same questions that are returning us to the Gospel.

The questions of Jesus are as present and primal as salt, piercing through the heavy, dark slumber of this world like unquenched constellations. In constant persistence, he humbles himself and offers a question that would transform our very souls.

His questions are the evidence of God's relentless engagement.

It is our choice to receive them, to hold them in our hands. It is also our choice to ignore them. Nothing, however, will keep him from asking.

We turn the final page of this book, but the journey begins in earnest. In the end, Ireland wasn't our final destination, although it will always represent home. After ten weeks, we returned to America, discovering that the adventure was so much more than the location. The adventure was God himself, his suitcase packed with questions.

The coordinates on the map change for each of us, but Jesus never will.

All along, he has been inviting us to bring our questions to his table. What if what's next is another question, a question we ask that Jesus alone can answer?

"What question are you asking me today?"

If we ask, he will answer in the stillness. He loves to engage us, for this is why he made us, and this is why he came. We can stay with the questions, holding them in our souls. He will keep asking his questions, no matter what.

He is, after all, the Inquisitive Christ.

FOR CONTEMPLATION AND DISCUSSION

Lectio Divina Exercise:

Imagine sitting on a soft bed of grass with Jesus. The hillsides around you overlook the sea far below. Look and see the thousands around you both, the ones who hang back from the circle of intimate trust. Notice the air: Can you smell the salt? Listen as Jesus breathes in deep and then speaks to your identity. *"You are the salt of the earth."* How do you respond? What do you see in the face of Jesus as he watches you ponder this metaphor and its meaning? Recognize, for a moment, that you cannot stay salty. Can you say this to Jesus? If so, what is his response to your confession, your shame?

For Reflection:

1. Have you ever considered the primal presence of salt? In creation? In the fall? In the Gospel?
2. When have you experienced a physical imbalance of your salt levels? What did you feel and observe?
3. How does it make you feel that *artuō*, the seasoning that elevates others, is what Jesus has in mind for you?
4. What does it look like for you to be the salt of the earth? How do Jesus's questions participate in this?
5. Have you ever experienced the conversational intimacy in his questions? If so, when? How?
6. What is your answer to Jesus's question: *"What if salt loses its saltiness?"*
7. What is the next step for you in this journey of questions? Will you ask Jesus about the questions he has for you today?

Appendix

100 Questions Jesus Asked[1]

1. Do you love Me? (John 21:16)
2. Do you also want to leave? (John 6:67)
3. What is your name? (Luke 8:30)
4. Could you not watch for Me one brief hour? (Matthew 26:40)
5. What do you want Me to do for you? (Matthew 20:32)
6. Do people pick grapes from thornbushes or figs from thistles? (Matthew 7:16)
7. Do you see anything? (Mark 8:23)
8. Can you drink the cup that I am going to drink? (Matthew 20:22)
9. My God, my God, why have You forsaken Me? (Matthew 27:46)
10. For who is greater, the one who is seated at the table or the one who serves? (Luke 22:27)
11. Why do you weep? (John 20:15)
12. Can none be found to come back and give glory to God except this outsider? (Luke 17:18)
13. Have you anything here to eat? (Luke 24:41)
14. Does no one condemn you? (Luke 8:10)
15. Can any of you by worrying add a single moment to your lifespan? (Matthew 6:27)
16. How many loaves do you have? (Matthew 15:34)
17. Who touched Me? (Luke 8:45)
18. Salt is good, but what if salt becomes flat? (Mark 9:50)
19. What did you go out to the desert to see? (Matthew 11:8)
20. What concern is it of yours? (John 21:22)
21. Do you really believe I can do this? (Matthew 9:28)

22. Do you see these great buildings? They will all be thrown down. (Mark 13:2)

23. How can anyone enter a strong man's house and take hold of his possessions unless he first ties up the strong man? (Matthew 12:29)

24. Have I been with you for so long and still you do not know Me? (John 14:9)

25. If all you do is love the lovable, do you expect a bonus? (Matthew 5:47)

26. Why are you testing Me? (Matthew 22:18)

27. Who is My mother? (Mark 3:33)

28. Do you not yet understand? (Matthew 16:8)

29. Why do you call Me good? (Mark 10:18)

30. Why are you trying to kill Me? (John 7:19)

31. Why do you make trouble for the woman? (Matthew 26:10)

32. Which is more important, the gold or the Temple that has made the gold sacred? (Matthew 23:17)

33. Is a lamp brought in to be put under a basket and not on a stand? (Mark 4:21)

34. What are you looking for? (John 1:38)

35. If I have spoken rightly, why did you strike Me? (John 18:23)

36. Why don't you judge for yourself what is right? (Luke 12:57)

37. Would I have told you that I'm on my way to get a room ready for you if it weren't true? (John 14:2)

38. Didn't the One who made the outside also make the inside? (Luke 11:40)

39. Who do people say the Son of Man is? (Matthew 16:13)

40. But who do you say that I am? (Matthew 16:15)

41. What are you discussing as you walk along? (Luke 24:17)

42. How can you ask, Where is the Father? (John 14:9)

43. Why are you anxious about clothes? (Matthew 6:28)

44. Do you believe this? (John 11:26)

45. How is it you seek praise from one another and not seek the praise that comes from God? (John 5:44)

46. Did you catch anything? (John 21:5)

47. When the Son of Man comes, will he find any faith on the earth? (Luke 18:8)

48. Why do you break the commandments of God for the sake of your tradition? (Matthew 15:3)

49. Friend, who appointed Me as your judge? (Luke 12:14)

50. Have you come out as against a robber with swords and clubs to seize Me? (Matthew 26:55)

51. What is written in the law? How do you interpret it? (Luke 10:26)

52. Why were you looking for Me? (Luke 2:59)

53. Which of you who has a sheep that falls into a pit on the Sabbath will not take hold of it and lift it out? (Matthew 12:11)

54. If you are not trustworthy with worldly wealth, who will trust you with true wealth? (Luke 16:11)

55. What do you think? Which of the three men became a neighbor to the man attacked by robbers? (Luke 10:36)

56. Does this teaching shock you? (John 6:61)

57. Why do you harbor evil thoughts? (Matthew 9:4)

58. What king, marching into battle, would not first sit down and decide with ten thousand troops he can successfully oppose another king marching upon him with twenty thousand troops? (Luke 14:31)

59. What are you arguing about along the way? (Mark 9:33)

60. Shall I not drink the cup the Father gave Me? (John 18:11)

61. Have you come to believe because you have seen Me? (John 20:29)

62. What profit would there be for one to gain the whole world and forfeit his soul? (Matthew 16:26)

63. Will God not secure the rights of his chosen ones who call out to him day and night? (Luke 18:7)

64. If I tell you about earthly things and you will not believe, how will you believe when I tell you of heavenly things? (John 3:12)

65. How many baskets full of leftover fragments did you pick up? (Mark 8:19)

66. Why do you call Me "Lord, Lord" and not do what I say? (Luke 6:46)

67. If people do these things to a live, green tree, can you imagine what they'll do with deadwood? (Luke 23:31)

68. Simon, are you asleep? (Mark 14:37)

69. Why do you notice the splinter in your brother's eye yet fail to perceive the wooden beam in your own eye? (Matthew 7:2)

70. Do you want to be well? (John 5:6)

71. Why does this generation seek a sign? (Mark 8:12)

72. How can you say good things when you are evil? (Matthew 12:34)

73. Can the wedding guests mourn when the Bridegroom is with them? (Matthew 9:15)

74. Do you think I cannot call upon my Father? (Matthew 26:53)

75. What are you thinking in your hearts? (Mark 2:8)

76. If you do not believe Moses' writings, how will you believe Me? (John 5:47)

77. Why are you terrified? (Matthew 8:26)

78. Will you be exalted to heaven? (Luke 10:15)

79. Can any of you charge Me with sin? (John 8:46)

80. Why are you sleeping? (Luke 22:46)

81. Are there not twelve hours of daylight? (John 11:9)

82. To what shall I compare this generation? (Matthew 11:16)

83. What did Moses command you? (Mark 10:3)

84. Where can we buy enough food for them to eat? (John 6:5)

85. If even the smallest things are beyond your control, why are you anxious about the rest? (Luke 12:26)

86. What can one give in exchange for his life? (Matthew 16:26)

87. You trust God, don't you? (John 14:1)

88. Do you understand what I have done for you? (John 13:12)

89. O faithless and perverse generation, how long must I endure you? (Matthew 17:17)

90. What if I want John to remain until I come? (John 21:22)

91. Where is your faith? (Matthew 14:31)

92. If I am telling you the truth, why do you not believe Me? (John 8:46)

93. Are you not worth much more than they? (Matthew 6:26)

94. How are you to avoid being sentenced to hell? (Matthew 23:23)

95. Do you not yet understand or comprehend? Are your hearts hardened? Do you have eyes and still not see? Ears and not hear? (Mark 8:18)

96. Are you saying this on your own, or did others tell you about Me? (John 18:34)

97. Did you never read the scriptures? (Matthew 21:42)

98. Why do you ask Me about what is good? (Matthew 19:16)

99. You are a teacher in Israel and you do not understand this? (John 3:10)

100. Was it not necessary that the Messiah should suffer these things and then enter his glory? (Luke 24:46)

Notes

CHAPTER ONE: "WHERE IS YOUR FAITH?"

1   John Eldredge, "5 Agreements That Are Killing Millennials," *Ransomed Heart* (blog and podcast), February 9, 2018, accessed via podcast April 2, 2018, https://www.ransomedheart.com/rhplay/podcast/5-agreements-are-killing-millennials-part-1.

2   Strong, James. *Strong's Expanded Exhaustive Concordance of the Bible* (Nashville: Thomas Nelson, 2006), s.v. 935, "Basileus." This and all other Strong's references include the last portion of the citation. Many of the references were found at https://www.biblestudytools.com/lexicons/greek/nas/.

3   Pearn, John Hemsley and Richard Charles Franklin. "'The Impulse to Rescue': Rescue Altruism and the Challenge of Saving the Rescuer." *International Journal of Aquatic Research and Education* Volume 6, Number 4, Article 7, November 1, 2012. https://scholarworks.bgsu.edu/ijare/vol6/iss4/7/.

CHAPTER TWO: "DO YOU NOT YET UNDERSTAND?"

1   This and other Socrates information comes from Nails, Debra, "Socrates." *The Stanford Encyclopedia of Philosophy* (Spring 2018 Edition), Edward N. Zalta, ed., https://plato.stanford.edu/archives/spr2018/entries/socrates/>.

2   Nails, "Socrates."

3   Nails, "Socrates."

4   Mark, Joshua J. "Socrates." Ancient History Encyclopedia, September 2009. https://www.ancient.eu/socrates/.

5   Tolkien, J. R. R. *The Hobbit* (Boston: Houghton Mifflin, 2001), 33.

6   Hugo, Victor. *Les Misérables* (New York: Barnes and Noble Classics, 2003), 40.

7   Shakespeare, William. *Romeo and Juliet*, in *A New Variorum Edition of Shakespeare, Volume 1*, Horace Howard Furness, ed. (Philadelphia: J. B. Lippincott

and Co., 1871), 287. https://books.google.com/books/about/A_New
_Variorum_Edition_of_Shakespeare_Ro.html?id=-wEuAAAAYAAJ.

CHAPTER THREE: "WHY ARE YOU SLEEPING?"

1   "Narcolepsy Fast Facts." Narcolepsy Network. https://narcolepsynetwork
     .org/about-narcolepsy/narcolepsy-fast-facts/.
2   "Sleep and Sleep Disorder Statistics." American Sleep Association.
     https://www.sleepassociation.org/about-sleep/sleep-statistics/.
3   "Torpor." A *Dictionary of Zoology.* Encyclopedia.com. (April 4, 2019).
     https://www.encyclopedia.com/science/dictionaries-thesauruses-pictures
     -and-press-releases/torpor.
4   Strong, s.v. 2523.
5   Strong, s.v. 3306.
6   Strong, s.v. 1569.
7   Strong, s.v. 85.
8   Thayer, Joseph and William Smith. "Greek Lexicon entry for Ademoneo."
     The NAS New Testament Greek Lexicon, 1999. https://www
     .biblestudytools.com/lexicons/greek/nas/.
9   Strong, s.v. 4036.
10   "Exhaust." Merriam-Webster.com. https://www.merriam-webster.com
     /dictionary/exhaust.
11   Lewis, C. S. *The Magician's Nephew,* in *The Complete Chronicles of Narnia.*
     (New York: HarperCollins Publishers, 1998), 67 (emphasis mine).

CHAPTER FOUR: "WHAT DO YOU WANT ME TO DO FOR YOU?"

1   Strong, s.v. 1937.
2   Melville, Herman. *Moby Dick* (New York: Barnes and Noble Books, 1993),
     135.
3   Lewis, C. S. *The Lion, The Witch and The Wardrobe,* in *The Complete Chron-
     icles of Narnia* (New York: HarperCollins Publishers, 1998), 86.
4   Tolkien, J. R. R. *The Return of the King,* in *The Lord of the Rings* (Boston:
     Houghton Mifflin Co., 1987), 925.
5   Strong, s.v. 2309.

CHAPTER FIVE: "WHY ARE YOU TRYING TO KILL ME?"

1   Smith, William, Dr. "Entry for 'Pharisees.'" *Smith's Bible Dictionary,* 1901.
     https://www.biblestudytools.com/dictionaries/smiths-bible-dictionary/phari
     sees.html.

2   "Pharisees." *Jewish Encyclopedia.* http://www.jewishencyclopedia.com /articles/12050-perushim.

3   Thomson, J. E. H. James Orr, gen. ed. "Pharisees." *International Standard Bible Encyclopedia,* 1915. https://www.biblestudytools.com/encyclopedias/ isbe/pharisees.html.

4   Smith, "Entry for 'Pharisees.'"

5   Thomson, "Pharisees."

6   Scott, J. Julius. Walter A. Elwell, ed. "Pharisees." *Baker's Evangelical Dictionary of Biblical Theology.* Baker Books: Grand Rapids, MI, 1996. https:// www.biblestudytools.com/dictionaries/bakers-evangelical-dictionary/phari sees.html.

7   Thomson, "Pharisees."

8   Thomson, "Pharisees."

9   Orr, James, M.A., D.D., gen. ed. "Entry for 'Christs, False.'" *International Standard Bible Encyclopedia.* 1915. https://www.biblestudytools.com /encyclopedias/isbe/pharisees.html.

10   Strong, s.v. 3985.

11   Strong, s.v. 2617.

12   Strong, s.v. 615.

CHAPTER SIX: "STILL YOU DO NOT KNOW ME?"

1   Walsh, Matt. *The Daily Wire.* https://www.dailywire.com/news/24137/ walsh-were-nation-porn-addicts-why-are-we-matt-walsh.

2   "Pornography." Enough.com. https://enough.org/stats_porn_industry.

3   Ibid.

4   Unless otherwise noted, social media statistics were found at the following online source: https://www.brandwatch.com/blog/amazing -social-media-statistics-and-facts/.

5   Shakya, Holly B. and Nicholas A. Christakis, "A New, More Rigorous Study Confirms: The More You Use Facebook, the Worse You Feel," *Harvard Business Review.* https://hbr.org/2017/04/a-new-more-rigorous-study confirms-the-more-you-use-facebook-the-worse-you-feel.

6   Shultz, Carl. Walter A. Elwell, ed. "Entry for 'Know, Knowledge." *Baker's Evangelical Dictionary of Biblical Theology,* 1997. https://www.biblestudytools .com/dictionaries/bakers-evangelical-dictionary/know-knowledge.html.

7   Strong, s.v. 6063.

8   *Vine's Expository Dictionary of New Testament Words,* "Ginōskō." https://www .blueletterbible.org/search/dictionary/viewTopic.cfm?topic=VT0001579.

9   Strong, s.v. 1097.

10   *Vine's,* "Ginōskō."

11 *Vine's,* "Ginōskō."

12 Willard, Dallas. *The Divine Conspiracy: Rediscovering Our Hidden Life in God* (San Francisco: HarperSanFrancisco, 1998), 324.

13 Willard, Dallas. *Hearing God: Developing a Conversational Relationship with God* (Downers Grove, Illinois: IVP Books, 1999).

14 Strong, s.v. 2048.

15 Adam, David. *A Desert in the Ocean* (Paulist Press: Mahwah, New Jersey, 2000), 3.

CHAPTER SEVEN: "HOW CAN YOU ASK—WHERE IS THE FATHER?"

1 Kruk, Edward. "Father Absence, Father Deficit, Father Hunger." *Psychology Today.* May 23, 2012. http://www.pscyhologytoday.com.

2 Rosiak, Luke. "Fathers Disappear from Households Across America." *Washington Times.* December 25, 2012. https://www.washingtontimes.com/news/2012/dec/25/fathers-disappear-fromhouseholds-across-america/.

3 Gretchen Livingston, January 8, 2018. https://www.pewresearch.org/fact-tank/2018/01/08/most-dads-say-they-spend-too-little-time-with-their-children-about-a-quarter-live-apart-from-them/.

4 Strong, s.v. 1166, from *Thayer's Greek Lexicon,* Electronic Database. https://biblehub.com/greek/1166.htm.

5 Strong, s.v. 714.

6 Elwell, Walter A. "Entry for 'Fatherhood of God.'" *Evangelical Dictionary of Theology,* 1997. https://www.biblestudytools.com/dictionaries/bakers-evangelical-dictionary/fatherhood-of-god.html.

7 Elwell, "Entry for 'Fatherhood of God.'"

CHAPTER EIGHT: "HAVE YOU ANYTHING HERE TO EAT?"

1 Lewis, C. S. *The Horse and His Boy,* in *The Complete Chronicles of Narnia* (New York: HarperCollins Publishers, 1998), 190.

2 Strong, s.v. 5584.

3 Strong, s.v. 5567, Entry for "psállō," Thayer's Greek Lexicon (online).

4 Strong, s.v. 5586, Entry for "psēphos," Thayer's Greek Lexicon (online).

5 Strong, s.v. 4151.

6 Lewis, C. S. *The Great Divorce,* in *The Complete C. S. Lewis Signature Classics* (San Francisco: HarperSanFrancisco, 2000), 477.

7 Lewis, *The Great Divorce,* 478.

CHAPTER NINE: "DO YOU WANT TO BE WELL?"

1   "About Chronic Diseases." National Health Council, July 29, 2014. http://www.nationalhealthcouncil.org/sites/default/files/NHC_Files/Pdf _Files/AboutChronicDisease.pdf.

2   National Health Council, "About Chronic Diseases."

3   Carson, D. A. *The Gospel According to John* (Leicester, England: Inter-Varsity Press, 1991), 242.

4   Kostenberger, Andreas J., Clinton E.Arnold, gen. ed., *Zondervan Illustrated Bible Backgrounds Commentary, Volume 2* (Grand Rapids, Michigan: Zondervan, 2002), 54.

5   Strong, s.v. 769.

6   Strong, s.v. 4599.

7   This connection is made by a number of Biblical commentators, though not all affirm its relevance.

8   Strong, s.v. 5199.

9   Lewis, C. S. *The Voyage of the Dawn Treader*, in *The Complete Chronicles of Narnia* (New York: HarperCollins Publishers, 1998), 326.

10 Keller, W. Phillip. *The Shepherd Trilogy: A Shepherd Looks at Psalm 23* (Grand Rapids, Michigan: Zondervan, 1996), 14.

11 Keller, 48.

CHAPTER TEN: "HOW MANY LOAVES DO YOU HAVE?"

1   Strong, s.v. 740.

2   Garrett, Duane A. Walter A. Elwell, ed. "Entry for 'Bread, Bread of Presence.'" *Evangelical Dictionary of Theology*, 1997. https://www.biblestudytools.com/dictionaries/bakers-evangelical-dictionary/bread-bread-of-presence.html.

3   Strong, s.v. 142.

4   "Jesus' Ministry." Bible Timelines.com. https://www.bibletimelines.com/timelines/jesus-ministry.

5   "Social Comparison Theory." *Psychology Today*. https://www.psychologytoday.com/us/basics/social-comparison-theory.

6   "Social Comparison Theory."

7   Strong, s.v. 1754.

CHAPTER ELEVEN: "DO YOU SEE THESE GREAT BUILDINGS?"

1   Pinero, Antonio. *National Geographic* Online. https://www.nationalgeographic.com/archaeology-and-history/magazine/2016/11-12/king herod-judaea-holy-land-rome-new-testament/.

2   "The Second Temple." Jewish Virtual Library, quoted in https://www.jewishvirtuallibrary.org/the-second-temple.

3 Jewish Virtual Library, "The Second Temple."
4 Jewish Virtual Library, "The Second Temple."
5 Jewish Virtual Library, "The Second Temple."
6 Strong, s.v. 4444.
7 Dates used from The Ring of Kerry. http://www.theringofkerry.com/cahergal-leacanabuaile-forts.
8 Some dates and building details were used from an Irish historical clan site: http://maccarthyclan.org/ballycarbery-castle/.
9 Strong, s.v. 4797.
10 Strong, s.v. 2647.
11 Strong, s.v. 3089.

CHAPTER TWELVE: "WHAT IF SALT LOSES ITS SALTINESS?"

1 Food and Agricultural Organization of the United Nations. Chapter 7 http://www.fao.org/3/r4082e/r4082e08.htm.
2 Fisher, Len. "How Much Salt Is in a Human Body?" BBC online science magazine. https://www.sciencefocus.com/the-human-body/how-much-salt-is-in-a-human-body/.
3 Schmeck, Harold M., Jr. "Hunger for Salt Found to be Powerful Instinct." *New York Times*, August 9, 1983. https://www.nytimes.com/1983/08/09/science/hunger-for-salt-found-to-be-powerful-instinct.html.
4 Schmeck, "Hunger."
5 Schmeck, "Hunger."
6 "Take It with a Grain of Salt." Harvard Health Publishing, Harvard Medical School. https://www.health.harvard.edu/heart-health/take-it-with-a-grain-of-salt.
7 Vines, W. E., MA. Entry for "Salt, Saltness." *Vine's Expository Dictionary of NT Words*, 1940.
8 Ryken, Leland, Jim Wilhoit, Tremper Longman, Colin Duriez, Douglas Penney, and Daniel G. Reid. *Dictionary of Biblical Imagery*, s.v. "Salt." (Downers Grove, Illinois: InterVarsity Press, 1998), 752.
9 *Dictionary*, "Salt."
10 *Ellicott's Commentary for English Readers*, "Leviticus 2:13" https://biblehub.com/commentaries/leviticus/2-13.htm.
11 Patch, James A. "Salt." James Orr, gen. ed. *International Standard Bible Encyclopedia*, 1915. https://www.biblestudytools.com/dictionary/salt/.
12 *Ellicott's*, "Leviticus 2:13."
13 Hirsch, Emil G. "Salt." *Jewish Encyclopedia*. http://www.jewishencyclopedia.com/articles/13043-salt.
14 Hirsch, "Salt."

15   Benson Commentary, "Leviticus 2." https://biblehub.com/commentaries/
     benson/leviticus/2.htm, *emphasis mine.*

16   Hirsch, "Salt."

17   *Ellicott's,* "Leviticus 2:13."

18   Lowman, Moses. *A Rational of the Ritual of the Hebrew Worship.* (London: J.
     Noon,   1748),   154.   https://books.google.com/books/about/A_Rational
     _of_the_Ritual_of_the_Hebrew_W.html?id=H0MVAAAAQAAJ.

19   Strong, s.v. 741.

APPENDIX: 100 QUESTIONS JESUS ASKED

1   This list was adapted from online lists, and the questions appear in the
    order in which I first studied them.

About the Author

Cara L. T. Murphy is an American-born, Irish-bred writer and teacher. An instructor with Liberty University's School of Divinity, Cara trains students toward a passion for knowing the God of the scriptures. With her husband and two daughters, she lives in Virginia and adventures in County Kerry, Ireland, seeking more of God in all the unveiled places. Cara is a pilgrim who reads constantly, cultivates both conversations and her roses, and in all things, desires journeying deeper into the wild country of the Living Word. Cara holds a master of arts in religious studies, specializing in Biblical languages.